HITLER'S NEMESIS

The Stackpole Military History Series

THE AMERICAN CIVIL WAR

Cavalry Raids of the
  Civil War
Ghost, Thunderbolt, and
  Wizard
Pickett's Charge
Witness to Gettysburg

WORLD WAR I

Doughboy War

WORLD WAR II

Armor Battles of the
  Waffen-SS, 1943–45
Armoured Guardsmen
Army of the West
Australian Commandos
The B-24 in China
Backwater War
The Battle of Sicily
Beyond the Beachhead
The Brandenburger
  Commandos
The Brigade
Bringing the Thunder
Coast Watching in
  World War II
Colossal Cracks
A Dangerous Assignment
D-Day Deception
D-Day to Berlin
Destination Normandy
Dive Bomber!
A Drop Too Many
Eagles of the Third Reich
Eastern Front Combat
Exit Rommel
Fist from the Sky
Flying American Combat
  Aircraft of World War II
Forging the Thunderbolt
Fortress France
The German Defeat in the
  East, 1944–45
German Order of Battle, Vol. 1
German Order of Battle, Vol. 2
German Order of Battle, Vol. 3
The Germans in Normandy
Germany's Panzer Arm in
  World War II
GI Ingenuity

Goodwood
The Great Ships
Grenadiers
Hitler's Nemesis
Infantry Aces
Iron Arm
Iron Knights
Kampfgruppe Peiper at the
  Battle of the Bulge
Kursk
Luftwaffe Aces
Massacre at Tobruk
Mechanized Juggernaut or
  Military Anachronism?
Messerschmitts over Sicily
Michael Wittmann, Vol. 1
Michael Wittmann, Vol. 2
Mountain Warriors
The Nazi Rocketeers
On the Canal
Operation Mercury
Packs On!
Panzer Aces
Panzer Aces II
Panzer Commanders of the
  Western Front
The Panzer Legions
Panzers in Normandy
Panzers in Winter
The Path to Blitzkrieg
Penalty Strike
Red Star under the Baltic
Retreat to the Reich
Rommel's Desert Commanders
Rommel's Desert War
Rommel's Lieutenants
The Savage Sky
A Soldier in the Cockpit
Soviet Blitzkrieg
Stalin's Keys to Victory
Surviving Bataan and
  Beyond
T-34 in Action
Tank Tactics
Tigers in the Mud
Triumphant Fox
The 12th SS, Vol. 1
The 12th SS, Vol. 2
The War against Rommel's
  Supply Lines
War in the Aegean
Wolfpack Warriors

THE COLD WAR / VIETNAM

Cyclops in the Jungle
Expendable Warriors
Flying American Combat
  Aircraft: The Cold War
Here There Are Tigers
Land with No Sun
Phantom Reflections
Street without Joy
Through the Valley

WARS OF THE MIDDLE EAST

Never-Ending Conflict

GENERAL MILITARY HISTORY

Carriers in Combat
Desert Battles
Guerrilla Warfare

HITLER'S NEMESIS

The Red Army, 1930–45

Walter S. Dunn, Jr.
Foreword by David Glantz

STACKPOLE
BOOKS

Published in paperback in 2009 by
STACKPOLE BOOKS
5067 Ritter Road
Mechanicsburg, PA 17055
www.stackpolebooks.com

HITLER'S NEMESIS: THE RED ARMY, 1930–1945, by Walter S. Dunn, Jr., was originally published in hard cover by Praeger, an imprint of Greenwood Publishing Group, Inc., Westport, CT. Copyright © 1994 by Walter S. Dunn, Jr. Paperback edition by arrangement with Greenwood Publishing Group, Inc. All rights reserved.

Cover design by Tracy Patterson
All photos from author's collection

Printed in the United States of America

10 9 8 7 6 5 4 3 2 1

Library of Congress Cataloging-in-Publication Data

Dunn, Walter S. (Walter Scott), 1928–
   Hitler's nemesis : the Red Army, 1930–45 / Walter S. Dunn, Jr.
      p. cm. — (Stackpole military history series)
   Includes bibliographical references and index.
   ISBN 978-0-8117-3543-8
   1. Soviet Union. Raboche-Krest'ianskaia Krasnaia Armiia—History—World War, 1939–1945. 2. World War, 1939–1945—Soviet Union. I. Title.
   UA772.D8 2009
   940.54'1247—dc22
                                        2008020350

Contents

Foreword

Fifty years have passed since the end of the Second World War, a conflict whose scope, ferocity, destructiveness, and consequences were unprecedented. Quite naturally, much has been written about the war. It has been analyzed repeatedly from the political, social, economic, and military perspectives. Guilt has been assessed and reassessed by historians and political scientists alike. Civilian and military participants have explained in their memoirs how and why they acted as they did. Biographies have laid bare the mind and soul of military leaders and dissected their feats and failures, and many novelists have tried to capture the challenges and horror of war from a human perspective. All but a few have failed.

Much has been written, as well, about the purely military realm. Campaigns and battles, leaders and the led, and military organizations from army to platoon have received their due. Yet, after all these years of close investigation and the publication of hundreds of volumes, both good and bad, two yawning gaps in our knowledge of the war remain to be filled. The first, analysis of the military science or art of war, or what makes forces function as they do, is quite natural and understandable. The victorious Western powers were democracies, and democracies classically are prone to forget conflicts once they have ended. Nor, by their very nature, do they dwell on the intricacies of war while at peace, for military establishments in democracies rapidly demobilize and attention shifts to postwar reconstruction. The other victorious power, the Soviet Union, did produce volumes of detailed military analysis (since Marxism-Leninism treated war as a rational subject for scientific analysis), but much of this analysis was treated as a national resource, classified, and withheld from public view. What Russian analysis that did appear was thorough but both inaccessible and mistrusted in the West. The few Soviet works published in English tended to be somewhat superficial and highly politicized.

The second gap, and the most damaging from the standpoint of understanding why the war turned out as it did, was the lack of detailed information concerning the actual course and nature of combat on the Eastern Front, or, what the Soviets call the Soviet-German Front. Here, for nearly four years, massive forces struggled in a contest that, to a great extent, determined the ultimate outcome of the war. By virtue of the constructive work of a host of war participants and postwar historians, we do possess a clear view of the war from the German perspective. The von Mansteins, Guderians, Mellenthins, and von Sengers wrote vivid memoirs and studies of campaigns and operations. More ambitious historical surveys by Albert Seaton, Carl Ziemke, Allen Clark, and others reflect the highest standards of scholarship and have become classics in their own right.

But all of these works suffer from the same shortcomings that characterize Western knowledge of the Soviet-German Front in general. The authors, participants or historians alike, have been denied fully half of the requisite sources upon which to base their accounts, specifically the Soviet half. Hence they portray the German Army in mortal combat against a faceless, featureless, and numerous foe, so numerous, in fact, as to mitigate against further analysis and to predetermine the outcome of conflict. Only the classic survey of Malcolm MacIntosh, and the epic tomes of John Erickson have captured the war from a Soviet perspective. And these works, although they have withstood the test of time, could not tell the entire story, for Soviet historians themselves did not know it.

Details on the Soviet conduct of war were available to a considerable extent in a vast collection of Soviet open source materials on the war—a veritable deluge of books, including general histories, memoirs, campaign and battle studies, unit histories, etc. Western historians, however, seldom used them, either because they were in Russian and were difficult to obtain, or because they did not believe them, given the highly politicized nature of the few English-language Russian sources that were readily available. In fact, and perhaps ironically, the mass of Soviet material was surprisingly accurate, although somewhat incomplete. Names (generally), dates, occurrences, and descriptions of military actions were correct; comparative strengths, outcomes, losses, and perspectives often were not.

Western historians who knew the Russian language, who had access to Russians works, and who possessed the patience to test what was said against German, Japanese, and other archival materials could fill in the gaps and reconstruct a more accurate view. However, these historians were, and still are, few in number. Walter Dunn is notable among these few.

Given these historiographical realities, Walter Dunn has employed time-tested methods of judging Soviet sources against German archival materials to prepare this massive work, which fills a major gap in our understanding of the Red Army at war. Through tedious and painstaking research in the German archives and a vast number of Soviet military books, some formerly classified, he has reconstructed the form and shape of the Red Army during the war years. By adding flesh and sinew to what had formerly seemed a gaunt skeleton, he has placed recognizable faces on that great grey mass of men whom the German Army fought against and of whom Western historians wrote.

Here, laid out in detail for the reader, are the infantry, armor, artillery, and cavalry formations which waged the war, and the multitude of supporting forces which enabled the Red Army to survive and emerge victorious after four years of struggle. Dunn relates the agonizingly slow and costly process of reforming and restructuring the Red Army, which transformed it from the ponderous and ineffective force that suffered devastating losses in Operation barbarossa to that potent armor-tipped force that traversed Poland in less than three weeks in early 1945. The message that proper force structure is a vital ingredient in victory should not be lost on historians or those who structure modern armies.

The detail and scholarship evident in this volume will earn for it the accolade of the "last word" in Red Army organization and structure until that day when the archive doors swing wide open. Even then, I am convinced there will not be much to add.

David Glantz

Preface

S*econd Front Now 1943*, published in 1981, presented the thesis that the second front was possible in 1943 and desirable from the Western point of view. The conclusion of this study is that the Soviets did not need, and Stalin did not want, a second front in 1943, at least in France. Although most Russians would have welcomed the assistance to reduce casualties, there is reason to believe that Stalin did not want an earlier invasion and subsequent movement far to the east of the meeting point of the two armies, even if more Russian casualties occurred. The underlying thesis of both books is the refutation of the charges that Franklin D. Roosevelt and George C. Marshall were tools of the Communist conspiracy in advocating the opening of the second front in 1943.

Military history takes three forms: operational, personal, and institutional. The best military history incorporates all three. Operational history relates the movements and the battles. Personal history emphasizes heroism, the horror of war, death, and destruction. Institutional history describes units—how and why they were formed, their function, and how well they performed. This work emphasizes institutional history, almost to the exclusion of the other two forms.

One must keep in mind when writing military history that the basic purpose of the military was to kill people and destroy property. Both actions are illegal in civilized society, but society grants the military the license to perform these acts either because of a need for a group to protect itself from another or to pursue its national self-interest. While defensive wars are easy to justify, conflicts entered for national self-interest are not. It must be proved that a condition exists that would in the long term result in harm to the nation. In both cases it is essential that a nation possess an efficient instrument to protect itself and carry out its national policy. The more efficient the army and its weapons, the quicker the war will end. Fewer casualties and less destruction result, as, for example, in the German campaign of May 1940. A long-drawn-out war of attrition results when the technologically superior force cannot quickly overcome the

weaker party, especially if the weaker party is highly motivated. The war
on the Eastern Front was an example of this.

Motivation and good morale are essential to an army. A highly motivated army may in the long run prevail over the better equipped rival.
Napoleon considered morale at a ratio of three-to-one over other factors.
Morale is not the exclusive property of one nation nor does it remain
constant. Morale varies from one individual to another and at different
times in the same individual. The United States, Germany, Great Britain,
and the Soviet Union all believed that the high morale of their troops in
World War II contributed to successful battles. In this study, references to
the morale of the Red Army have been made when known and when
appropriate to explain the failure or success of a unit. However, the
major concern is the material aspect.

Because operations were the test and battles were decided on the
basis of effectiveness, frequent references have been made to battles and
campaigns, but without detail. The author assumes that the reader has a
working knowledge of the events of World War II and references are
made to operations on that assumption. The book is organized topically
rather than chronologically, resulting in a certain amount of repetition.
For example, the Battle of Kursk appears on many pages; if the battle was
fully described each time, the book would become very tedious.

Reconstructing the evolution of the Red Army was a challenging
endeavor, as information was voluminous but fragmented. Various sources
were often contradictory. The major task was to scan thousands of pages,
cards, and microfilm frames and assemble the information in a con-
densed and concise form that could be interpreted. Some of the data
have been summarized in tables in the book, but they represent only a
small fraction of the vast detail accumulated, recorded, and indexed in a
computer database.[1]

Enormous amounts of information were available, but the quality
varied. Soviet sources included the *Soviet Military Encyclopedia*, several
multivolume histories, the *Military History Journal*, and hundreds of unit
histories and memoirs.[2] Over forty rolls (about 40,000 frames) of the
Captured German Records Microfilm dealt exclusively with the Red
Army.[3] The British still classify the Red Army files because the means of
obtaining the information during the Second World War are still sensi-
tive. The few items that have been made public were based on German
sources. American intelligence files have not been opened. The U.S.
Army published TM 30-430, a technical manual describing the Red Army
in 1945 and 1946, based on German intelligence files.

Many excellent monographs have been published on various branches of the Red Army, on weapons, and on the economic development of the Soviet Union. The information in the monographs has been compared with Russian publications and German intelligence data. A computer database of over 6,000 unit histories including all armies, corps, divisions, brigades, and tank and artillery regiments was assembled. These units constituted most of the Soviet combat strength. The task was made easier because the Soviets usually assigned unit numbers in consecutive order, and blocks of numbers were used for specific types of units. Random five-digit numbers were used for field post office numbers. Changing the number or name of a unit was limited by the amount of confusion created—for example, with mail delivery. The German Fremde Heer Ost (FHO), the German intelligence service, maintained a card file of Soviet Field Post Office numbers that remained constant even though the designation of a unit might have been changed. The level of accuracy of the database, including assumptions based on patterns, is well over 95 percent, based on the percentage of changes resulting from new information. Most changes were of minor significance—for example, a division may have moved from one army to another a month earlier than previously assumed.

The practice of maintaining unit histories of both friendly and opposing forces was formalized by Napoleon. His staff maintained detailed records of every regiment including officers, history, and state of readiness. Poirier and Conner's *Red Army Order of Battle*, an outstanding pioneer work on the Red Army in World War II, used the files of FHO, the *Soviet Military Encyclopedia*, and German and Russian published materials to create unit histories of divisions and larger units.[4] However, information in printed publications cannot be manipulated to find patterns.

The computer provides flexibility and simplifies the accumulation of data. A single published source may yield over a thousand possible new entries. One source alone provided the writer with over 50,000. However, most entries were already in the file and needed only verification, a matter of a few seconds. Very little documentation was possible. To create footnotes for each entry would have resulted in over 1 million footnotes! Even with the use of two-, three-, and four-character codes for most of the entries, the file contains seven megabytes (7 million characters)—the equivalent of nearly a million words.

The FHO maintained a similar file of unit histories on KARDEX cards. In early 1943 the Germans replaced the first set of cards started before June 1941. The number of cards used for each unit in the first set was reduced to two by the elimination of many sections—for example, the ethnic composition and the name of the commanders. A synopsis of the information on the first card was transferred to the new cards. Because many cards were filling up in late 1944, a third set presumably was created that formed the basis for many of the surviving summaries. The cards were filed in KARDEX file cabinets that made adding data convenient but sorting into new arrangements difficult. Summaries were made by flipping through the cards and counting, a time-consuming and relatively inaccurate process.

The German information came from spies, prisoners of war, intercepts of radio transmissions by units, Soviet publications and broadcasts, and captured documents. The level of accuracy is very high and the file is excellent from an historical point of view. The data pass the tests of historical validity, as the records were made at the time by persons familiar with the events with no motive to distort the facts and in a form that could not be altered without detection. When the German information was checked against available Soviet data, remarkably few irregularities surfaced. Some conflicting data from prisoners of war were indicated on the German cards as of doubtful veracity. Most disagreements resulted from the omission of data in the Soviet publications.

The FHO compiled the data for operational purposes, to provide the German high command with a up-to-date picture of the Red Army. However, much of the data came from cooperative prisoners or captured documents relating to conditions days or months earlier, too late for use by field commanders. Gehlen, the chief of the FHO, used the data to develop forecasts of Russian intentions and potential strength, conclusions often ignored. For historians the German intelligence files were a viable substitute for access to the Russian archives. Although far from complete, the German records provided valid data to verify or discredit Soviet publications.

Many individuals have been of immeasurable assistance in completing this work. The consultations with Col. David Glantz and Prof. James Goff have been invaluable. My many conversations with Gen. Albert C. Wedemeyer concerning the military-political situation in 1942 and 1943 provided an insight that could come from no other source. David McNamara, Robert Volz, Douglas Burgmeister, and many others have provided information and encouragement.

No scholarly work could succeed without resources. The librarians of the Memorial Library of the University of Wisconsin were unstinting in their support. Perhaps no one has contributed as much as my wife, who has read the manuscript many times and helped turn the mass of detail into a readable piece.

Introduction

The Red Army was the only army that could defeat the Wermacht in World War II by conventional means. To defeat a foe as skillful as the Germans required advanced weapons in sufficient quantity and an army of at least 5 million men in Europe willing to take enormous losses. The British and the Americans could never have accepted such heavy casualties to defeat the Germans. Public opinion in both countries would have balked at a war dragging on for years with millions of casualties. The Russians suffered heavy casualties, nearly 6.9 million killed and died of wounds and sickness; and 4.6 million missing, of whom only 2,775,000 returned after the war. It took a concerted effort by the British and the Americans to overcome about 100 German divisions from 1943 to 1945. If the other 200-plus divisions had come from the Eastern Front, the Allies would have been in dire straits. The question remains whether the atomic bomb would have been used in Europe.

On the other hand, the Red Army was able to cope with the full power of Germany and its satellites. In the summer of 1943 practically the entire German Army was on the Eastern Front. The occupation force in France had only one combat-worthy division and the few divisions in Sicily had only recently organized. With this knowledge Stalin saw that he would be the victor and his main concern turned to the postwar world. Even though Allied assistance would have reduced Russian casualties, he had little concern. In April 1945 the Red Army could have waited on the Oder and let the Americans take Berlin, saving the Russians 250,000 killed and wounded. Instead, Stalin insisted on a race to be first between the First White Russian Front and the First Ukrainian Front, needlessly increasing casualties.

The three keys to Soviet victory in World War II were the strength of its organization, the availability of weapons and supplies, and the powerful presence of supporting combat units. This study details the first key—the units and how, when, and why they were formed. The cohesion of units from rifle group to army group enabled poorly educated and unsophisticated Russian peasants and workers, often much older and less physically fit than their counterparts in other armies, to defeat the German Army. The symbols of the unit's significance in the Red Army abound: the swearing-in ceremony in the presence of the regimental flag, the awarding of honorific names to regiments and divisions commemorating the taking of a city, and the passing of unit traditions to new formations after the original unit disappeared. The honorific titles remained with a division even though it changed its number and function.

The other keys—supply and supporting arms—are mentioned in developing the central theme but require separate studies. The purpose of this work is to relate how the Red Army was organized and functioned in World War II. As a result of the study, it will become apparent that by early 1943 the Red Army was able to defeat the German Army without military action by the West. Russian strategy from then on was dictated by politics and by the position of the Soviet Union in the postwar world.

A Soviet military writer has outlined the factors that determined a nation's ability to win a war:[1]

1. The economic base
2. Technological competence
3. Military doctrine and tradition
4. Geographic environment
5. Ability and experience of personnel
6. The comparative power of the enemy

An advantageous position in a majority of these areas was necessary for victory. The Soviet government addressed all of these factors in the 1930s and early 1940s, and by early 1943 had achieved an advantage in all areas.

A strong economic base was created by the five-year plans that developed heavy industry and adopted mass-production techniques. In June 1941 Germany, with the addition of the economic power of its occupied countries, was far stronger than the Soviet Union. The loss of western Russia in 1941 further depleted the Soviet economic base. However, by Draconian measures and concentrated effort, Russian military production surpassed German production by early 1943.

Industrial technological competence, the second factor, was acquired from technical assistance contracts with the Americans in the 1930s. Military technology was gained through cooperative activity with the German Army in the 1920s at air bases and tank training grounds in the Soviet Union. Battlefield competence was strengthened by experience in the first two years of the Great Patriotic War. At Kursk in July 1943 the Russians seized the initiative and held it until the end of the war.

Tradition came from a blend of the czarist army and the revolutionary armies of the new government. During the war more and more of the prerevolutionary traditions were reintroduced to the Red Army. Doctrine was developed during the 1930s and in the first two years of the war. Soviet military leaders learned from the concepts being developed in the West and from actual experience fighting the Japanese and the Finns.

The fourth factor, geographic environment, was fixed, but Soviet strategy and tactics were developed to make the fullest use of the environmental advantages and to compensate for the disadvantages. The ability and experience of the personnel, the fifth factor, was improved through the reformation of the Red Army in the 1930s, though it did not reach the point of equality with the Germans until 1943.

With regard to the last factor, comparative power, the Russians began an armaments race with the Germans in the early 1930s. After eight years of investing in heavy industry, Russia switched to manufacturing weapons in 1937. The Germans had a significant head start and retained their superiority in quality and quantity in 1941. The Russians overcame their deficit by early 1943. In early 1943 five of the six factors turned in favor of the Soviet Union, leading to eventual victory. The sixth, geography, had always been favorable to the Russians, but full advantage was taken of the climate and the terrain in offensive operations in the last two years.

Two major elements led to Russian victory: production and manpower. The strength of the Soviet economy, created in large measure by American technical assistance in the 1930s, enabled the Russians to outproduce the Germans. An efficient military organization placed the fruits of production in the right place at the right time. The production methods were learned from the Americans, but the organization of manpower was homegrown.

Little has been written of the war on the Eastern Front by Western authors because of a lack of access to the Soviet archives. There is little doubt that the war was lost for Germany on the Eastern Front. By the end of 1943 the Germans had little hope for a victory, even though the Allied invasion was six months away. How could a backward country, the Soviet Union, defeat Germany, one of the greatest industrial powers of the world, having probably the finest trained and equipped army of World War II? The most popular opinion in the West has been that masses of Russian soldiers attacked the German defenses until the Germans were overcome. The Soviets, on the other hand, emphasize the superiority of the socialist system and the heroism of the individual inspired by Communist fervor.

The popular Western image of the Red Army during World War II was a huge army of illiterate, ill-trained, ill-clad, poorly equipped, subhuman soldiers who fought because they feared the NKVD machine guns at the rear. Victory for the Red Army as viewed by the West came only by trading ten Russian lives for one German life. This image continues in popular Western literature.

The Soviet image of the Red Army is almost as distorted. In communist publications, the Red Army was composed of super-patriotic, idealistic young men who had to be restrained from forfeiting their lives by needless acts of personal bravery. According to the Soviets, the real problem was not urging the troops to sacrifice their lives but restraining them from doing so needlessly. The task of the officers was to instruct them to be better soldiers and to give their lives for a reason. The Soviet position was that the soldiers were imbued with patriotic fervor based on faith in the socialist system and the Communist Party.

Closer to the truth was that the Soviet Union outproduced the Germans and, willing to take losses, overwhelmed them. Was it possible for a country with less than half the steel-making capacity of Germany and its satellites to win the battle of production? Lend-lease was part of the answer, as it provided Russia with trucks, locomotives, rails, and other goods that would have absorbed much of Soviet production capacity.

The question still remains: How could a country that was not able to provide rifles for its army in World War I outproduce most of Europe only 25 years later? In the intervening period Russia had been devastated by many crises: defeat in World War I, foreign occupation from 1917 until 1919, a civil war that lasted until 1921, and a Communist regime that eliminated the professional class, including army officers, engineers, government officials, transportation specialists, and almost every other person with the skills necessary to make an economy work smoothly—not once, but twice, after the Revolution and in the purges of the late 1930s. The Soviet Union was in chaos by the late 1920s with millions dying of starvation and industry at a standstill.

During the 1920s, the Communist leadership swallowed its pride and invited foreign concessions, encouraging companies to come into Russia and operate coal mines, gold mines, factories, the telegraph system, and other businesses. Although this system spurred economic activity, the basic concept of giving foreign capitalists the right of exploitation was not acceptable, plus profits flowed out of the Soviet Union. Cancellation of the concessions began in the late 1920s, and by the early 1930s most of the concessions were gone.

Replacing the concessions were technical assistance contracts. Coincidental with the first five-year plan, designed to modernize the Soviet economy, the Russians began signing technical assistance agreements with Western companies, primarily American, some German, and a few British, French, Swiss, and others. The agreements generally called for the company to design, build, and equip a plant and train Russians in its operation. These plants were then copied by the Russians with limited foreign help. Under these agreements the entire auto, tractor, and steel industries were expanded and modernized. Other industries also benefited from foreign expertise. By 1936, although most of the technical assistance contracts had expired and the foreigners had left, the Soviets continued to import machinery for their factories.

Foreign assistance enabled the Soviet Union to advance technologically over a half-century in the course of about eight years. Copying Western technology catapulted Russian manufacturing acumen into the twentieth century by eliminating the need for research and development and standardizing almost everything from blast furnaces to lathes. Multiple-unit construction reduced manufacturing time and cost. By the late 1930s the Soviet Union had the latest designs and the largest factories, primarily copied from the best in the United States. After the foreigners left, young Soviet engineers with little experience operated existing plants and produced copies, not only of machines but of entire plants. These factories, although plagued by inefficient operation in the late 1930s, formed the basis for the Soviet war industry in World War II, making the tanks and other weapons that defeated the Germans.

In addition to production, the other factor was manpower, which was not an exclusive Soviet advantage. There were 80 million Germans versus 200 million Soviet citizens. However, the Germans had the manpower of allied European nations and the population of the occupied zone of Russia. Russia lost over 60 million people in the first six months of the war, equalizing the ratio of manpower, 140 million Russians versus 80 million Germans plus 60 million Russians, many of whom cooperated in the German war effort. Although Russia's allies made a substantial contribution to defeating the Germans with the air war and lend-lease supplies, until June 1944 the Allies did not tie up considerable numbers of German troops. Germany's allies—Finland, Roumania, Hungary, and Italy—made major contributions to the armies on the Eastern Front.

The manpower equation was balanced by Germany's extremely wasteful and inefficient management of both industrial and human resources. Whereas the Russians extracted the last drop from their potential, the Germans only talked of total war until late in 1943. From the very beginning Russia demanded incredible sacrifices from its people. Fourteen-year-old boys, women, and invalids were employed in factories working ten-hour shifts six or seven days a week to replace men in the army. Every possible ounce of human and industrial capacity was devoted to winning the war, stripping the civilian economy of all but the barest essentials. In contrast until the very end the Germans still had the highest ratio of personal maids of any country in World War II. German women were not employed in industry to any appreciable extent and factories worked only one shift. Some teenagers served part time in antiaircraft units, but the high schools remained open. On the other hand, the Germans continued to manufacture luxuries such as furniture and other civilian goods and obtained more nonessential products from the occupied countries. Even in the captive nations, life was probably more palatable than it was for a Russian transferred to one of the new industrial centers in the Ural Mountains.

The Red Army seldom had more than 6.5 million troops directly involved on the Eastern Front. The total in the armed forces was usually about 10 million. The German and satellite armies facing the Russians varied from period to period, but seldom were below 3 million and sometimes exceeded that number. The Russians did enjoy a two-to-one margin overall and a higher margin in select areas. The cost of winning a war against an opponent as powerful and skillful as Germany was high. Ten million Russian soldiers died, compared to about 3 million Germans and their allies killed on the Eastern Front. Russian losses of three-to-one were the price of attacking a highly proficient defender.[2]

When the regular divisions were destroyed by the Germans in 1941, thousands of young Communists were dispatched from the cities to instill patriotic fervor and to gain time through heroic action, sometimes fighting to the last man.[3] On the other hand, many Russian soldiers, hating the Stalinist regime, surrendered readily, believing that the Germans were liberators.[4] The Soviet soldier did not have an unquenchable patriotic love for the Communist Party and the socialist system. The fact that the Germans were able to recruit hundreds of thousands of Soviet citizens to serve as service troops in the rifle divisions, as well as to fight the partisans, to work as laborers in Germany, and even to serve as soldiers in Ost Battalions in France, indicated that there was disaffection with the Soviet system, especially in the Baltic States, the Caucasus, and the Ukraine.

The Red Army men fought as most soldiers, not with outstanding brilliance but with persistent determination. The Soviet soldier fought in all likelihood because of national pride and hatred of the Germans.[5]

Knowledge that the Germans treated prisoners inhumanely became widely known after the first few months of the war.[6] In the early months of the war the Germans had captured millions of prisoners with ease. After the record of brutality and atrocities became known, the prisoner bag dropped appreciably. The brutal policies of the Germans revealed in towns recaptured in the winter of 1941–42 also instilled a desire for revenge in the troops.

Production and manpower were brought into play by the Red Army. In the early months of the war the Red Army leadership was inexperienced and the men untrained. By 1943 combat experience had changed the Red Army into a professionally led, capable, trained army. By the end of the war it was equipped with the most cost-effective weapons used by any army during World War II. To believe otherwise is to be faced with an anomaly. How could subhuman masses defeat what was undoubtedly the best tactically trained army of the war, the German Army?

To make use of the production and manpower, the Russians had to improve their military skills beginning in the 1930s. First a doctrine for the overall strategy on the conduct of war had to be devised. Considerable debate followed on tactics resulting from experience in Spain, the Mongolian border, and Finland. Then weapons had to be designed to implement the tactics, and units organized to utilize the weapons. Finally, and equally crucial, a system was planned to provide manpower and produce the weapons, munitions, and other supplies to create units and to replace losses.

The keys to victory were the organization, support, and supply of the Red Army. All three had to be accomplished in the most cost-effective manner. Although the industrial base of the Soviet Union was but a fraction of the potential industrial base of the combined industrial nations of Europe under Hitler's sway, what made the difference was the Russian ability to reduce every weapon and organization to the minimum standard to accomplish the mission. The Soviet government had learned the value of utter simplicity through necessity during the period following the Revolution of 1917 and the Civil War. The need to restore the devastation and the enormous effort to reconstitute the country under the two five-year plans taught the lessons of maximum return for investment; the resources used to accomplish an objective had to be reduced to the bare minimum.

Russian weapons were simple, not because the soldiers were too stupid to operate complex weapons but because anything that could not offer advantages to compensate for the cost was eliminated. An example of minimum quality to accomplish the task was the T-34 tank that was extremely uncomfortable for the crew. The men in the turret perched on seats suspended from the turret side because there was no floor. The base of the tank was filled with shells covered with mats. After firing the first few rounds, the loader jumped from his seat and scrambled around on the bottom of the tank while the turret revolved above him. However, the gun and the armor were excellent and the tank was considered the best one used during World War II.

Throughout the war the number of man-hours and material needed to produce a T-34 steadily declined by simplifying the design. Few changes were made to improve the performance at the cost of production. In contrast, German weapons became increasingly complex. Six months passed from the time the Tiger was first used in battle until it was comparatively free of technical flaws. The Panther was still not free of problems at the Battle of Kursk, yet both tanks were marvels of technical innovation.

German commanders, with large service organizations, continually complained about the lack of engines and other spare parts to keep their tanks and motor vehicles running. Hitler was castigated for being more concerned about making large numbers of new tanks rather than maintaining the existing ones. The Russians concentrated on making simple, easy-to-maintain tanks with a limited service life, replacing worn or damaged ones with new. Crippled vehicles were stripped of usable parts and scrapped or sent to the rear to be remanufactured in repair plants. Service units were kept to a minimum. Rarely if ever did a prisoner mention the lack of spare parts as being a factor in the shortage of equipment available to the front.

Prisoners did comment on the marvelous engine in the British tanks, but the average life of a tank on the Eastern Front was only six months. What was the point of putting a beautiful engine designed to last for years in a tank that would be destroyed before the engine was broken in? English tanks were used for training where long engine life paid off in training drivers. The "root of the matter" was cost-effectiveness. In what manner could human and physical resources be used to the greatest advantage? The choice was either a single beautiful tank with excellent optics and comfortable crew facilities or four ugly giants. The Germans opted for the former and lost the production battle, one of the keys to victory.

Another key to Russian victory was organization. Again the objective was to obtain the most cost-effective method of employing men and weapons under the prevailing conditions. During the 1930s the Russian military organization was in a constant state of flux, reflecting the radical changes in strategic and tactical thinking. Changes were still under way in mid-1941 and contributed a great deal to the early Russian defeats. However, a steady stream of new organizations were developed, tried, and if faulty, discarded, but if successful, replicated endlessly. Organizations were drastically altered to reflect the increasing number of weapons and the means to employ them versus the limited manpower position. While the number of riflemen in the division steadily dropped arithmetically, the number of weapons multiplied geometrically. The Red Army of April 1945 was a far more powerful instrument than in June 1941.

Keeping constantly in mind the matching developments in the German, British, and U.S. armies, one can see the emergence of a powerful machine devoted to the defeat of Hitler. In the end success was achieved by overpowering numbers of weapons, not men, but paid for by tragic losses of the latter. By the spring of 1943 the Red Army had halted the Manstein counteroffensive that had drained the Germans of their strategic reserve, the occupation army in France. The final defeat of Hitler was merely a matter of time.

How much time was more a political than a military decision. The Western Allies could have hastened the end but chose not to. Stalin was afforded additional time to position the Red Army in the heartland of Germany to prevent a second *Cordon Sanitaire* similar to that created by the Treaty of Versailles in 1919. When the war finally ended in May 1945, the Soviet Union was able to erect an iron curtain, holding captive millions of people of Eastern Europe for more than forty years.

Protracting the war favored the Soviet Union and worked to the disadvantage of Britain and the United States. Prolonging the war gave Hitler an additional year or more to pursue the Final Solution. Most of the Jews killed in the Holocaust died in the last two years of the war. How many could have been saved by ending the war earlier? Churchill and Roosevelt made many choices during the war. Most were not dictated by circumstances, as many would argue, but came from a careful weighing of resources and desirable outcomes. Gross underestimation of the power of the Soviet Union and the Red Army was a major flaw in the calculations of the Western leaders. Rather than being worn down by the Germans, the Red Army grew stronger in the final years. The heavy Russian civilian casualties came in the early years of the war; there were no Soviet civilian casualties after the Germans were driven out in 1944. The goals of the West would have been best served by ending the war promptly in 1943 or early 1944. One of the reasons it failed to do so was a misconception of the Red Army. This study seeks to correct that misconception.

CHAPTER 1

Soviet Military Doctrine

Soviet military doctrine incorporated strategy, operational art, and tactics. Strategy was designed to achieve long-range objectives and was based on a realistic assessment of resources, strengths, and weaknesses, as well as potential enemies. Operational art was the Soviet term for the methods and between grand strategy and small-unit tactics. Tactics were the means to achieve short-range goals necessary to reach the long-range objectives.

Should a strategic theory be defective (for example, Hitler's far too ambitious objectives for the resources at his disposal), a nation would be defeated. If commanders lacked skill in the operational art and could not make the best use of their resources (for example, at Izyum in 1942), disaster occurred. If the tactics did not match the abilities of the troops, repeated tactical defeats ensued.

Strategy, operational art, and tactics were each a means to attain objectives and were subject to a realistic appraisal of resources. A blitzkrieg could not be conducted if an army had only a few tanks and no means of production. Keying weapons and units to established theory was complex. The French Army attempted to change its tactical use of tanks in 1940 from supporting the infantry to acting as an offensive force in newly created armored divisions. French tanks, designed for infantry support, had neither the speed nor the fuel capacity to work independently. The newly formed armored divisions lacked adequate service units to provide fuel, supplies, and transport. Therefore, the divisions failed to make a significant contribution. Strategy, operational art, and tactics were dictated by available resources.

Soviet strategic doctrine treated peace and war as integral parts of a whole. Success in averting or conducting a war depended on the status of the army before an outbreak of war and on the efficiency of mobilizing additional men and material during a war.[1] During the 1920s the Soviet Union was weak, lacking many resources, even sufficient food. In 1926, A. A. Svechin, chief of staff of the Red Army, advocated the strategic defense. A strategic defense absorbed the first blow with covering forces

1

and then the reserves would attack. The 1929 Soviet field regulations established the strategic defense as doctrine.[2]

Svechin fell out of favor in 1931 when he attacked the commissar system that shared command of a Russian unit between the military commander and the political officer. Stalin sent Svechin to a labor camp and promoted Tukhachevskii, who had objected to Svechin's defensive ideas, from command of the Leningrad Military District to the General Staff in May 1931.[3] To correspond with the growth of industrial strength, Tukhachevskii developed a doctrine for deep penetration with a mechanized army that he had proposed in the 1920s. V. K. Triandafilov and G. S. Isserson had published the doctrine in a book in 1929.[4] Isserson outlined a strategy that had the objective of surrounding and destroying large bodies of the enemy as follows:[5]

1. Gain local superiority of from three-to-one to five-to-one by thinning out dormant sectors and concentrating forces in the decisive sector.
2. Demoralize the enemy defensive forces with a massive artillery barrage.
3. Follow up the artillery with a tank-supported infantry assault to open a gap in the enemy line.
4. Send in a second echelon with engineers to make the gap passable for mobile units.
5. Send in mechanized and cavalry units to exploit and attack deep defenses.

The major controversy centered on the objective of the mechanized and cavalry units. The conservative doctrine was to turn in quickly and encircle the enemy in the forward defense line. In a blitzkrieg the tanks penetrated deep into the enemy communications zone, destroying the rear services, and finally turned to surround entire armies. Tukhachevskii supported the theory of deep penetration. The more traditional approach called for tactics to destroy the enemy forces piecemeal.[6] The conservatives feared that the exploiting forces with open flanks would be exposed to counterattack by enemy reserves. Therefore, the exploiting force should turn in quickly while it still had sufficient forces to guard its flanks. The organization of the Red Army would be profoundly influenced by the choice of theory. The Field Regulations of 1936 reflected Tukhachevskii's ideas of deep penetration.

Military doctrine was revolutionized by the tank and the "elastic defense" developed on the Western Front in World War I. An elastic defense abandoned the continuous line of trenches and substituted a main line of resistance with mutually supporting strong points far enough apart to weaken the effect of artillery barrages. Attacking infantry were gradually worn down as they encountered one strong point after another. Experiments with new weapons in the 1930s also modified Soviet military doctrine rooted in czarist traditions. Based on an evolving doctrine in the 1930s, the Soviet Union created weapons, units, logistical organizations, and military productive capacity. Tukhachevskii began the task of retraining the army in 1935, forming military academies to teach the new doctrine. In the same year the Kharkov Tank Factory began mass producing tanks to provide the weapons.[7]

In 1931 Stalin said that Russia had been defeated in World War I because it was backward. The Soviet Union's military, culture, political system, industry, and agriculture lagged behind the other European powers. Other nations recognized Russia's weakness and could attack without fear. Stalin recognized that the new Soviet Union had to change, and Russia began to prepare for war in the 1930s with the five-year plans.[8] By 1937 Russia, with 10 percent of the world's industrial production, had become the third greatest industrial power behind the United States and Germany.[9]

The threat of German invasion was very real to the Soviets. They anticipated the three elements of Barbarossa, the drive via Kaunas and Riga to Leningrad, the drive north of the Pripet marshes via Smolensk to Moscow, and the drive south of the Pripet marshes, bypassing Kiev on the south, to the bend of the Don River.[10] If the three drives were successful, the Germans would cripple the Soviet Union, politically and economically, and control much of the population. Soviet organization, training, prewar dispositions, and mobilization plans anticipated the three-pronged attack on its political, economic, and military centers.

The conservative group opposed to Tukhachevskii was still powerful. In 1934 Voroshilov had proposed a system of fortifications along the entire border to ward off the German attack and construction was initiated. The line would absorb the first blows and give the Red Army time to mobilize according to Svechin's ideas of strategic defense. Still, the emphasis was on offensive action. Any defensive action would be limited and would soon give way to the offense.

The purge in the late 1930s removed Tukhachevskii and advocates of the large independent tank force. Under a law passed in December 1934 a suspected traitor could be arrested, tried, and, without appeal, executed in forty-eight hours. Stalin feared the growing authority of the army, and therefore in May 1937 reinstated the commissars who had been abolished in 1934. The German Gestapo had forged documents accusing Tukhachevskii of treason and sent them to the NKVD via

President Benes of Czechoslovakia. In May 1937 Tukhachevskii was arrested and later executed.[11] At the same time many other political, military, and industrial leaders were imprisoned or killed.

By the end of 1938 the senior members of the officer corps were either in prison or dead. The effect of the purge was comparable to the 1917 revolution. Most of the political, managerial, and military elite were replaced by new men, many of whom rose from obscure positions to places of power. Some succeeded—for example, Zhukov—but others failed. The atmosphere was fearful as men were forced to accuse one another to protect themselves. Men who had foreign contacts were most suspect. Officers who had gained valuable combat experience in Spain were also under suspicion.[12] The conservative friends of Stalin led by Voroshilov dominated the army.

Marshal B. M. Shaposhnikov became chief of the Soviet General Staff in 1938. A new military doctrine called for offensive rather than defensive action, but the emphasis was on turning in quickly rather than deep penetration. In 1938, S. N. Krasil'nikov wrote "A Prospective Plan for the Development of the Red Army between 1938 and 1942." The plan, approved by Shaposhnikov and Voroshilov, called for an increase in offensive forces. Large tank units were created for strategic purposes. Parachute troops, additional infantry, and artillery were designed for offensive use.[13] On March 24, 1938, Shaposhnikov completed his strategic plan calling for an offensive strategy and reshaping the army to accomplish this goal by 1942.[14]

In November 1938 the Main Military Council approved a strategic deployment plan submitted by Shaposhnikov. The plan, anticipating an attack by both Germany and Japan, would contain the Japanese in the east while the main force defeated the Germans in the west. To accomplish the objective, a large, well-equipped force would be maintained in the west aided by a belt of fortifications. The covering force would defend until the mass of the army mobilized and launched a counteroffensive. The anticipated scenario called for the infantry in their fortified line to stop the German attack and the tank forces to launch a massive counteroffensive.[15]

A major setback to strategic planning occurred when General D. G. Pavlov returned from Spain in 1939 and, based on his experience, recommended the elimination of large mechanized units.[16] After the German campaigns in Poland and France proved the efficacy of the blitzkrieg, Stalin reversed course and authorized the creation of a deep-penetration tank force. In 1940 Stalin ordered the formation of twenty-nine mechanized corps including sixty tank divisions with a total of

30,000 tanks. In May 1940 the German panzer force had only ten panzer divisions with 3,000 tanks. The grandiose Russian plan would have produced a tank force much more powerful than the Germans, but it was far from complete in June 1941. Even though Hitler had formed ten additional panzer divisions by June 1941, he reduced by half the number of tanks in each division, leaving the total at about 3,000 tanks.

In 1941 the Soviet military position was weak. Although the large size of the Red Army had a deterrent effect on Hitler, the rapid expansion had resulted in a low level of training. New Russian units were equipped with obsolete weapons because production of modern weapons could not match the increased requirements. In 1941 Soviet industry was still testing new weapons and shifting to mass production of new models. In 1941, 78 percent of the aircraft and 50 percent of the tanks in the border districts were either obsolete or obsolescent.[17] Another disadvantage was that the purge had removed most of the leadership of the army. Overconfidence further impaired the Russians. Even in March 1941 the Russians believed that they could halt the German attack and assume the offensive. This confidence led to offensive troop dispositions unsuitable for defense in June.[18]

In the 1930s strategy and tactics were evolving in Germany as well. German strategic planning also dictated that the offensive was the optimum strategy. Only through rapid, decisive campaigns could Germany win a world conflict before a British blockade strangled the country. Two tactical schools emerged—one, supported by Guderian and agreeing with Fuller, advocated a breakthrough followed by deep penetration to disrupt communications and destroy the enemy's cohesion. This theory rightly deserves the descriptive name of blitzkrieg, for it led to the rapid collapse of the enemy with few casualties on either side. The campaign in Belgium in 1940 and the drive to the channel ports were classic examples.

The official offensive doctrine supported by most of the senior German commanders was wedge and pocket, "*keil und kessel*," or encircle and destroy the enemy.[19] The tank forces broke through the defense line at two points, and after a limited advance the two points turned in and forged a pocket. The tanks remained on the outer ring to prevent rescue from the outside, while the infantry formed an inner ring to reduce the pocket. The result was the capture of large numbers of enemy troops.[20]

The German plan for the invasion of the Soviet Union called for both deep penetration and wedge-and-pocket tactics. The three separate drives toward Leningrad, Moscow, and Rostov sought to paralyze the country's political and economic base, a blitzkrieg strategy. However, the major objective was the destruction of the Red Army by wedge and pocket. The

Germans used the wedge and pocket in the advance toward Moscow. Unlike the lightning strokes in the West that disintegrated the French and British with few casualties and many prisoners, in Russia the German infantry reduced the pockets by bitter fighting with heavy casualties on both sides.

While primarily concerned with offensive actions, the Germans developed a defensive doctrine in the 1930s that was a revised form of the World War I elastic defense. The objective was to spread the troops to make them less vulnerable to artillery barrages. A defensive line involved four areas. First came the advance position, then the outpost zone, followed by the main line of resistance (*Hauptkampflinie*, or HKL in German), and finally a reserve line. The advance position concealed the location of the HKL and prevented advances by small enemy forces to the HKL. The troops in the advance position withdrew in the face of a major attack.

Next, the outpost positions were two or three kilometers behind the advance position and held by weak detachments of infantry to shield the HKL from enemy reconnaissance. Again, the troops withdrew in the face of heavy attack. The HKL, located two to five kilometers behind the outpost positions, was four to six kilometers deep with individual strong points constructed for all-around defense with barbed wire and mines. The reserve position, located behind the HKL, served as a second line in the event the enemy drove through the HKL. Counterattack troops waited in the reserve position.

Ideally, the HKL was located on a reverse slope—the side of a hill away from the enemy lines, protected from direct fire and observation. The theory was that the defense would wear down an attacker gradually as he penetrated the first three zones. A counterattack by reserve troops would repel the attacker before he broke through the final zone. Counterattacks were launched immediately to restore the situation if any penetration took place.[21]

The elastic defense had worked well in World War I until the tank appeared. The tanks equipped the attacker with sustained firepower through the entire system and enabled the Allies to penetrate the deep defensive zones. The major issue in the late 1930s, therefore, was to adjust the elastic defense to tank attacks. The goal was to separate the infantry from its supporting tanks. The defenders concentrated small-arms fire on the attacking infantry while evading its tanks. Once the defenders drove away the infantry, the isolated tanks were destroyed by antitank guns located in the rear of the HKL or antitank rifles. Natural and prepared obstacles channeled the tanks into killing grounds and minefields also destroyed unsuspecting tanks.[22]

The German and Soviet doctrines shared many ideas. In June 1941 the major problem for the Russians was how they could stop the Germans when everyone else had failed. The Soviet strategy in June 1941 was to halt the invasion as close to the border as possible and to launch a counteroffensive. The Red Army stationed forty-eight divisions in the tactical zone (10–50 kilometers deep) near the border and fifteen divisions in the intermediate zone (50–300 kilometers deep) to delay the enemy and allow the country time to mobilize.[23] The troops on the border failed to hall the Germans in June 1941. The Russian units lacked training, leadership, men, and weapons. The defenses were being moved from the pre-1939 border to the new border covering the acquisitions in the Baltic States, Poland, and Bessarabia. Surprise denied the Soviet troops enough time to occupy defensive positions.[24]

Stalin accepted the loss of the frontier armies and the armies in the operation zone. Units were ordered to hold positions when threatened on the flanks instead of retreating. When a pocket resulted, the Russians held the remaining front and attempted to create an all-around defense. The Red Army units in prepared positions who had not retreated when their flanks were threatened were more difficult to dislodge. Usually the rear of the pocket collapsed first, making it difficult to escape from the pocket later. Generally the Russians held their positions until ordered to withdraw and filter through the German lines.

The second series of pockets around Smolensk resisted even longer and the German advance bogged down. The Russians stopped the Germans on the Desna River at Yelna on July 15, 1941. Russian morale improved when told that they were defending Moscow. Soviet artillery and antitank guns were better than their German counterparts and played an important role in the battles. The Katusha rocket launchers were used for the first time on July 15, giving the Germans a disagreeable surprise.[25] On August 11, 1941, the Russians launched furious counterattacks in the center, attempting to relieve the surrounded troops around Smolensk. The attack at Yelna against a thinly held line penetrated the German defenses. A counterattack by the 10th Panzer Division restored the situation by August 30. However, on September 5, the Germans gave up the Yelna salient, the first operational withdrawal by the German Army in World War II.[26] The Germans went on the defensive, and the doctrine of elastic defense came into play.

The German field commanders assumed that they would have flexibility to select positions and conduct an elastic defense that would be an infantry responsibility. They also assumed that there would be sufficient infantry available for defense in depth, creating the four zones described above. The principal threat would come from the Red Army infantry. German tanks would be held in reserve for counterattacks. These German assumptions proved wrong.[27]

At Yelna, as at other locations, the German divisions held sectors more than thirty kilometers wide. Instead of an elastic defense, there was a thin belt of widely spaced strong points defending improvised lines on unfavorable ground. Russian artillery fire destroyed the strong points, killing many German troops. Soviet attacks penetrated the thin German lines and the counterattacks faced comparatively fresh Russian forces, rather than troops weakened by driving through a deep defensive zone. The Germans did not have sufficient infantry even in August 1941 to prepare an elastic defense.[28] The Russians also halted the drives on Leningrad and Rostov. The breakthroughs there did not result in large pockets.

The final drive on Moscow in November employed a blitzkrieg strategy to break through with little concern for forming pockets. When finally stopped, the Germans had even less infantry to establish an elastic defense than in August. Any defense in depth was hindered by the critical shortage of men, supplies, and equipment, and Hitler's orders preventing withdrawal to favorable ground. The terrain and weather hampered the construction of fortifications.[29] The Russians concentrated their forces in selected areas and broke through the German defense lines. Large Russian units penetrated enemy lines, and though the Germans were able to assemble reserves and destroy most of the Russian units, the Germans lost considerable ground.[30]

In the face of Soviet attacks, the Germans began to retreat, but intense cold and reliance on horses to transport artillery and heavy weapons meant the loss of equipment. On December 16, Hitler ordered the army to hold its positions. They did not have enough troops to hold a continuous line. They held the villages and road junctions as strong points, leaving the Russians in the fields. The Russians were able to infiltrate between the strong points, but German reserves drove out the infiltrators. The tactics succeeded in part because the Russians attacked the strong points rather than bypassing them. When driven back, the Germans destroyed the villages to prevent use by the Russians.

Temperatures dropped to -4 and -13 degrees Fahrenheit in January 1942, very cold even for Russia. The snow was also unusually deep and movement off the roads was possible only on skis. The unusual weather was an advantage to the Germans, forcing the Russians to attack the villages on the roads and favored the German defenders occupying the built-up areas. The Russians had to either withdraw at dusk or spend the night in the open.[31]

The Soviets were very critical of both strategy and tactics during the winter campaign shown in a study made in 1942. The conduct of multiple offensives required more resources than were available. The reserve armies were distributed along the entire length of the front. Tanks were not concentrated in large units, but were parceled out to the field armies. As a result the Russians did not attain decisive superiority anywhere. Poor leadership and the practice of mass attacks by infantry led to unnecessary losses. The troops lacked training. Logistical arrangements were defective and promising advances were stopped for lack of supplies. Shortage of artillery shells prevented the destruction of the strong points by artillery fire.[32] Other weaknesses in Soviet tactics were evidenced by the ease with which the Germans were able to separate the infantry from tanks by small arms fire. Left alone, the tanks stopped and turned back because they were vulnerable without the infantry.[33]

Even without the infantry, the Russian tanks were difficult to destroy. The available German 37mm antitank gun could penetrate only the weaker side armor at close range. When the German antitank guns were behind the forward line, the Russian tanks could attack the German infantry before coming under fire. When the Germans placed the antitank guns too far forward, the Russian infantry shot the crews. The 88mm guns then in use were difficult to conceal because of their high silhouette. These guns had to be sited well behind the front line and therefore could not destroy Russian tanks before they reached the German lines. In the end, the infantry often had to destroy Russian tanks with explosives, a dangerous task.[34]

Field Marshal Manstein wrote after the war that the achievements of the Red Army in the winter of 1941–42 were the result of several advantages: improvement in senior and middle level commanders, a superior organization for the field army (six divisions and no corps headquarters), greater use of mortars, increased production of tanks and guns, and an efficient antitank system. The smaller rifle divisions and the new rifle brigades were within the capabilities of new inexperienced commanders.[35]

German commanders were critical of their own winter tactics. The isolated strong points were merely an expedient. The Russians infiltrated through the gaps and emerged in the German rear at full strength. When a strong point was taken, the Russians opened a large gap. German counterattacks usually came on the second day after a breakthrough, giving the Russians a full day to entrench. The German counterattack then found a powerful force. The most dangerous facet of the strong-point tactic was that it concentrated men and equipment, forming excellent targets for

Russian artillery and tanks. Although the Russians did not take full advantage of the enemy weaknesses in the winter, the Germans could not expect that lack of reaction to continue.[36]

The spring thaw halted the winter offensive, but by May 1942 the mud had dried and operations had resumed. The Russian strategy was to preempt the German offensive in the south, while maintaining a powerful defensive force in front of Moscow. Ten or more Soviet reserve armies were forming but were not ready for battle in May. Although the Russian attack at Izyum broke through, the German elastic defense was successful and halted the Soviet drive. The German forces cut the salient off at the base using conventional World War I tactics. A large pocket was formed around thousands of Russians. The Red Army had a gaping hole in the line. The Germans immediately launched their planned Operation Blau, a drive aimed at Stalingrad and the Caucasus.

German strategy in Operation Blau in the summer of 1942 was blitzkrieg in character with two divergent spearheads aimed at economic objectives. Destruction of Red Army units was not a major pan of the plan. As a result there were few pockets.[37] New Russian tactics called for withdrawal when threatened with encirclement. The Russian motorized artillery regiments escaped along with the infantry. On the negative side for the Russians, incompletely trained reserve armies thrown into the battles in the Don bend suffered heavy casualties. There were not enough antitank regiments to form adequate antitank gun lines, so tank brigades were used to reinforce the antitank defense. The German drives halted at Stalingrad on the Volga and at Mozdok in the Caucasus at the end of a slender logistical lifeline.

German defensive doctrine in 1942 was determined by the lack of infantry. The forward position in the elastic defense was eliminated because of the shortage of troops. Greater efforts were made to resist penetration of the HKL and to counterattack sooner. These changes made containment of attacks more costly in German lives. Too many troops and weapons were forward where they were subject to artillery fire, and counterattacks were launched against comparatively fresh Soviet troops.[38] Hitler's order of September 8, 1942, demanded that the troops stand and fight in the HKL, instead of withdrawing and allowing the attacker to strike at thin air.[39]

Soviet tactics were revised by Stalin's Order #301, October 8, 1942, that made fundamental changes in tactical doctrine. Tanks were concentrated at crucial points, not spread across the entire front. Tanks were not to be used in the antitank role. The primary task of the tank corps was the destruction or enemy infantry, not enemy tanks. Artillery (emphasized in the original document) was to be the primary defense against tanks. In attack, close cooperation between tanks and infantry with heavy artillery and air support was obligatory.[40] Emphasis was placed on large-scale attacks by tanks and infantry. To make these attacks possible the number of tank corps was increased from eighteen in July 1942 to twenty-five in November. Four tank armies were created along with new mechanized corps. Independent tank brigades and regiments under field army command supported the rifle divisions. Heavy tank regiments and infantry joined to break through the German lines.[41]

The Russian offensive tactics used in November 1942 began with a long artillery bombardment of the German lines. The first wave of heavy tanks and infantry destroyed German antitank guns and engaged enemy tanks. From 500 to 1,000 meters behind the first, the second wave of medium tanks carried infantry. These units eliminated any remaining strong points and passed through the first wave. The third wave had more medium tanks carrying infantry to destroy remaining strong points and to exploit the breakthrough, destroying communications and isolating units. Additional forces with light tanks protected the flanks of the breakthrough and performed reconnaissance during the exploitation phase.[42] The Red Army applied the tactics with admirable efficiency in the winter of 1942–43. The Russians followed the classic tactic of cutting off the German salient at its base and encircling the enemy forces at the tip in Stalingrad.

In February 1943 Stalin believed that he had defeated the German Army and that Germany was about to collapse. He threw all of his reserves into reckless offensives. The attempts to cut off more Germans with drives toward the Black Sea were defeated. The offensives were poorly planned and lacked strategic reserves. The Russian units were worn down by previous battles. There was little coordination between the fronts as each launched individual attacks. The field armies lacked sufficient firepower and the tank units had poor logistical support.[43]

In response to Stalingrad, Hitler denuded the forces in France and transferred 20 divisions to the Russian Front by March 1943, leaving the West open to invasion. Manstein used the fresh divisions to repulse the February offensives. Tactically, the Germans were still masters in the use of antitank gun lines and counterattacks by panzers to repulse the Russian attacks. The Russian could not cope with panzer counterattacks because they failed to move antitank guns forward with the attacking troops. The spring thaw brought operations to a halt.

In April 1943, anticipating the German offensive at Kursk, Stalin favored a preemptive strike, but Zhukov, Vassilevsky, and others argued for a strategic defense. The Russians created a complex defensive system at Kursk to absorb the German attack. After the German attack was repulsed the Red Army would launch several offensives. Kursk was a land-mark in the development of Soviet strategy, tactics, and operational skill based on experience. Better weapons, more efficient organization, and closer coordination of tanks, artillery, and infantry all contributed to the victory at Kursk.[44]

A major improvement at Kursk was the development of defense in depth, the Soviet version of the German elastic defense. The tactical defense zone consisted of two lines of defense with a total depth of fif-teen to twenty kilometers. A battalion defense area was two to two and a half kilometers wide and one and a half to two kilometers deep, and con-sisted of strong points with all-around defenses and interlocking fare with other strong points. A regimental sector was only four to five kilometers wide and a division sector eight to fourteen kilometerse wide. Compared to the defenses in front of Moscow in 1941, there were two to three times as many troops per kilometer. At Moscow there was only half a battalion of infantry and seven to twelve guns per kilometer; at Kursk, a battalion of infantry, twenty-six to forty guns and mortars, and three or four tanks or SUs per kilometer.[45]

The first goal of the defensive system was to divide the attacking tanks from the infantry and then destroy each separately before the infantry could dig in. Although the Russian defenses sapped the strength of the German attackers, some tanks penetrated the Russian forward defenses only to be counterattacked by Russian reserves. When the Ger-mans penetrated the line on the south side of the bulge, the Soviets attacked the open flanks of the advancing Germans, while the second echelon and the reserves prevented any exploitation of the break-through.[46]

By mid-July 1943, the Germans were on the defensive. German posi-tions in late 1943 consisted of two defensive lines, the HKL and the reserve, with a total depth of fifteen kilometers. The Soviets used new tac-tics to break through. On the first day of an attack the Russians breached the HKL with rifle divisions, then broke through the second line of defenses, and finally captured favorable ground from which the tank corps could launch attacks. On the second day the tank corps exploited the breakthrough, embarking on deep penetration attacks.

As more armored vehicles and guns became available, the attacking forces became more powerful. An attacking division with four to six bat-talions had a front only two or three kilometers wide with seven to twenty tanks and more than 100 guns and mortars per kilometer.[47] Fire support for the infantry increased dramatically. Artillery and mortars moved very near the front to neutralize the German defenses. In the attack the artillery barrage rolled forward, followed by the tanks about 200 to 400 meters ahead of the infantry. An attacking division had either a tank brigade or a tank regiment and an SU regiment in support. If the German defenses were too strong, a tank corps could be called forward to provide the final punch.[48] The major concern for the Russians was breaking through the strong German defenses. Once they were through, the tank forces either plunged ahead to disrupt German communications and cause broad withdrawals or the spearheads would turn to meet and enclose a pocket.

As the rifle strength of the Soviet divisions dwindled from 1943 on, new tactics were devised. In 1944 the Soviet doctrine for attack called for the formation of storm groups consisting of a rifle company, two or three tanks or SUs, two antitank guns, two divisional artillery guns (either 76mm guns or 122mm howitzers), and detachments of engineers and chemical warfare troops. At the battalion level, the storm group consisted of three of the above company storm groups, a tank company, one or two 76mm gun batteries, a battery of 120mm mortars, and one or two heavy-caliber guns (203mm howitzer) or SUs, and an engineer company.[49]

Support of this magnitude for Russian rifle companies of 100 men was quite different from the massed infantry attacks of 1941. The dramatic increase in the use of material to replace manpower was demonstrated by the shrinking width of the attack zone. In 1941 a rifle division zone was sixt to eight kilometers wide; in the second period of the war, from two to six kilometers wide; and in the final years of the war, only one to two and a half kilometers wide. By 1945 a rifle battalion attacked on a 300-meter to 700-meter front.[50] On a frontage of only 100 meters, the Germans would be faced with about 100 infantrymen, two or three tanks, and four pieces of artillery in close support!

The Red Army had improved considerably by the spring of 1943, based on the experience of 1941 and 1942 and more plentiful weapons. The field army was increased in size from seven divisions in 1942 to twelve in 1943. The corps headquarters was revived in late 1942 and by early 1943 most armies included two such headquarters. The number of army troops was increased, including four artillery regiments and service units. The average manpower of an army increased from 90,000 to 130,000 men. Meanwhile the army commanders had acquired more skill in the employment of large forces.[51]

The major increase in the ratio of Soviet tanks and artillery to men was the result of increased production based on careful use of available resources. The Soviet high command designed weapons, created units, and developed logistical systems based on theories that were continuously tested and revised in the light of experience. Considering the complex relationship among strategy, tactics, weapons, organization, and supply, the remarkable aspect was not how many mistakes were made, but how few. Poor practices were followed, sometimes knowingly, because of the lack of any practical alternative, but ended when a solution was found. For example, tanks were used in 1942 as antitank weapons, but tank-destroyer brigades were formed as quickly as possible to eliminate the practice. Other examples abound as the Red Army matured and evolved. By early 1943 the Red Army had developed the doctrine to employ its troops successfully against the German forces at any time or place that it chose.

CHAPTER 2

Creating the Red Army, 1918–41

Beginning with a few worker battalions in 1918, twenty-five years later the Red Army had expanded to more than 500 divisions. This mass-produced army, beginning without tradition or doctrine, and deprived of leadership by the purges in the late 1930s, defeated the German Army, the most skillful army of World War II. The efficient organization and use of manpower by the Red Army contributed much to the victory. However, even by 1941 the Russians had much to learn.

Lenin had created the Red Army in 1917, soon after the Communist-led revolution to replace the Russian Army of the czars. Its first goal was to defend the new Bolshevik government against its enemies, including Russians and foreign troops intent on restoring the czarist regime. The officers of the new Red Army included former noncommissioned officers of the czarist army and a few professional officers. Fearing betrayal by the former czarist officers, the Bolsheviks assigned a reliable Communist to each unit as a commissar. Without the commissar's approval, no order could be carried out.

Foreign intervention in the civil war had left a legacy of suspicion of the Western powers. In the 1920s both the Soviet Union and Germany were outcasts in Europe. As Russia was not a signatory to the Versailles Treaty, the German Army, violating the treaty, proposed to carry out experimental military programs in the Soviet Union. The programs included aircraft manufacture, poison gas development, training of air crews, and development of tanks and training crews. The Germans shipped prototypes of tanks and aircraft to the training grounds provided by the Soviets. Exercises and experiments were conducted to develop new doctrines, to learn methods, and to solve problems. As part of these programs, the Germans provided some training to the Red Army. The association created a pro-German clique among the Red Army officer corps. However, cooperation ended when Hitler came to power with his anti-Bolshevik program in the 1930s.

At the end of the civil war in the early 1920s, the Soviet government demobilized most of the Red Army. The war had devastated the country's economy. The Soviet Union could not retain men in the army who were needed on the farms and in the factories. The Red Army maintained some regular divisions, but reformed most as territorial divisions in 1923 to provide reserves and training units. In February 1923, the 57th Rifle Division became a territorial division in the Urals Military District.[1] In 1924, the Red Army included thirty-four regular divisions and fifteen territorial divisions.

Frunze, Voroshilov, and Tukhachevskii replaced Trotsky in command of the army in 1924 and reorganized the army, adding twenty-seven territorial divisions. The new organization included eight military districts plus an independent army in the Caucasus. Some divisions recruited their men in one area and used the local language—for example, the men in the 1st and 2nd Georgian Divisions spoke the local language. Divisions were assigned to districts as follows in 1925:

District	Rifle Division	Cavalry Division
Moscow	10	1
Leningrad	7	1
White Russia	10	2
Ukraine	17	4
North Caucasus	5	3
Transcaucasus (army)	7	
Volga	5	1
Central Asia	3	1
Siberia	7	1
TOTAL	71	14

Included in the totals were twenty-nine regular divisions, forty-two territorial divisions, twelve regular cavalry divisions, and four territorial cavalry divisions. The total strength of the army was 562,000 men.[2]

The Law on Universal Military Service of 1925 subjected all men between nineteen and forty to military service. A conscript received two years of pre-induction training and five years of part-time service. Most of the draftees served in the territorial divisions, drawing their personnel from a limited area.[3] The army added thirty reserve divisions in the late 1920s. Should war break out, reservists would fill the territorial and reserve divisions, making them available for operations within a short time.

In 1927 the Red Army included twenty-eight active divisions at reduced strength, forty-five territorial divisions with training cadres and part-time soldiers, and thirty reserve divisions with small cadres, for a total of 103. The Military Law of 1928 changed the draft age to twenty-one years, but exempted many men from service. By 1931 the number of rifle divisions had declined to seventy-one, of which forty-one were territorial formations, and all were under strength. The active division had 9,000 men—50 percent of wartime strength—and the territorial divisions had only 1,400 full-time soldiers.[4]

Determined efforts to build the Soviet economy under the five-year plans made the government reluctant to tie up manpower and resources in the military when not faced with an immediate threat. The conscription age was raised to twenty-one. The Red Army made significant improvements in weapons in the early 1930s and by 1934 it was receiving modern equipment. The major problems were the lack of professionally trained officers and poor morale. The peasant soldiers hated the regime because Stalin was forcing their families into collective farms.[5]

The Red Army was primarily a training army from 1924 to 1935 with from twenty-six to thirty regular divisions, thirty-seven to forty-seven territorial divisions, and thirty reserve divisions. Organization was in a constant flux during these years. In 1924, the 57th Rifle Division was redesignated the 57th Ural Rifle Division; and in June 1931, the division provided the cadre for the 85th Chelyabinsk Rifle Division. The divisions had names reflecting their origin—for example, the 2nd Turkestan Division and the 2nd Pre Amur Division. Three Kolkhoz divisions in the sparsely populated areas in the Far East had one unit of reservists in each town.[6]

With the rise of Adolf Hitler to power in Germany as an avowed enemy of communism, the Soviet military could not ignore the danger. In 1935 Hitler openly discarded the Versailles Treaty that had limited the German Army to 100,000 men and prohibited conscription. As Germany rearmed, a new threat emerged. The threat of German invasion became stronger when Hitler began expanding his army. The Soviets reacted by increasing the size of the Red Army.

In 1936 the government amended the conscription law, reducing the draft age to nineteen. All citizens became eligible in addition to the workers and peasants. The low birth rate during World War I had reduced the number of men reaching military age throughout Europe. The number in the Soviet Union dropped from 1.8 million in the class of 1915 to 1.4 million in 1916. By taking in one and a half classes each year, the Red Army increased its annual intake to 2.7 million in 1936, 2.3 million in 1937, and 2.1 million in 1938 and 1939.[7]

In 1935 the reserve divisions were reorganized as territorial divisions or abolished, leaving twenty-six active divisions and fifty-eight territorial divisions.[8] Four more divisions were formed in 1936 and all received numbers, abandoning the regional designations.[9] The number of military districts was increased to thirteen in 1936, with varying numbers of divisions detailed on the following table.[10]

COMPOSITION OF MILITARY DISTRICTS IN 1936

District	Rifle Divisions	Cavalry Divisions
Moscow	10	1
Leningrad	6	3½
White Russia	12	6
Kiev	13	6
Kharkov	6	
North Caucasus	6	2½
Transcaucasus	7	1
Volga	4	
Ural	3	
Siberia	4	
Central Asia	3	2
Transbaikal	5	2
Far East	11	2
TOTAL	90	26

During 1937 and 1938 the Red Army suffered a major setback. Stalin had ordered a purge of the army's leadership. The reason for the purge may have been the emerging strength of the officer class. The army leadership, concerned with the morale of the peasant soldiers whose families were suffering from the collective farm movement, had urged Stalin to relent in the campaign, causing a rift between the Communist Party and the army officers.

The purge removed all of the deputy commissars for defense as well as all of the military district commanders, 13 of 15 army commanders, all but 28 of 85 corps commanders, and 110 division commanders. Some were shot and the rest sent to prison. From one-third to one-half of the army officers were arrested. To fill the vacancies, Stalin promoted young officers rapidly although they lacked training and experience.[11] After the purge, division commanders were from thirty-five to forty years of age, regimental commanders thirty to thirty-five, and companies were commanded by lieutenants.[12] The shortage of officers with staff training was a major cause of the defeats in 1941. Stalin had placed his cronies in the high command, including G. I. Kulik (charged with artillery and rifle units) and E. A. Shchadenko (responsible for mobilization) on the General Staff.[13]

The Red Army was transformed from a training army in 1935 to a professional army in 1939, gradually replacing the territorial divisions. By 1938 there were sixty-two active divisions and only thirty-four territorial divisions. While providing a structure for training, the territorial divisions were not a viable military force. The last territorial divisions were abolished in March 1939 and converted into active divisions to provide full-time training. By 1939 the relationship of divisions to regions had ended. Regiments from regional divisions formed new divisions with men from various parts of the Soviet Union.[14]

The infantry regiments of the divisions were renumbered, replacing the old system that numbered regiments in a regular pattern. The new system used arbitrarily numbered regiments, mostly below 400.[15] The 57th Rifle Division had the 169th, 170th, and 171st Rifle Regiments in 1923. In 1941 the regiments were numbered 80, 127, and 293. As intended, the renumbering scheme confused foreign intelligence. The British had not learned the new system by January 1940.[16]

The Law of Universal Military Conscription of September 1, 1939, again strengthened the Red Army. Increasing the length of military service provided men to create 125 new divisions as well as fill the active divisions and convert territorial divisions to active status. All citizens of the Soviet Union from age nineteen to fifty were eligible for military service. Active service began at age nineteen except for those who finished middle school at eighteen. Recruits reported between September 15 and October 15. Active service was two years for the army, three years for NCOs, three years for the air force, four years for the coast guard, five years for the navy, and two years for internal troops. Training in the reserves continued at ten hours per month following active service. The reserves consisted of three classes: up to thirty-five years, thirty-six to forty-five years, and forty-six to fifty years of age.[17]

The Red Army expanded rapidly from 1938 to August 1940 as the German threat became more apparent. The number of divisions in Europe increased from 98 in January 1939 to 120 in March 1939, plus 16 cavalry divisions. The number of tanks increased to over 9,000.[18] A British intelligence source estimated the growth in total divisions over three years as follows:[19]

	1938	1939	Aug. 40
Rifle divisions	95	110	158
Cavalry divisions	33	35	43

The new divisions were formed from cadres, reservists, and new recruits added to the army under the new conscription law. Although existing divisions might have been required to surrender some trained men as cadres for the new divisions, they remained as fighting units. The new divisions had few low-numbered regiments, substantiating the assumption that units did not receive full regiments as cadres. Most of the regiments had numbers between 300 and 700. The later divisions all had regiments numbered between 800 and 1090.

In the summer of the 1939, the Russians defeated the Japanese at Khalkin-Gol, showing some competence in the use of tanks.[20] On September 17, 1939, a practice mobilization added reserves to divisions. On the same day, the Red Army entered Poland with little resistance.[21] The Finnish War of 1939–40 exposed many weaknesses in the Red Army caused by the rapid expansion. Poor leadership resulted from the loss of officers in the purge.[22] Voroshilov took the responsibility for the Finnish defeat. He had little understanding of modern war and had opposed the formation of tank corps in 1934, believing the tank brigade was the maximum size. In May 1940 Timoshenko replaced him. Timoshenko was a realist with professional training who recognized that the Red Army had to be retrained.[23]

The leadership of the Red Army was still conservative. In May 1940 the marshals of the Red Army included Voroshilov, Timoshenko, Shaposhnikov, Budyenny, and Kulik. Shaposhnikov was an excellent theorist and a good staff planner, but weak and subject to the others. Kulik, a close friend of Stalin, preferred towing guns with horses rather than trucks or tractors and objected to new artillery pieces because they were ugly. Budyenny, another close friend of Stalin from the Civil War, was a cavalry officer who favored cavalry over tanks. In December 1940 the conservative marshals rejected the idea of a tank army or tank divisions with combat and logistical supporting units.[24] However, Timoshenko initiated some basic reforms. He promoted officers to fill the vacancies created by the purge, revived military discipline, and reduced the power of the commissar.[25]

By the summer of 1940 a wartime mobilization plan existed and the strength of the active army continued to grow. In May 1940 there were 161 rifle divisions, 23 cavalry divisions, and 38 tank brigades.[26] Of these, 34 divisions were in the Far East and 17 divisions were on the Turkish border.[27] Most of the 161 rifle divisions were below strength. There were eight tables of organization for infantry divisions and three for cavalry, as follows:

14,000-man division	3
12,550-man division	15
12,000-man division	80
Motorized rifle division (12,000 men)	3
Motorized division (12,000 men)	4
9,000-man division	3
Mountain division (9,000)	10
6,000 man division	43
Total rifle divisions	161
6,560 man cavalry division	16
Mountain cavalry division	5
3,543 man cavalry division	2
Total cavalry divisions	23

Although one-quarter of the divisions were well below strength, all had nearly full wartime allotments of machine guns and artillery.

Of the 38 tank brigades, 1 had T-35 and KV heavy tanks, 3 had T-28 medium tanks, 16 had light BT tanks, and 18 had light T-26 tanks. There were three armored car brigades.[28] By September 1940 tank divisions had been formed from some of the brigades. Ten tank divisions and 8 tank brigades were assigned to the western border, along with 124 rifle divisions and 4 motorized divisions.[29]

The Soviet move toward a mechanized striking force was well under way by January 1941. The Germans estimated that the Russians would mobilize 150 rifle divisions (including 15 motorized divisions) and 6 mechanized corps for service in Europe after a war began. The first wave would consist of 107 divisions, most of which were already active; the second wave, 77 divisions, available in three months; and the third wave, 25 divisions, available in six months; for a total of 209 divisions when fully mobilized. In addition, the Russians would mobilize 32 cavalry divisions and 36 mechanized brigades, of which 24 were already active.[30] The Germans anticipated that the first and second waves would be distributed as follows:[31]

	Europe	Caucasus	Asia/East	Total
Rifle divisions	100	6	29	135
Motorized divisions	15			15
Cavalry divisions	25		7	32
Mechanized brigades	31		5	36

The Germans seriously underestimated the Russian resources. On March 11, 1941, the Red Army had a third more units than the Germans expected. The twenty new Russian mechanical corps began to assemble in February and March 1941, formed from existing tank brigades.[32] In June 1941 the situation was as follows:[33]

	Europe	Finland	Asia/East	Total
Rifle divisions	158	13	23	194
Motorized divisions	27		6	33
Tank divisions	53	1	7	61
Cavalry divisions	7		1	8
Rifle brigades	2		1	3

Beginning in May 1941, the Germans began a rapid buildup of forces on the Eastern Front and the Russians made comparable moves. From May 1 to June 21, German strength in the east rose from 72 divisions to 168 compared to 170 Soviet rifle and cavalry divisions.[34] However, none of the Soviet divisions was at full strength in June 1941. The average strength of 144 rifle divisions was only 8,000 men (compared to full strength of 14,483) and 19 other rifle divisions had only 600 to 5,000 men. The seven cavalry divisions averaged only 6,000 men.[35]

On June 22, 1941, the Red Army on the western frontier had 170 divisions and 2 rifle brigades in five military districts.

Leningrad Military District	14th Army
	7th Army
	23rd Army
Baltic Special Military District	8th Army
	11th Army
	27th Army
Western Military District	3rd Army
	10th Army
	4th Army
Kiev Special Military District	6th Army
	5th Army
	26th Army
	12th Army
Odessa Military District	9th Rifle Corps

An additional sixty divisions were in the second echelon.[36] More Russian divisions were moving to the frontier.[37] On April 26, 1941, the

Transbaikal and Far Eastern military districts sent a mechanized corps, two rifle corps, and two airborne brigades to Europe. The Ural Military District sent two rifle divisions. The 22nd, 21st, and 19th armies came from the Ural, Volga, and North Caucasus military districts. The 16th Army came from Transbaikal.[38]

On June 21, 1941, the total Red Army on all fronts included the following: 178 rifle divisions, 18 mountain divisions, 2 motorized rifle divisions, 61 tank divisions, 31 motorized divisions, and 13 cavalry divisions, a total of 303 divisions. In addition the Red Army included 74 independent artillery regiments, 5 airborne corps, 10 antitank brigades, 120 fortified regions, and 11 NKVD divisions.[39]

In only twenty-five years, the Red Army had grown from a few untrained battalions to an army of more than 300 divisions. In the first four years, the army concentrated on defeating the enemies of the Soviet state. During the next fifteen years, the army was primarily a training organization with most of its troops in territorial divisions. In 1936 the Red Army began a rapid transformation into a professional force. Unfortunately the combined effects of rapid expansion, changing doctrine, and loss of leadership from the purge resulted in poor performance. Although the structure had been created and the weapons designed, the Red Army needed more time and experience to defeat the Germans. The Russians would learn the necessary lessons at great cost in combat in the first two years of the war. The Germans destroyed most of the prewar divisions in the initial onslaught, but those divisions delayed the Germans long enough for the reserve armies to be assembled.

CHAPTER 3

Wartime Mobilization

On June 22, 1941, the Germans launched operation Barbarossa with three drives directed at Leningrad, Moscow, and Rostov. The Red Army was not ready and suffered enormous losses. The Russians had ample warnings, including one on March 5, 1941, from Richard Sorge, a Soviet spy in Tokyo with access to the German embassy, but Stalin refused to believe that the Germans would attack.[1] The first four months of combat had reduced the Red Army from 4.4 million men to 2.3 million.[2] To replace these losses and create an army to defeat the Germans, Stalin planned to mobilize 350 divisions.[3]

In early June, before war broke out, the Russians had mobilized 790,000 reservists to fill existing divisions. The classes of 1919 to 1922 were already in the service. The Russian war mobilization plan detailed the formation of new divisions from 1.5 million young soldiers of the class of 1923 who were completing their training and recalled reservists.[4] By June 30 the Russians had mobilized about 5.3 million reserves from fourteen classes, 1905 to 1918 (men aged twenty-three to thirty-six years), who had previous military training.[5] Inductions continued to replace losses and create new units. Between July 1 and December 1, the army had received an additional 3,544,000 new recruits.[6]

Many details of the mobilization plan can be assumed by an analysis of the division histories. The first table outlines the doubling of the Red Army from 1940 to June 1941 from 117 divisions to 232. The second table details the formation of 260 new divisions in the second half of 1941.

DIVISIONS EXISTING BEFORE JUNE 22, 1941

GROUP District	A	B	C	Total June 22, 1941
Archangel	3	4	—	7
Baltic	—	5	—	5
Central Asia	1	3	—	4
Far East	17	1	—	18

DIVISIONS EXISTING BEFORE JUNE 22, 1941 *continued*

GROUP

District	A	B	C	Total June 22, 1941
Kharkov	6	6	1	13
Kiev Special	13	10	11	34
Leningrad	7	3	2	12
Moscow	15	12	4	31
North Caucasus	7	6	3	16
Odessa	4	3	2	9
Orel	3	4	2	9
Siberia	5	6	—	11
Transbaikal	5	1	—	6
Transcaucasus	8	3	2	13
Ural	4	4	2	10
Volga	7	2	1	10
West Special	12	11	1	24
TOTAL	117	83	32	232

Note: Includes rifle, motorized, and mountain divisions. The approximate formation dates of the groups are:

A: Before January 1940	117
B: During 1940	83
C: Before June 1941	32
Total Active June 1941	232

DIVISIONS FORMED IN THE SECOND HALF OF 1941

GROUP	D	E	F	G	H	I
Archangel	2	1	6	9	16	
Baltic				1	1	6
Central Asia	4	4		3	11	15
Far East	2		3	6	11	29
Kharkov	7	1	5	2	15	28
Kiev Special	2		1	1	4	38
Leningrad	5			9	14	26
Moscow	33	7	1	26	67	98
North Caucasus	3	12	3	3	21	37
Odessa	8		1	2	11	20
Orel	12	3	1	5	21	30
Siberia		12	1	2	15	26
Transbaikal			1	1	2	8

DIVISIONS FORMED IN THE SECOND HALF OF 1941 *continued*

GROUP	D	E	F	G	H	I
Transcaucasus	2		16	3	21	34
Ural	2	11		1	14	24
Volga		13	2	1	16	26
West Special				3	3	27
Reformed Brigade				3	3	3
Ethnic				1	1	1
TOTAL	85	64	40	74	260	492

D: June–August 1941   85
E: August–November 1941   64
F: July–November 1941   37
G: Divisions re-formed July–December   74
H: Total divisions June–December   260
I: Total divisions prewar and June–December   492

Groups A, B, and C represent the 232 divisions formed before the war. Groups D, E, F, and G constitute the mobilization plan carried out in the six months following the outbreak of war, a total of 260. The new divisions (including DNO divisions later given regular army numbers) in Column G received the numbers of destroyed divisions. The numbers compare closely to the totals presented in Soviet published sources: 229 divisions active on June 22 and 237 raised in the next six months.[7] The difference likely resulted from the definition of "new division." A rehabilitated division may have been identified as a new division. The table excludes DNO divisions except those later reformed into regular divisions.

German intelligence records and published Soviet information gathered in a computer database provided the information for the table. Many divisions raised in the second half of 1941 had a distinctive regimental numbering scheme, suggesting that they were part of a plan. There were eighty sets of numbers, each with two to four divisions having related regimental numbers. Each set of numbers followed a pattern related to the military districts. The Soviets usually numbered the regiments in each set in one of the following sequences:

1	3	5	1	4	7	1	5	7
2	4	6	2	5	8	2	6	8
			3	6	9	3	9	10
						4	11	

Consecutive artillery regiment numbers formed the relationship between some divisions. Other divisions had random groups of regimental numbers within a limited range. Most sets came from one military district. A few sets had one division from the North Caucasus and the other from the Volga district or one from the Ural and one from the Siberia district. The preceding tables indicate that the mobilization plan was altered by the invasion that swept aside many of the existing 232 divisions far more quickly than anticipated.

The Soviet Union was divided into military districts, which were administrative organizations charged with inducting and training men, forming new units, and other duties, similar to the German Wehrkreis. In the mobilization plan the number of divisions allocated to each district was proportionate to the population of the district. In the eighteen months before the war, each district created a number of divisions almost equal to those existing before 1940. The military districts of Archangel, Far East, Kharkov, Orel, Odessa, North Caucasus, Siberia, Transcaucasus, Volga, and Ural produced about the same number of divisions before 1940 and in the eighteen months following. The Baltic District produced six divisions based on the existing units of the three former independent nations. The Germans had incorporated units of the Austrian Army into the German Army in 1938 in a similar fashion. The Germans occupied the Baltic District and only one new division came from the area in 1941.

After June 1941 the districts occupied by the Germans produced very few divisions. These heavily populated districts had a consistent pattern of forming large numbers of divisions before the war, but played a much smaller role in later mobilization plans. The Western Special formed twenty-four divisions before the war and only three after. Orel formed nine before the war, twelve in the early months, and five after that; Kiev Special, thirty-four before the war, four after. Leningrad produced only seven divisions during the second half of 1941, but much of the available manpower probably was assigned to the ten Leningrad *Opolchenye* divisions. The Moscow District formed thirty-one before the war and sixty-seven divisions after—far more than usual. The Moscow District may have formed divisions from recruits and reservists evacuated from the districts overrun by the Germans.

The sparsely populated districts, Central Asia and Transbaikal, made a small contribution before the war but sharply increased their activity after the war began. Central Asia formed four divisions before the war and eleven after. The Volga District raised ten before and sixteen after. The Transcaucasus Military District formed thirteen before June 1941 and twenty-one divisions between July and December 1941.[8]

The mobilization plan succeeded with some problems. An example of the mobilization process was the formation of nineteen rifle divisions and five cavalry divisions in the Kharkov and Odessa military districts at the end of July 1941. Despite the urgency, more than a month's time elapsed before the divisions were organized. The divisions lacked part of their artillery, small arms, signal equipment, engineer equipment, and even uniforms. The military district headquarters obtained some material locally. When the divisions were ready, eight rifle divisions and two cavalry divisions went to the Southwestern Front. Nine rifle and three cavalry divisions went to the Southern Front, and two rifle divisions and two tank brigades to the Stavka reserve.[9]

The Soviets said that between July 22 and December 1, 1941, they had created 227 rifle divisions to replace lost formations, including 84 reformed rifle divisions and 143 new rifle divisions.[10] The number of reformed rifle divisions (84) was greater than the 74 reformed divisions. The difference may be because some divisions were reformed without the knowledge of the Germans. There were many divisions in the 400 series that simply disappeared, ten more of which may have been used to re-form lost rifle divisions.

The 143 new rifle divisions were fewer than the 189 new divisions listed in Groups D, E, and F in the table on page 37, but the table includes the additional month of December. At least 11 divisions were formed in December. The Soviets mentioned "400 divisions formed" (of all kinds) elsewhere in the source and "291 sent to the active army." Divisions held in reserve armies and not sent to the front may not have been included in the Russian total.

The GUF, the Reserve Armies Administration, created in July 1941, supervised the formation of strategic reserves.[11] The GUF created new divisions and entire armies to replace those destroyed. By July 15 the Reserve Front had six armies with thirty-one divisions.[12] Additional armies were forming in the east. On October 10, 1941, the Reserve Front was abolished, and the armies were added to the Western Front.[13]

By October 1, 1941, the Red Army had received substantial reinforcements. The army then included 213 rifle divisions, 30 cavalry divisions, 5 tank divisions, and 7 airborne brigades. The rifle divisions averaged only 7,500 men and the ground forces opposing the Germans had only 3,245,000 men. The Red Army had 2,715 tanks and 20,580 guns and mortars.[14] The renewed attack on Moscow cost the Russian forces heavy casualties, but GUF provided replacements.

Some units came from Siberia. On October 13, 1941, the 312th and 316th Rifle Divisions arrived at the front from Kazakh, the 313th Rifle

Division from Turkestan, and the 178th Rifle Division from the Siberian Military District.[15] A few Far Eastern divisions went to Europe, but most of the divisions from the east came from the Siberia, Ural, and Central Asia districts. The Far East sent many replacements to Europe in march companies, but there was no large movement of divisions.

The mobilization program continued through the winter of 1941–42. In October 1941, the formation of nine reserve armies was ordered.[16] One of the reserve armies, the 10th, was formed in October 1941. The experienced regular army cadre made up 15 percent of the army. Most of the men were reserves without combat experience. The unit was 90 percent Russian; 4 percent were Ukrainians; and the rest were various nationalities, including 3,245 Mordvins in the 326th Division. Five percent were Communists and about 3 percent were Komsomols, or Young Communists. In November the army commander requested additional Communists to stiffen the army. More than 700 arrived, mostly wounded men with combat experience discharged from hospitals.

One-third of the officers were regular army, the rest reserves. The division commanders had training and experience. The staff officers and regimental commanders were regulars, many of whom had been recently promoted. Only a few of the officers were graduates of the military academy, but most had attended advanced training schools. The rifle and artillery battalions were commanded by reserve officers, few of whom had combat experience.

The nine rifle divisions of the 10th Army came from the Moscow and Orel military districts. The military district and formation date were as follows:

Division	Military District	Formation Date
322nd	Moscow	July 1941
323rd	Moscow	August 1941
324th	Moscow	October 1941
325th	Orel	October 1941
326th	Moscow	August 1941
328th	Moscow	September 1941
329th	Orel	September 1941
330th	Moscow	August 1941
332nd	Moscow	July 27, 1941

The 57th Cavalry Division came from Central Asia and the other cavalry division, the 75th, came from Siberia.

The divisions were comparatively well armed for training units. There were over 65,000 rifles for 100,000 men, 1,209 machine pistols, and 2,000 heavy and light machine guns. In June 1941 most regular divisions had only 400 machine pistols and 600 machine guns. The 10th Army had about 100 machine pistols and 200 machine guns per division. The army had 249 regimental and divisional artillery pieces, about half the authorized number, but adequate for training. The army had few mortars, antiaircraft guns, or antitank guns, items that were scarce in Russia at the time, but sufficient in number for training. The most serious lack was signal equipment. The army had only one signal company, an impediment to training as messages had to be delivered by couriers on horseback.

The divisions had trained before assignment to the 10th Army. One of the better divisions, the 328th, had six weeks' prior training. However, only 60 percent of the men had completed their rifle marksmanship training and only 25 percent had learned to throw grenades. After three weeks in the 10th Army, the 328th Division was still providing individual training to men, noncommissioned officers, and junior officers. Artillery and heavy weapons crews lacked experience. The 324th and 325th Divisions were even further behind.

In November the army practiced unit maneuvers, marching, and antitank defense techniques. On November 24, 1941, about a month after forming, units of the army left for the front. Although one division had four months' training, two divisions had less than two months'. The high command ordered that three divisions—the 322nd, the 323rd, and 330th—be given priority in preparation for combat. The 322nd went to the 50th Army at Kaluga. The 329th went to the 26th Army at Volkhov. The rest of the divisions remained with the 10th Army except the 330th, which later served with the 49th Army. On the way to the front, the 10th Army picked up tanks, motor vehicles, and artillery. On November 28, only four days after the order to move to the front, German air reconnaissance spotted trains at Ryazan that were carrying elements of the army. One cannot fault the Russian's efficiency in pulling together reserves.[17]

The Soviets also rebuilt armies weakened in combat. The 50th Army reformed at Tula. In mid-October, three extremely depleted rifle divisions (293rd, 413th, and 239th) arrived from the front, each with from 500 to 1,000 men. The men were exhausted, with uniforms in tatters and very little equipment. Within two months, the divisions had been refitted and raised to strength. Additional divisions arrived. By December 1941, the 50th Army had seven rifle divisions, three cavalry divisions, a depleted tank division, and independent tank regiments.[18] The rapid reconstruction of the 50th Army was probably typical of many armies in the fail of 1941.

Total reserves increased dramatically—four divisions in October, twenty-two in November, and forty-four in December.[19] Despite the severe dislocation and the devastating losses inflicted by the Germans in the first six months, the Soviets restored their army and launched a counteroffensive. By November the Red Army stood at 3.4 million men resulting from the large reinforcements, but only 1,954 tanks were at the front.[20] The winter offensive battered the unit strength of the Red Army, but did not result in the destruction of units.

Formation of new divisions continued in 1942, as shown in the following table:

NEW DIVISIONS FORMED, 1942–45

	41	42	43	44	45	Total
Archangel	16	5	3	3		27
Baltic	6					6
Central Asia	15	4				19
Far East	29	17	3	1	5	55
Kharkov	28	1				29
Kiev Special	38		2			40
Leningrad	26	1	1	1		29
Moscow	98	31	5	1		135
North Caucasus	37	22				59
Odessa	20					20
Orel	30	7	2			39
Siberia	26	12				38
Transbaikal	8	1				9
Transcaucasus	34	5	2	4		45
Ural	24	13				37
Volga	26	15				41
West Special	27			1		28
Unknown	1			1		
TOTAL	488	134	18	12	5	657

Note: Includes divisions with new numbers and replacements for destroyed divisions and divisions redesignated as Guards

NEW DIVISIONS FORMED BY REORGANIZING EXISTING UNITS

	41	42	43	44	45	Total
From brigades	3	15	41	5		64
From NKVD		8	1			9
Ethnic divisions	1	1				2
SUBTOTAL	4	24	42	5		75
TOTAL	492	158	60	17	5	732

German intelligence estimated that Russia began the war with 225 rifle divisions in June 1941 near the 232 in the tables above. The Germans estimated 448 new formations compared to 455 (subtracting the 37 divisions raised in the Far East from the total of 492). The Germans missed by only seven divisions in four years. The German total of 673 new and existing formations compared to the 677 (732 minus 55 in the Far East) in the tables.[21]

Professor Goff estimated 229 rifle and motorized divisions available on June 22, 1941, and 483 new divisions for a total of 712.[22] Colonel Glantz estimated that the total reached was 707.[23] Both estimates were based on totals published in Soviet sources. Poirier, in his excellent work on the Soviet order of battle, gave 724 as the total number of formations as follows:

Divisions	Poirier	Tables
In existence June 1941	242	232
Formed in the second half of 1941	251	260
Formed in 1942	158	158
Formed in 1943	49	60
Formed in 1944	21	16
Formed in 1945	3	6
TOTAL	724	732

The additional eight divisions were primarily 400-series divisions that Poirier had not identified.[24]

The difference between the German and Soviet sources was probably the result of differing interpretation of the redesignated divisions and the DNO (the *Opolchenye*, or workers' volunteer) divisions. The database included some divisions in the 400 series later renumbered using numbers of abolished divisions, resulting in a double count. The 438th Division was formed in Magnitogorsk in December 1941 and renumbered

the 169th in January 1942. The 426th division became the 147th, the
427th the 149th, and the 469th the 244th. Information is very sparse on
many 400-series divisions.

However, even with the lowest number, the Soviets mobilized over
700 divisions. More than 100 divisions were renumbered as part of the
total or disbanded within a short time. Despite the incursion of the Germans that seriously disrupted the mobilization, the Russians were able to
form 260 divisions in the first six months of the war and 158 in 1942.
Unfortunately, the Germans were efficiently destroying considerable
numbers, but the steady stream of new divisions enabled the Soviet Union
to remain in the war.

In 1942, the Red Army reorganized following the heavy losses
incurred in the winter offensive, replacing manpower and creating new
units. The Soviets formed additional rifle divisions with a reduced
authorized strength of 10,000. They eliminated the corps organization in
late 1941 and reduced the strength of the field army to six rifle divisions.[25] The Red Army had accumulated considerable reserves by May
1942. A German intelligence report estimated the Red Army at from 394
to 414 divisions.

	Division	Brigade	Cavalry Division	Tank Division	Tank Brigade
On German front	239	81	14	1	25
Army reserves	32	19	23	1	39
TOTAL	271	100	37	2	64
Front reserve		4	4		6
Refitting	19	16			
Finland	24	2	10	2	
Caucasus	29		1		
Iran	5				
Inside Russia	5		6		1
Far East	21	5	1	2	5
In formation	20–40	6–12	3–6		4
TOTAL	399–414	133–39	62–65	4	82

The units had 6 to 6.5 million men.[26] The Germans estimated that
the Russians formed sixty new divisions in the first four months of 1942.
The additional men were made available by several measures. Women
replaced men in factories and the army trained seventeen-year-olds to be

ready for combat when they reached eighteen. Older men, foreigners, and men previously considered unfit also were conscripted.[27]

In March 1942, Shaposhnikov and Vassilevsky reviewed the strength of the Red Army, its equipment, and its supply situation. Lacking reserves, the two members of the Stavka decided to remain on the defensive in the summer, prepare defenses, and concentrate in the Moscow area.[28] In May, Timoshenko, in command of the southern armies, presented a new plan for a major offensive in the south to reach the line Gomel-Kiev-Cherkassy-Pervomaisk-Nikolayev, but the Stavka objected. Timoshenko then presented a plan to envelop Kharkov with two drives, one from Izyum and the other farther north at Volchansk. Stalin approved the latter plan.[29] Disaster followed at Izyum, and the Germans launched their drive on Stalingrad and the Caucasus. To counter the German offensive, the Red Army had enormous reserves, but the units lacked training. In the spring of 1942 the Russians had formed ten new reserve armies numbered 1 through 10 with an average strength of six rifle divisions, each with 7,000 men.[30]

The 1st Reserve Army formed at Tula in April 1942. In June it had the 13th, 18th, 29th, 112th, 113th, and 229th divisions. In July the army, redesignated the 64th, went to Stalingrad with the 29th, 112th, 113th, 164th, and 229th. There, the army picked up additional divisions. The 13th Division went to the Leningrad Front 42nd Army, and the 18th to the Stalingrad 4th Tank Army. In August, after intense combat, the 64th Army had only the 29th Division remaining of the original reserve army.

The 2nd Reserve Army formed at Vologda in April 1942 and was redesignated the 1st Guard Army in July. Also in July, the army included the 37th, 38th, 39th, 40th, and 41st Guard Divisions formed in June and July from airborne corps and the 397th Rifle Division. These divisions had superior manpower, but were short on infantry unit training. The army traveled from Vologda to Stalingrad in early August.[31]

The 3rd Reserve Army formed at Tambov in April 1942. It probably included the 159th, 232nd, 237th, 195th, 107th, and 303rd divisions. Redesignated the 60th Army, in July it went to the Voronezh Front. The 237th went to the new 38th Army in the Southwestern Front; the remainder stayed with the 60th Army.

Little is known of the 4th Reserve Army formed at Kalinin. It may have included the 165th, 167th, and 169th divisions and 242nd Rifle Brigade, among other units. The 167th had been redesignated from the 438th Division formed in Magnitogorsk from Communist volunteers. The army headquarters formed a new 38th Army Headquarters, but few, if any, divisions went to the 38th. In August the 38th Army had the 237th from the 3rd Reserve Army, the 296th from the 9th Army, the 193rd and 340th from the 40th Army, the 240th and 284th from the 48th Army, and the 167th from the 60th Army.

The 5th Reserve Army formed at Novo Annenski on the Don, northwest of Stalingrad in April 1942, including the 1st, 127th, 153rd, 181st, 184th, and 196th divisions. In July it was redesignated the 63rd Army. Three divisions stayed with the 63rd Army and two went to the 62nd Army at Stalingrad.

The 6th Reserve Army, formed on the Don River northwest of Stalingrad in April, may have included the 141st, 160th, 206th, 212th, 219th, 309th, and 350th divisions. The 6th Reserve was redesignated the 6th Army in the Southwestern Front in June 1942 and four of the divisions stayed with it.

The 7th Reserve Army formed at Stalingrad in May 1942 with the 147th Division and possibly the 62nd, 98th, 192nd, 214th, and 308th divisions and the 124th and 149th brigades. The army was redesignated the 62nd, and all of the above units remained with it in July. After heavy fighting in the Don basin, only the 98th and 192nd divisions from the reserve army remained; the rest were replaced by new divisions.

The 8th Reserve Army formed at Saratov in April. It may have included the 49th, 120th, 231st, and 315th divisions. In August, redesignated the 66th Army, it went to Stalingrad. There, additional divisions joined the army, the 42nd from the Northwestern Front 34th Army, the 99th from the Southwestern 6th Army, and the 316th from the 9th Reserve Army.

The 9th Reserve Army was formed with ten rifle brigades from the Gorki, Ivanov, and Vladimir oblasts of the Moscow District as cadres. The ten brigades became the 32nd, 93rd, 180th, 207th, 238th, 279th, 292nd, 299th, 306th, and 316th divisions. Two hundred march companies of replacements (20,000 to 40,000 men) from the eastern oblasts of the Moscow District, the Caucasus, and Central Asia reinforced the new divisions.[32] In July, five of the divisions plugged gaps in the Southwestern front. On August 27, 1942, the army headquarters, redesignated the 24th Army, went to the Stalingrad area, but its five divisions (32nd, 93rd, 238th, 279th, and 316th) were sent to other fronts.[33]

Of the five divisions assigned to the 9th Reserve Army before August 27, 1942, the 32nd and the 279th went to the Western Front, 43rd Army; the 93rd went to the Kalinin Front, 41st Army, and the 316th went to the Don Front, 1st Guard Army. The 238th was identified at Rshev in October, probably with the 30th Army. The dispatch of the four divisions of the 9th Reserve Army to the Moscow area revealed a continued interest in offensive action at Rshev.

The new 24th Army entered the front line and took control of the 173rd, 207th, 221st, 292nd, and 308th divisions plus the 217th Tank Brigade. Of these divisions, the 207th, 292nd, and 308th had been in the original 9th Reserve Army.[34] The 221st had been part of the 8th Reserve Army and the 173th came from the 10th Army on the Western Front.

The 10th Reserve Army formed at Ivanovo in April. In July or August it was redesignated the 5th Shock Army and took part in the Stalingrad offensive. The 297th and 315th Divisions were in the army in November and may have been assigned earlier. The assignments of the reserve armies and their divisions revealed the many demands on the Red Army in 1942. The crushing defeats in the south in the summer of 1942 created a crisis requiring the employment of reserve armies before their training was complete. The overwhelming majority of the divisions of the reserve armies went to the south, most as early as July 1942. The Red Army reserves had grown from twenty-four divisions in April to forty in June and sixty-two in July. In June the high command began to commit the reserve divisions in the south and by August the reserves decreased to only twenty-three rifle divisions, one rifle brigade, and two mechanized corps. By September most reserves had been absorbed in the battles in the south and only seventeen divisions remained in reserve in October.[35]

During the summer of 1942 the Germans identified increasing numbers of new rifle divisions—twenty-seven in May, five in June, and fifty-four in July, a total of eighty-six. Eight of the divisions from the Caucasus lacked combat experience and previously were unidentified. Nine were new formations with the numbers of divisions destroyed at Izyum and Kerch, and the rest were new formations.[36]

The new divisions arrived at the front from three to four months after formation. Seven divisions from the Far East, Transbaikal, and Siberia were sent to Stalingrad in July and August. The 399th formed in Transbaikal in March 1942; the 321st and 422nd in the Far East in April; the 204th in the Far East in June; and the 126th, 205th, and 208th in Siberia in June 1942. None of these divisions had appreciable unit training, Pive arriving in Stalingrad a month after formation. The divisions sent to withstand the German offensive in the summer of 1942 were new and few had prior combat experience. The older divisions remained in the center and in the north. The poor performance of the Red Army in the spring and summer of 1942 resulted from inadequate unit training, despite Stalin's order in March 1942. After August few of the newly formed divisions entered combat prematurely, as Stalin released only enough divisions to delay the Germans at Stalingrad. Most were reserved for the counteroffensive.

By November 1942 the new divisions had six or more months' experience. The Soviets refer to November 1942 as the beginning of the Second Period of the war. The remarkable aspect of the 1942 rebuilding program was its responsiveness to tactical and strategic lessons learned since the beginning of the war. The previous two rebuilding programs in 1941 and early 1942 emphasized rifle and light tank units because of the shortage of weapons, not poor doctrine. The third rebuilding in mid-1942 reflected the new strategy and tactics. Experience was translated into doctrine that, in turn, determined production schedules and mobilization. The increased production of weapons, tanks, artillery, and automatic weapons, and the formation of a wide variety of units, was not haphazard but rather part of a comprehensive plan.

For the remainder of the war, except in a few months, the Russians had a substantial reserve that could be used to obtain local superiority anywhere on the line. The Germans, on the other hand, seldom had many reserves and had to thin out less threatened sectors when they needed troops to counterattack. In the time required to accomplish the thinning process, the Russians made substantial gains.

The changing composition of the Red Army from 1942 to 1945 is outlined in the table "Combat Units for Select Months." Four months have been selected, May 1942, just before the German summer offensive; November 1942, on the eve of the encirclement of Stalingrad; July 1943 during the Battle of Kursk; and January 1945, the beginning of the final offensives. The number of rifle formations (divisions and brigades) remained stable from May 1942 to the end of the war. By July 1943 the number of rifle divisions increased as rifle brigades formed new divisions to replace those redesignated as Guards.

Despite the heavy losses inflicted by the Germans in the second half of 1941, the Soviets were able to mobilize divisions not only to replace those lost but to add more than sixty to the total. A further forty were formed in the first half of 1942 and another forty in the first half of 1943. Smaller increases occurred from then to the end of the war. Airborne divisions added about thirty divisions by the end of the war. Instead of being worn down by the Germans, the Red Army grew stronger as the war progressed.

In preparation for the Battle of Kursk, the Russians accumulated an enormous reserve of eight armies and two tank armies, including fifty-seven rifle divisions, nine cavalry divisions, twenty-one rifle brigades, four mechanized corps, and seven tank corps.[37] The reserves took part in the end of the Kursk battle and then launched the Russian offensives.

COMBAT UNITS FOR SELECT MONTHS[38]

Type	May 1942	Nov. 1942	July1943	Jan. 1945
Rifle divisions	442	436	471	529
Rifle brigades	139	172	99	36
Tank corps	24	27	29	27
Mechanized corps		11	12	14
Tank brigades	172	202	166	177
Tank regiments		81	170	222
Artillery divisions		7	27	35
Antiaircraft div.			33	59
Tank destroyer reg.			110	351
Self-propelled artillery regiments			53	367
German Front only				
Men (in millions)		6.1	6.4	6.5
Tanks and SPs		6,900	9,900	12,900
Guns and mortars		77,700	103,100	108,000

The supporting arms, tanks, and artillery experienced the greatest growth in 1943. During 1943 the tank forces grew to 5 armies, 37 corps, 80 independent brigades, and 149 independent tank and mechanized artillery regiments. Artillery increased to 6 corps and 26 divisions.[39] For the remainder of the war, the Red Army concentrated on creating new armored and artillery units. Rifle brigades formed rifle divisions or were abolished.

After the Red Army crossed the old Soviet border at the end of 1944, the bonus manpower of men drafted in reoccupied Soviet territory ended. The young men in the annual classes tended to go to the new armored artillery formations that required longer training and greater skills. Manpower resources were not used to replace the losses in the divisions and the rifle strength of the divisions declined steadily. The sixteen rifle divisions created in 1944 and 1945 were primarily new divisions formed in the Far East (nine) and divisions formed from brigades (four).

The shift in the structure of the Red Army was made possible by the prodigious production of weapons. Firepower, not manpower, won the final battles. The number of weapons in the rifle divisions increased as the number of riflemen decreased. Recruits went to hundreds of new artillery, self-propelled artillery, and tank regiments. The number of guns in the self-propelled artillery regiments increased from twelve to sixteen or twenty-one. Tank regiments had more tanks and more than compensated for the abolition of some tank brigades. The total number of men at the front remained about 6 million, but more were serving heavy weapons, guns, and armored vehicles and fewer were serving in the rifle companies.

The Soviet Union had a prolific mobilization machine—far greater in capacity than the U.S. and German systems, both of which produced well-documented dramatic results in World War II. While the U.S. system raised 90 divisions (and countless other specialized units) and the Germans mobilized over 400 divisions, the Soviet Union formed over 700 divisions.

The more one studies the details of mobilization of the Red Army, the more impressive is the magnitude of the accomplishment. The Red Army in June 1941, in the midst of expansion, was poorly trained, equipped with obsolete weapons, and led by inexperienced commanders. The army surprised in June 1941 despite the warnings was destroyed at the frontiers. New armies were hastily but efficiently mobilized between July and December 1941. The new divisions, despite anecdotes of cavalry without saddles and shortages of all kinds, halted the vaunted Germany Army at the gates of Leningrad, Moscow, and Rostov. Most of these divisions had less than six months' training or had provided cadres for other divisions. The Red Army switched from defense to offense in the winter offensive of 1941–42.

Ground down by the winter offensive, the Red Army reformed a second time beginning in March 1942, but suffered serious defeats during the German summer offensive of 1942. By November 1942 a third program had developed a powerful force that defeated the Germans at Stalingrad, and went on to victory. By mid-1943 the Red Army was well-trained, well-equipped, well-supplied, and well-led.

Winston Churchill did not believe that General George Marshall could create a 100-division U.S. army within eighteen months after Pearl Harbor and train the force well enough to take on the Germans in France in 1943. With a much smaller industrial base, the Russians created more than 500 new divisions with far less time to train (usually three to six months), and defeated the Germans in the bloodiest campaign in history.

CHAPTER 4

Manpower

The prevalent image of the Red Army during World War II is that of a mass army, poorly trained and inadequately equipped, with a few exceptions, such as the T-34 tank. The general interpretation has been that this inexhaustible mass of men had overwhelmed the German Army through sheer numbers while absorbing huge losses. The true picture was more complicated. Because of heavy losses in the opening months of the war and the occupation of the most populous regions of the country by the Germans, the Red Army did not have unlimited manpower after 1941. The demands for labor on the farms and in the factories competed for the available men.[1] The shortage of men had forced the Soviet Union to adopt cost-effective use of manpower. The Russians had to learn to use their men in the most efficient manner. By early 1943 the Russians had over 6 million well equipped and trained men in the field against the Germans. The methods used to attain that goal led to sacrifices greater than demanded in any other nation.

Four factors determined the war potential of a nation in a war of attrition.

1. The industrial capacity to manufacture weapons and other equipment
2. The labor force
3. Raw materials
4. The skills to employ and manage the first three

Given time, industrial capacity could be expanded and managerial skills learned, so the primary components were people and raw materials. The Russians had large quantities of both, but manpower became a serious problem after the Germans occupied the western region.[2]

There were four stages in the mobilization of manpower. In the first stage the unemployed and underemployed reentered the workforce. In the second stage people moved from leisure and consumer-oriented activity to war-related activity. In both the first and second stages the military had an unlimited supply of men from nonessential activity. In the third stage, with no surplus in the civilian economy, the government had

41

to set priorities, balancing the needs of industry and the army. In the fourth stage the military appropriated workers from essential weapons production. Should the fourth stage continue too long, the war would have been lost because of the lack of replacement weapons.[3]

The Soviet Union was already in the second stage in June 1941; there were few unemployed or underemployed workers. In 1942 the position moved to the third stage, where priority decisions had to be made concerning the labor force. However, when the Russians moved to the fourth stage late in 1942, taking men from war industries, military production did not suffer because women and children replaced the men.[4] The first major loss was the population in the occupied area. Some adult males did escape, either through service in the army, by evacuation with factories, or by fleeing. The occupied area had included 40 percent of the population—about 80 million persons. Perhaps 20 or 30 million escaped, leaving about 60 million under German tale. The Germans estimated that 66 million lived in the occupied zone.[5]

The impact of the loss on the economy was enormous. The large number of men entering the army intensified the economic crisis. From 1940 to 1942 the Soviet armed forces increased from 4.2 to 10.9 million. By December 1942 6.5 million were killed or missing and nearly 5.5 million had been wounded, all of whom were replaced. The number of persons in farming, industry, and other occupations fell from 70.8 million to 44.4 million. Farming alone dropped from 35.4 to 15.1 million; industry fell from 11.0 to 7.2 million; and other employment from 20.2 to 11.2 million.[6]

Although the total population had been reduced, the primary source of military replacements was the class of young men who turned eighteen each year. A class represented the physically fit men born in a specific year eligible for induction into the army. Men born in 1920 (nineteen years of age in 1939) formed the class of 1920. The number of men in the annual classes of recruits increased steadily during the war as shown in the table "Potential Military Manpower." The Germans estimated the annual recruit intake at 1.9 to 2.2 million men.[7]

POTENTIAL MILITARY MANPOWER[8]

Birth Year	Birth Rate per Thousand	Males A in millions	Males B in millions	Male & Female in millions
1906	—	—	1.5	3.0
1907	—	—	1.5	3.0
1908	—	—	1.5	3.0
1909	—	—	1.5	3.0

POTENTIAL MILITARY MANPOWER *continued*

Birth Year	Birth Rate per Thousand	Males A in millions	Males B in millions	Male & Female in millions
1910	—	—	1.5	3.0
1911	—	—	1.5	3.0
1912	—	1.8	1.5	3.0
1913	47.0	1.8	1.5	3.0
1914	46.9	1.8	1.5	3.0
1915	39.7	1.8	1.5	3.0
1916	29.9	1.433	1.5	3.0
1917	23.9	1.4	1.5	3.0
1918	32.0	1.4	1.6	3.2
1919	31.0	1.4	1.6	3.2
1920	31.2	1.468	1.6	3.2
1921	32.6	1.76	1.6	3.2
1922	33.4	1.76	1.6	3.2
1923	38.8	1.76	1.6	3.2
1924	43.1	2.121	1.9	3.2
1925	44.7	2.122	2.2	3.2
1926	43.6	2.122	2.2	3.2
1927	43.2	2.122	2.2	3.5
1928	44.3	—	—	3.5

Note: There are two sources of estimates on male births, reflected in columns A and B. Blank spaces indicate no data available.

According to German estimates, the class of 1923 would have had about 1.6 million men minus any deaths, but the German estimates were low. With improved conditions after the Civil War, the birth rate had increased dramatically from 30.9 in 1920 to 44.3 per thousand in 1928. Based on a population of 147 million persons in 1926, the result was about 6.5 million children and 3.25 million males in the class of 1928. Of these, 90 percent were fit for service under Soviet rules, producing a class of nearly 3 million seventeen-year-olds in 1945.[9] The classes of 1921 and 1922 (men reaching eighteen in 1939 and 1940) were probably a little more than 2 million each year. The classes 1923 through 1927 probably increased to nearly 3 million annually from the area of pre-1939 Russia. However, German occupation would have reduced the number of available men to about 2 million annually from 1941 to 1943. The liberation of the occupied area in 1944 made an additional 1 million youths available each year in 1944 and 1945.

The low birth rate and high death rate in the 1930s was a result of economic conditions. After 1929 the forced collective-farm movement disrupted village life and agriculture. Famine resulted, reducing the birth rate and increasing the death rate. The birth rate was decreased by migration from country to city, the shortage of housing, and free abortion until 1936. The rate of population growth from 1926 to 1939 was only 1.1 percent, so the number of available men of military age had remained stable. The impact of the low birth rate was intensified in the postwar years when combined with the deaths caused by the war.[10]

The Soviet Union in 1941 had a high proportion of young people in its population. The Russian male population was divided as follows:[11]

Under 20 year of age	43.0 million	45.0%
20 to 39 years of age	31.5	33.0%
40 to 59 years of age	14.7	15.4%
60 and over	6.2	6.6%

Additional men came from the population of eastern Poland, the Baltic States, and Bessarabia, which had been acquired in 1939 and 1940. The total Soviet population had increased to 198 million. However, the Germans occupied these areas in 1941. Even the men drafted before the war from the recently acquired areas of the Soviet Union were not always reliable. The Germans were able to recruit hundreds of thousands of Lithuanians, Estonians, and Latvians to serve in security units of the German Army. Roumania and Finland reincorporated the captured lands into their homelands and conscripted the men into their armies. Few of these men would have made desirable Soviet soldiers. The 22 million added to the Russian population by the acquisitions of 1939 and 1940 did not translate into many additional troops.[12] Not all of the men previously under Communist control made reliable soldiers. Laplanders from the far north, Mongolians from the Far East, the disaffected nationalities of the Caucasus, and some Central Asian nationalities were not good prospects.[13]

The Red Army needed men to replace the 4,473,000 lost in the first six months of the war and to fill new units.[14] The Russians created new divisions and replaced losses from four sources: reserves called up in 1941, the annual class of young men reaching 18 years of age, returning wounded, and later in the war, men recruited in the areas liberated from the Germans. Most men of military age were in the reserve and had prewar military training. New recruits passed through an elaborate replacement training system. Wounded men were an enormous source of replacements. If possible they returned to their original units. The rest entered the replacement pool and joined other units. Severely wounded men trained recruits in the replacement units, relieving fit men for combat. Men from the reoccupied areas, "booty soldiers," included former partisans and liberated prisoners of war. Only the new recruits needed additional training in the divisional replacement battalion.[15]

Unlike Germany, Great Britain, and the United States, the Soviets had continuous compulsory military training between the wars. However, in the 1930s the Soviets disqualified one-third of the 1.5 million men in each annual class for health and other reasons. The training structure could absorb only 650,000 of the remainder, leaving 350,000 more untrained. The other 350,000 received only a minimum amount of training.[16] Many men of the classes 1896 through 1904 had combat experience in World War I and the Civil War. These men, in their late thirties and early forties in 1941 and 1942, provided the Soviets with a large pool of trained soldiers and combat-experienced noncommissioned officers.

Determining the number of potential Soviet soldiers was a matter of prime concern to Fremde Heer Ost. In October 1941 a civilian demographer compared available Russian statistics to similar German statistics to estimate Soviet manpower resources. He assumed that the Russians had 2.2 times as many men of military age as Germany and therefore could mobilize and maintain 469 divisions (2.2 times 213 German divisions). This number was very near the number active from 1942 on. Germany had 17.2 million men aged nineteen through forty-five on September 4, 1941, as follows:

Combat Fit		7,331,000	42.6%
Army	5,200,000		
SS	140,000		
Total	5,340,000		(31.0%)
Limited Service		5,574,000	32.4
Not combat fit		3,336,000	19.4
Replacements		965,000	5.6
TOTAL		17,206,000	100.0%

The Soviet Union had 46 million men fifteen through fifty years of age. Using the German percentage of men in the army, 31 percent of the total was 14,260,000. The study subtracted 2 million killed, 2.5 million wounded, and 3.5 million prisoners of war as of October 1941 from the 14,260,000. The study concluded that the Red Army had about 6,260,000 men to oppose the 3.4 million Germans on the Eastern Front.[17] This estimate was near the actual number in the later years of the war.

Another study made in March 1942 estimated that there were 47 million men of military age (sixteen to fifty years), of which 80 percent, or 38 million, were fit for service. Of these:

Estimated number on the front	5,000,000
Casualties (killed, POW, invalids)	6,000,000
Limited service	6,000,000–8,000,000
Air force and navy	2,000,000
TOTAL	19,000,000–21,000,000

There were 17 to 19 million men from which the Russians could draw replacements and create new units.[18] The computation did not include the impact of the nonavailability of the men in the occupied zone of the Soviet Union. Gehlen corrected this deficiency in a report to the German War Academy in June 1942. In the report, Gehlen noted that in January 1939 the Soviet Union had 170.5 million people. Occupied areas, parts of Finland, the Baltic States, Poland, and Roumania added 23 million. The natural increase of 6 million brought the total to 199.5 million in June 1941. As of June 1942, the Germans had occupied Russian territory with about 66 million people, reducing the base to 133.5 million.

Gehlen also introduced another significant factor: the average Russian was younger than the average German. Half of the Russians were under twenty years, whereas only one-third of Germans were under twenty. The difference was the result of heavy Russian losses during World War I, the Civil War, and to a lesser extent the Russo-Japanese War of 1905 and famine in the 1920s. Another effect of the combat deaths was that 52 percent of the older population were female. Being younger, the Russian population had more combat-age men. Gehlen concluded that 17 million additional Russians were available for military service in 1942.[19]

The Germans analyzed the Soviet population again in 1943. The study increased the potential number of men of military age to 40.3 million in June 1941, but reduced the total by half a million lost in the Finnish War and a further 12.4 million in permanent casualties since June 1941. The report concluded that as of June 1, 1943, the Russians had 12.9 million in the armed forces. The navy and the air force absorbed some men and the Far East diverted others, leaving 5.8 million on the German-Russian Front.[20] All three of these studies produced totals that were very close to the mark.

A study made in September 1944 listed the permanent losses since the beginning of the war:

Prisoners of war	5.8 million
Evacuated to Germany	1.7 million
Killed and invalids	6.6 million
TOTAL	14.5 million

In September 1944 the following diversion of men reduced the total available for military service:

War production	4.8 million
Railroads, farmers, etc.	2.7 million
NKVD	0.6 million
Labor camps	0.7 million
Unfit for service	4.5 million
TOTAL	13.3 million

These totals were subtracted from an estimate of 44 million available from the beginning of the war, leaving 16.2 million. Of these, 10.6 million were in the armed forces, of which 5,154,000 were in units on the German-Russian Front.[21] The conclusion of the study was off by more than 1 million men, as the Russians had over 6 million on the German Front in 1944.

In the closing weeks of the war, the Germans estimated that the permanent losses had risen from 14.5 million in September 1944 to 20.5 million in February 1945, including men evacuated to Germany to prevent their employment by the Red Army. The total potential men of military age, including those born between 1888 and 1927, was 50.4 million. Permanent losses and unfit men subtracted 28 million. An estimated 12.5 million were in the armed forces, of which at least 6.5 million were in the army.[22]

A summary of the five German studies showed that despite heavy Soviet losses, the Red Army grew stronger.

Date	Cumulative Losses (millions)	Total Armed Forces (millions)	European Front (millions)
October 1941	5.5	14.26	6.26
March 1942	not available	17.0	5.0
June 1943	12.4	12.9	5.8
September 1944	14.5	10.6	5.154
February 1945	20.5	12.5	5.5

The cumulative losses for February 1945 were high and likely
included many men evacuated from the liberated regions. Fremde Heer
Ost made other studies with slightly different totals, but the general conclusion was the same: the Russians were able to replace losses and add to
their strength. All of the German studies after 1942 underestimated the
number of Russian troops facing the Germans. Russian published data
for the period from 1942 on showed more than 6 million men on the
European Front:[23]

Date	European Front (millions)
November 1942	6.1
June 1943	6.4
January 1944	6.2
June 1944	6.4
January 1945	6.5

The chief of staff of the Red Army, Shtemenko, writing after the war,
compared the degree of mobilization of Russia and Germany. He wrote
that at its peak the Soviet armed forces had 11 million men representing
6 percent of the population of 194 million. The figures for losses were
edited from Shtemenko's work before publication. Soviet military losses
were 6.9 million dead, 4.5 million missing, and up to 4 million invalids.[24]
The total of 26.4 million was 13.6 percent of the population of 194 million. Shtemenko stated that the Germans mobilized 13 million, including
their losses, out of 80 million, or 16 percent, which he believed was far
too high despite the availability of foreign labor. In fact, the rate of mobilization for both countries was almost identical.[25]

Some losses, particularly in the rifle divisions, were replaced with booty
troops. Most of the Soviet Union had been liberated by mid-1944, and the
German evacuation program was not too effective. The British estimated
that only 1.5 million potential soldiers from all classes had been evacuated
by January 1945.[26] When the Soviets reoccupied an area, they immediately
extracted any available manpower. The Germans called these soldiers
"booty troops" as they were part of the booty obtained from the recapture
of the territory. In 1944 the Germans captured an order published by the
Russian 6th Army on April 27, 1944. The document had ordered the complete mobilization of men in the occupied zone. With these added men,
rifle divisions were reinforced to a strength of 6,000 or more each.[27]

Another human source was the enlistment of over 2 million women
in the Soviet armed forces, 400,000 in the air force and 1.6 million in the
army. Women made up 74 percent of the home defense antiaircraft regi-

ments, freeing over 100,000 men for other service. Women served as transport plane pilots, military police, and service and communications personnel. Volunteers served as snipers on the front lines and a few flew combat aircraft. The medical units had large numbers of women.[28] In February 1944, the 176th Guard Rifle Regiment had women serving as medical aides and as telephone operators in the signal units.[29]

Women also replaced men in industry, allowing more men to serve in the armed forces. In 1941 half a million housewives entered the workforce.[30] The percentage of women in industry increased from 41 percent in 1940 to 53 percent in October 1942. In the rural workforce, the proportion changed from 52 percent in 1939 to 71 percent in early 1943. The factories and farms were being run by women, older men, and youngsters, as the military-age men left for the army.[31]

The returning wounded made up many of the replacements for the army. Comments concerning the care of wounded men vary, but the Red Army had many medical units. Alexander Werth, writing during the war, described the death of a Russian soldier. The soldier died "in one of those terribly overcrowded field hospitals in which it was physically impossible to give the wounded all the individual attention and care that they needed."[32] Only the seriously wounded men were sent to the rear. Walking wounded returned to their units immediately after treatment in field hospitals. There was no evacuation for psychological reasons. The political officers dealt with chronic complainers.[33] The Russians adopted the pragmatic approach of considering a recovered wounded man as an asset. Several prisoners reported that badly wounded men were instructors in the training schools.

Given the large classes of incoming recruits, as well as the booty soldiers and the returning wounded, the Soviets did not exhaust their manpower in 1945, as many authors have stated. The Red Army received over 2 million recruits in 1943 and 3 million in 1944 and 1945—more than enough to replace losses. The Red Army lost 2.3 million killed and missing in 1943, 1,760,000 in 1944 and 800,000 in 1945—far fewer than the number of new recruits.[34] According to an estimate by British intelligente probably based on German sources, the Soviets lost about 1,450,000 permanent casualties (killed, POW, and wounded not returned) in 1944.[35] Replacements more than made up for the losses, permitting the formation of new units and reinforcing the existing units even in the final year of the war.[36] According to Soviet sources, the Red Army facing the Germans increased from 6.1 million men in 1942 to 6.5 million in 1945. Gehlen made an erroneous estimate showing a declining strength of the Red Army by January 1945.

Russians on the Eastern Front[37]

Date	(millions)
May 1942	4.0
January 1943	6.1
July 1943	5.9
January 1944	5.7
April 1944	5.5
January 1945	5.4

Gehlen's estimates were less than the actual numbers by a half million or more from the summer of 1943 until the end of the war. The official published Soviet figures showed more than 6 million men assigned to the German front from early 1943 to the end of the war.[38]

Winter 1941–42	4.2
Winter 1942–43	6.1
Late fall 1943	6.44
Winter 1943–44	6.2
Late fall 1944	6.5
1945	6.0

Soviet military strength on the Eastern Front was more than 6 million men from 1942 on. The reduction of men at the front in 1945 resulted from a partial demobilization. Because some men were not urgently needed to fight the collapsing German Army, the Red Army discharged them to begin rebuilding the civilian economy.

Determining the extent of the losses incurred by the Soviet Union is difficult. The changes in boundaries complicated the matter. The official figure for many years was 20 million military and civilian dead. In an article in Pravda on April 6, 1966, Kosygin said that the loss was over 20 million. A Soviet demographer in 1967 estimated the wartime deaths at 21 million. In 1989 Gorbachev raised the total to 27 million killed during World War II. Other computations estimated a loss of 19.6 million men and 6.1 million women. Nearly 2 million Russian prisoners of war died during the war. In 1993, military losses were published in thousands:

Killed and died of wounds	6,885
Missing that did not return	1,783
TOTAL DEAD	8,668
Prisoners that returned	2,775
TOTAL DEAD AND PRISONERS	11,444

After the war, 5,458,000 former prisoners and civilians returned to the Soviet Union. Many did not return, especially those from the Baltic States and the Ukraine. There were 45 million fewer people in the Soviet Union in 1959 than there would have been if ratio of birth-to-death rates of 1940 had continued. The loss included 10 million military deaths, 15 million civilian deaths, 10 million children who were not conceived because of dead potential parents, and 10 million persons who left the Soviet Union and prisoners of war who did not return.[39]

A detailed study published in 1971 by Urlanis concluded that the final death toll was the official 20 million, including 16.5 million males and 3.5 million females, plus the normal death rate of 2 million per year, a total of 28 million. Using tables of children enrolled in schools in the 1950s, it is clear there were 10 million fewer children because of the war.[40] Urlanis listed the civilian war-related deaths as follows in millions:[41]

Ukrainians	4.5
White Russians	2.2
Russians	1.8
Lithuanians	0.7
Latvians	0.6
Estonians	0.1
Moldavians	0.06
TOTAL	9.96

If civilian men and women in the occupied area died in near equal numbers, it is likely that at least 5 million women died because of the war. Urlanis probably altered his conclusion to agree with official policy in 1971.[42] Urlanis also supported the figure of 10 million military dead. The enormous Soviet losses in the war had a traumatic impact on the country. Every effort was made to conceal the facts and the resulting weakness of the Soviet economy from the West in the postwar world.

However, equally important to the number of men in the army was their quality physically and emotionally. The improved living conditions in the Soviet Union in the 1930s had a dramatic upscale impact on the health of the population and specifically on the health of potential soldiers. During World War I, 30 percent of the men called up were rejected for medical reasons. By 1933, improvement in health was already evident. Of the men examined prior to induction in Moscow in 1926, 38 per 1,000 had tuberculosis; in 1933, only 5.7 per 1,000. Heart disease dropped from 78 per 1,000 to 18.6; and "poor physical development" dropped from 25.7 per 1,000 to 4.4 per 1,000 during the same years. Similar improvements in the health of those called up were recorded for other regions: for example, heart disease in the Ukraine dropped from 73.5 per 1,000 to 5.1 per 1,000.[43]

The Germans estimated that of the 50.4 million Russians in the classes of 1888 through 1927, 7 percent were unfit for service.[44] The classes of 1926 and 1927 were called up in the last two years of the war. Of the class of 1926, 90 percent were inducted; 5 percent were considered unfit; and 5 percent had been evacuated to Germany before the Russians liberated the area. Of the class of 1927, 90 percent were inducted; 5 percent were unfit; 2 percent had been sent to Germany; and the remaining 3 percent were unknown.[45] The health of the average Russian citizen was good enough for him to qualify as a soldier under the Soviet criteria.

Of great significance was the age of the combat soldier. In the first six months of the war the Red Army included the regular army professionals as well as the classes that were in the army undergoing their regular training, the class of eighteen-year-olds called up for 1941, and several million older reserves. In 1942 Stalin had to dip more deeply into the reserves to replace the losses of 1941. Reserves thirty-two to thirty-six years of age made up most of the 358th Division in January 1942. The 360th Division had thirty-five- to forty-five-year-olds and most of the 21st Rifle Brigade were about thirty years.[46] In August 1942 the 1st Guard Army, the 24th Army, and the 66th Army were manned by old reservists.[47] A Russian general, Nekrasov, told the correspondent Alexander Werth that shortly after the Battle of Stalingrad, the replacements were "really pathetic." He said that the men were "either old chaps of fifty or fifty-five, or youngsters of eighteen or nineteen. They would stand there on the shore, shivering with cold and fear." Those that survived the first few days quickly became hardened soldiers.[48]

The manpower position improved in 1943 because of fewer losses and larger classes of recruits. The 226th Rifle Division formed in June and July in Lgov with men aged twenty-one to forty-six. More than 70 percent were twenty-one to twenty-seven, and 90 percent were Russian.[49] Even at the end of the war men as old as fifty-two years were fighting, but there were the exceptions.[50] The younger men went to the mechanized and technical units, while the infantry often received the older men.

The morale of the troops was important. Napoleon stated that morale was twice as important as material factors. The Soviet soldiers were sturdy and able to endure hardships that would have sapped the energy of other troops. Most of the Russian infantry had been farmers who were accustomed to hard physical labor and the outdoors. In 1937 the population was 57.9 percent collective farmers and handicraftsmen organized in cooperatives, 5.9 percent individual peasants, and 36.2 factory and office workers.[51] In 1940, 68.4 percent of the population lived in rural areas and only 31.6 percent in urban centers.[52] The average Russian soldier was strong enough to dig trenches without complaining.

The Russians were not robots but individuals with dissimilar emotions. The Germans considered the Soviet riflemen very cruel. The Germans believed that Russians and men from the Asian republics were the best soldiers. The White Russians, Ukrainians, and the various Caucasian nationalities were not as reliable and formed the major source of Hiwis and Ost troops who fought for the Germans.[53]

The forced collectivization of agricultural land left many farmers with a lingering hatred of the Communist regime.[54] Early in the war, the leadership realized that the Russian soldiers would fight harder for Russia than for the Communist Party. The propaganda directed at the troops therefore stressed fighting for "Mother Russia," national patriotism, and hatred of the Nazis. Ilya Ehrenburg was the major spokesman for the campaign of anti-German hatred.[55]

The Communist Party had considerable influence in the army. The political officers maintained discipline. The Party considered the commissars great contributors to the success of the army. These Communists were supposed to build up self-confidence and foster love of country, as well as indoctrinate the men with Communist ideology. They encouraged soldiers to join the Communist Party, which would give them valuable perquisites in the postwar world. By the end of the war there were 3 million members of the Party in the armed forces. The army consisted of 25 percent Communists and 20 percent Komsomols in May 1945. The highest award, Hero of the Soviet Union, was given to 6,437 Communists, 74 percent of the recipients of the award.[56] Most of the Communists were in the elite units—the tank and mechanized units and the airborne divisions. In September 1943, fifty-four men in the mortar company (almost all) of the 1st Battalion of the 3rd Guard Parachute Brigade were Komsomols.[57] Toward the end of the war, Hitler emulated the commissar system with the requirement that units appoint officers to be charged with political indoctrination.

The morale of the Red Army was still uncertain in 1942 despite the official propaganda and evidence of German atrocities in recaptured villages. In July and August 1942 in the Don Bend entire units disintegrated, while others fought to the last man. The causes of disintegration were poor leadership, insufficient training, and lack of unit cohesion. Reserve divisions sent into battle before they were ready were unable to withstand the German attacks. Tenacity resulted from good leadership and harsh punishment of deserters by the NKVD guarding the rear.[58]

Soviet morale improved in 1943 and 1944, as suggested in a German report on the average daily number of men deserting from the Red Army.[59]

July 1943	209
August 1943	130
September 1943	43
October 1943	43
November 1943	30
December 1943	28
January 1944	23
February 1944	19
March 1944	15
April 1944	10
May 1944	11
June 1944	11
July 1944	12
August 1944	26
September 1944	41
October 1944	74
November 1944	27

There was no apparent explanation for the sudden jump in the rate of desertions in September and October 1944. The sharp decline after the Russian victory at Kursk and the counteroffensives was clearly the result of knowledge that the Germans were beaten. Nothing helped morale more than defeating the enemy.

A careful analysis of a paper found on the body of an unidentified Russian officer produced a case study for comparison to the recurrent generalizations concerning the Red Army. The document listed the names and ranks of fifteen men (presumably in that officer's platoon), including military specialty, year of induction in the army, membership in the Communist Party, civilian occupation, previous combat experience, any convictions, date of birth, birthplace, nationality, education, and whether they had lived in the occupied zone.[60]

The document was a microcosm of the composition of the Red Army. The platoon was a mixture of many nationalities speaking a variety of languages. Achmetov, the sergeant, was from Fergana in Uzbek. Saarkalov, the sniper, was from Tashkent, also in Uzbek where the language resembled Turkish. Kibayev came from Dzhambul, about 125 miles northeast of Tashkent in Kazakh. Vassilyev, Kvatschow, Lavrenov,

Gonscharov, and another person whose name was illegible came from Mogilev in the White Russian republic and spoke a Slavic language. Gremev and Avilov spoke Russian and came from Ryazan.

Uchanov, Amyankov, and Stepezov came from the central area. Uchanov was Russian but came from the Tatar Republic. The language was related to Turkish, and he may have been bilingual. Amyankov was a Chuvash; the Chuvash language was related to Finnish. Stepezov was a Russian born in Moscow. Smirnyagin was a Russian from Sverdlovsk. Romazov was also a Russian, probably from Berdiansk. Although the platoon represented a broad spectrum of nationalities and languages, the men came from three distinct areas: the south around Tashkent, the center east of Moscow, and Mogilev.

The ethnic makeup of the platoon was six Russians, five White Russians, two Uzbeks, one Chuvash, and one Kazakh, an unusually high percentage of non-Russians and White Russians. The document was dated August 30, 1944, and was presumably found earlier in the month. Mogilev, the home of five men, was retaken in June 1944 by the 49th Army of the 2nd White Russian Front. The five White Russians probably were taken into the platoon after that time.

The platoon had soldiers age forty-two or older and two aged fifty and fifty-one. Only four of the men were under twenty-four years of age, and eight were over thirty-five. Two birth dates were illegible. Of the six men drafted in 1941, one was fifty-one, and others were forty-three, forty-six, and thirty-seven, although they were three years younger when drafted. All four were White Russians born in the Mogilev area and had lived in the occupied zone. Presumably they had been left behind the lines in 1941 and had returned to their homes around Mogilev on the Western edge of the Pripet Marshes, an area that harbored many partisans during the German occupation. The other two 1941 draftees, both young Russians, were submachine gunners and presumably the best soldiers in the platoon, based on the weapon assigned and experience.

There was another White Russian from Mogilev, age forty-four, who had been drafted in 1943. He had also lived in the Mogilev area during the German occupation, but had no combat experience. Of the fifteen men in the platoon, six were identified as booty troops, given a few days training, issued parts of a uniform and a rifle, and assigned to a rifle company.[61] To restrict the number, the Germans shipped as many men as possible to Germany before relinquishing territory.

Besides the four elderly White Russians, there were four other men over thirty-five; three were Russians and one was an Uzbek. Two of the Russians, ages forty-nine and fifty, had been drafted in 1942, one from

Ryazan and the other from the Tatar Republic. These two were part of the callup of 1942. The third Russian, age forty-two, had lived in an occupied zone, was first drafted in 1943, and had previous combat. He was probably another booty soldier picked up by the platoon. The last man over age thirty-five was an Uzbek. Trained as a sniper, he had been in combat twice before. Along with the platoon sergeant, also from Uzbek, he was one of the more well-trained soldiers in the platoon.

Younger men in the platoon generally had received better training. The thirty-seven-year-old was a Russian trained in the artillery who had been reassigned to a rifle platoon. As riflemen became scarce, divisions were ordered to reduce the number of men in the artillery gun crews and retrain the younger artillerymen as riflemen. The thirty-year-old was a Kazakh drafted in 1942 and, though twice in combat previously, had no listed military specialty. The twenty-three-year-old, a Russian born in Sverdlovsk, was a machine pistol man. The twenty-two-year-old was an Uzbek who had been drafted in 1942. The two twenty-one-year-old men were a Russian born in Moscow who carried a machine pistol, and a Chuvash who was trained as a mortar man.

Without fail, the younger soldiers were better trained; and the older men and the booty soldiers were the riflemen with the least amount of weapons training. The sergeant was only twenty-two; the artilleryman, thirty-seven; the mortar man, twenty-one; the sniper, forty; and the two machine pistol men were twenty-three and twenty-one. All of the riflemen were forty-two or over. The platoon had extensive combat experience. Of the fifteen men, one had four previous combat assignments; two had three; five had two; and six had combat experience at least once. Only one man had no previous combat experience—a White Russian booty soldier.

The year in which the men were drafted verified that older men were called up throughout the war. Of the six drafted in 1941, the age range was twenty-one (only eighteen when drafted) to fifty-one. The six drafted in 1942 ranged from twenty-one to fifty; the three drafted in 1943 were in their forties. Two Russians had been drafted in each of the three years; four of the White Russians had been drafted in 1941 and one in 1943. The men from the eastern provinces were all 1942 draftees, indicating that as manpower grew short, the net spread to areas not previously gleaned. The major expansion of the Red Army in 1942 drew heavily on eastern areas.[62]

The civilian occupations of the men provided an insight into Soviet society in 1940. The sergeant had been an office worker; two men had been workers presumably in factories both from Mogilev; and the rest had been collective-farm workers. Skilled men were in such great demand for the elite units and technical branches of service that a high percentage of the infantry was from the farms. Even the office-worker sergeant was from Uzbek rather than Russia. Those men born near the large cities of Moscow, Ryazan, and Sverdlovsk listed their occupations as collective-farm workers.

The men of the platoon were not well educated. The sergeant had some technical school education, and one private had eight years of grammar school. Of the other thirteen, only three had five years of schooling, probably leaving school at the age of eleven or twelve. Four had four years; three had three years; and two had only two years of schooling. The lack of education revealed that Soviet strides in improving education had not reached the age group in the army. Soviet statistics stated that 20 percent of the Red Army in 1939 had completed secondary school or beyond, and 60 percent had completed grammar school. The better educated men apparently were siphoned off to the technical services.[63] In the platoon most of the men had left school before the end of the Civil War, when the children would have begun to enjoy more schooling. Some of the soldiers came from the more remote and less settled areas of the Soviet Union, and most were collective farmers. The two members of the Young Communist League had four and five years of school, respectively. The two Komsomols were young, twenty and twenty-three, and both came from the east, from Sverdlovsk and Chuvash.

The men could scarcely read and write and spoke various languages, though probably all knew some Russian. The platoon leader would have had serious difficulty in training them and developing sophisticated tactics. The median age in the platoon was forty years. A rifle platoon with men aged forty-nine, fifty, and fifty-one was inconceivable to Western armies. All of the men forty-two and over were either not designated or listed as riflemen. With one exception, all of the men under forty-two had received special training. The poor quality of the infantry explained Russian tactics. A fifty-year-old rifleman with limited education could not be expected to carry out tactics relying on personal initiative as practiced by the Germans. Instead, the Red Army conunanders had to rely on carefully rehearsed plans.[64]

Three other documents provided useful comparisons, revealing the makeup of a mechanized brigade, a tank destroyer battalion, and an artillery battery in 1943. The first document described the 51st Mechanized Brigade on November 25, 1942. Although the table of organization called for 1,156 men, there were only 841 in the brigade. The brigade, formed on September 16, 1942, at Kosterovo, had no previous combat experience. In November it had been in the Caucasus as part of the 6th Mechanized Corps. The age breakdown was:

19 to 21 years	171
23 to 25 years	323
26 to 30 years	223
31 to 35 years	84
36 to 40 years	37
Unknown	3
TOTAL	841

The men were well trained; 646 had specialized training, including 198 who had attended regimental schools. Only 195 had no special training. The men were experienced; 222 had previous commands but only 164 had combat experience. The predominance of young men and the Lack of combat experience was a consequence of the recent organization of the brigade. The brigade had an excellent cadre.[65] The youth, experience, and training differed a great deal from the rifle platoon above.

The second document described the 261st Tank Destroyer Battalion of the 340th Rifle Division. The 340th Division formed in September 1941 in Balachov in the Volga Military District. The only data in the document were the age groups of the 268 men in the battalion. Compared to the elderly men of the rifle platoon, most of the men in the battalion were under thirty-five, as was case in the mechanized brigade:

Age	Number of Men
18	15
19	17
20	13
21 to 25	40
26 to 35	139
36 to 45	30
46 to 48	4

The spread in ages was as expected. Divisions formed in September 1941 were made up of reservists, many of whom were in the twenty-six-to-thirty-five age group. The casualty rate in a tank destroyer battalion was lower than in a rifle platoon, and many of the original men may have been in the battalion in 1944.[66]

The third document described a battery of the 615th Howitzer Artillery Regiment. The regiment was probably the howitzer regiment of the 197th Rifle Division, formed in April 1941 in Kiev. In July 1941, the regiment was withdrawn from the division and became the corps artillery regiment of the 29th Rifle Corps at Vilnyus. In December 1942, the regiment formed part of the 47th Howitzer Brigade of the 13th Artillery Division. As part of a prewar division, the battery had many younger men:

Age	Number of Men
19	2
20	9
21 to 29	44
30 to 35	8
36 to 46	8

Only thirty of the men were married; the other forty-one were single. Although originally part of a division formed in Kiev in 1941, the unit did not have many Ukrainians, as might be expected.

Nationality	Number of Men
Russian	51
Ukrainian	12
White Russian	3
Tartar	1
Armenian	1
Jew	1
Kazakh	1
Other	1

The probable date of the report was January 8, 1944. From the date of formation, April 1941, to January 1944 most of the Ukrainians had probably transferred to other units. A regiment using 122mm howitzers would have suffered few combat casualties.

The education level was quite high compared to the rifle platoon. Six had attended and nine had graduated from high school. Twenty-one had attended, and thirty-five had graduated from elementary school. The rate of Communist Party affiliation was very high: thirty-six were Party members, eighteen were Young Communists, and only sixteen were non-Party members.[67] The Young Communists, a man who had attended a technical school, and the men who had graduated from high school and elementary school were examples of the artillery receiving better manpower. All three documents confirmed that the younger and better qualified men had been taken by the technical units and that the infantry received the others.

The rifle platoons suffered the heaviest casualties during the grinding offensives that drove back the Germans. The Germans extracted heavy casualties as they slowly gave ground after 1943. On the other hand, the Russians were able to sustain the combat value of the rifle divisions with a steady stream of replacements though many were of inferior quality. The number of men in rifle platoons decreased while the available men formed new supporting units. The combat value of divisions was increased through more and better weapons. The Soviets continued to form additional units of all kinds throughout the war while constantly improving the armament. The Russians maintained about 6 million men at the front from January 1943 until the end, while the number of guns and mortars increased from 72,000 to 91,400. The number of tanks and self-propelled artillery pieces increased from 6,000 to 11,000.[68] The Soviet Union had not exhausted its manpower in 1945; instead more troops were used to operate heavy weapons while the number of riflemen declined.

CHAPTER 5

The Evolution of the Rifle Division

The evolution of the Soviet rifle division from 1930 to 1945 offered an insight into the intricate process of developing the optimum organization of a military unit. The process was dynamic, as the evolution was subject to continually changing factors. Influencing the changes were weapons technology, manpower, strategic and tactical doctrine, the potential or actual enemy, logistical capability, transportation, and environment. The changes had a direct impact on how many such units the Soviet Union could create and support as effective fighting units.

The triangular composition prevalent at all levels in the German, U.S., and British armies provided one element in reserve for each pair at the front, a 33 percent reserve. A division with only two component units—for example, the U.S. divisions and brigades in World War I—provided either no reserve or 50 percent reserves. An option was to break up organic units, taking one regiment out of one brigade as a reserve and leaving two regiments of one brigade and one regiment of the other brigade at the front, a 25 percent reserve at the cost of disrupting the chain of command. The command structure suffered with that arrangement. Four component units would have provided the same option: 25 percent or 50 percent reserves. Neither result was satisfactory as a 25 percent reserve was not enough. The triangular composition providing 33 percent reserves was preferable because either of the front-line sectors could be doubled in strength without breaking up organic units or disturbing the chain of command. A platoon would have two groups or squads forward and one in reserve. The rifle company would have two rifle platoons forward and one in reserve, and on up the ladder.

The smallest administrative and tactical unit was the rifle company. The rifle company has a long and varied history, but essentially the term has referred to a unit of 100 to 200 men under the command of a captain. The company was divided into two to four platoons commanded by lieutenants. The rifle company performed administrative, tactical, and

61

psychological functions. The company provided all of the essential human requirements. It fed, clothed, and equipped the infantrymen. The company cooks prepared the food; the supply sergeant issued equipment and ammunition; and the company commander paid the troops. When not in the field, the company lived together in one or more barracks. In the field both Germans and Russians usually provided two hot meals per day prepared by the company kitchen.

The relationship among the company commander, the platoon leaders, the section leaders, and the individual riflemen involved mutual trust, respect, concern, and devotion to duty. The company was an extended family for the soldier. The company commander knew all of his group or squad leaders and the platoon leader knew all of his men. Unit loyalty and personal relationships did more than any abstract feelings of patriotism to hold men together and reverse the normal intelligent response to flee from danger. If the company became too large, personal relationships deteriorated and performance suffered.

The number of men that one individual could control in a stressful situation limited the size of the rifle group. Few men could lead more than a dozen individuals, knowing what they could accomplish and what their limitations were. Most leaders could effectively control only a half-dozen. The basic building block in World War II was a light-machine-gun team supported by a few riflemen. A group usually had two fire teams of four or five men each, a leader with a machine pistol, a machine gunner, an ammunition carrier, and a rifleman. With two extra riflemen, the team leader could still maintain control.

In June 1944 the Russian rifle platoon consisted of a platoon leader, a messenger, and four groups, each with a group leader, a light machine gunner, an assistant gunner, a sniper, and five riflemen.[1] Toward the end of the war a second light-machine-gun team and one or more men responsible for antitank defense had replaced the riflemen in the group. The group seldom numbered more than ten men after 1941.

It was difficult for one to lead more than three or four subordinates. A leader had to control not only his own direct subordinates but, to understand a situation fully, also had to be aware of the men serving under his direct subordinates. A platoon leader commanded three or four group leaders with a total of about thirty men. A company commander led three platoons with administrative and heavy weapons support. The battalion commander directed the company commanders, but he had to know the platoon leaders and where the platoons were to maintain tight control of the whole group.

The most efficient rifle company had from 100 to 120 men armed with 18 light machine guns and a few mortars and antitank weapons. Firepower came from the light machine guns. As long as there were enough men to operate the machine guns, the company remained efficient in defense and at least functional in offense. The company could increase to 140 to 160 men, but any more added little to its combat value. A company of fewer than 80 men was also inefficient because of the high ratio of leaders to men. When a company was reduced to two rifle platoons, the triangular formation was lost.

The company was the basic administrative unit and formed an "organic" part of larger units. An organic component of a unit was part of its table of organization and remained permanently assigned. From time to time other units would be attached, but they remained only as long as needed. The largest unit made up of organic components was the division.

The term division had come into use under Napoleon to describe an integrated tactical and administrative unit capable of independent action. In World War II the Russian rifle division usually had three rifle regiments and an artillery regiment. The rifle regiments included two or three rifle battalions plus heavy weapons companies. The rifle battalion consisted of two or more rifle companies.

The Russians operated on a very lean service component compared to the German and U.S. armies. The Russians strived to create a division that had maximum combat effectiveness and minimum service overhead. A minimum level of service support was required to supply rations and ammunition. The Germans used hiwis—Soviet prisoners of war who had volunteered to work for the Germans—to carry out many service functions. Each German rifle division had up to 2,000 hiwis, about one-fifth of its total strength. The hiwis cared for the horses, drove the wagons, handled supplies, prepared food, and did other noncombatant tasks.

The Russians used women to replace men as snipers, communications personnel, and service personnel even at the company level. When fighting in their own country until 1944 the Russians used the civilian population to dig trenches, move supplies, and provide other services—for example, running the railroads—reducing the need for service units. The availability of civilian support reduced the administrative tail of the Red Army. Nondivisional troops were more likely to be combat, not service troops. The increase from 25 percent in 1942 to 60 percent in 1945 in nondivisional troops consisted mostly of supporting weapons units, not service.

Many of the service and supporting weapons units were not part of
the division but were essential to its operation. The term *division slice*
referred to the total number of men in a theater divided by the number
of divisions. The slice included all the troops needed to maintain a division in combat. The American division slice in January 1945 in Europe
was 43,400 men.[2] The U.S. slice included a large service element; less
than a third of the troops were in the division. The German division slice
dropped from 34,873 in 1939 to 21,895 in 1944, while the infantry division decreased from 16,626 to 9,985.[3] About half the troops were in the
divisions.

In June 1941, the Russian field armies on the border had a division
slice of 16,600 men with about 8,000 to 9,000 men in the division.[4] The
slice varied from about 13,400 in 1942 to 12,300 in 1945 (including rifle
divisions and tank and mechanized corps). The Soviet rifle division
strength dropped from about 10,500 in 1942 to 5,000 or less in 1945,
while supporting arms increased. The rifle division made up 50 percent
of the division slice in 1941 and had risen to 75 percent in 1942, but by
1945 the rifle division made up only 40 percent or less of the division
slice.[5] The Russian division slice had only half as many men as the German, but had almost as much firepower provided by the many supporting artillery and tank units.

The size of the division determined the number of rifle divisions that
could be created and supported. The Germans made some poor decisions, creating more divisions than could be supported. The result was a
waste of trained leaders with too few men to lead. The Soviets limited the
number of rifle divisions to about 500. The number of riflemen in the
division dwindled when recruits went to new artillery and armored units
in the last years of the war, but the new weapons added firepower. By the
time of the Battle of Berlin there was a tank or mechanized gun plus two
or more artillery pieces with every platoon of infantry.

The restructuring of the Soviet rifle division had begun in earnest in
1938. The territorial divisions were eliminated. The plan approved by the
General Staff in March 1938 called for the creation of ninety-six rifle divisions of four types: two levels of divisions on the borders, one level for the
interior, and the mountain division. The reorganization was to be completed by the end of the year.[6] The two levels on the borders were the
wartime with a *shtat* (table of organization and equipment) of 14,483
men and the "12,000" with a *shtat* of 10,291 men. The interior divisions,
the "6,000," had a *shtat* of 5,864 men and the mountain divisions had a
shtat of 8,829 men.[7] The four tables of organization were retained until
June 1941.

The wartime division *shtat* included three rifle regiments, two artillery regiments, an antitank battalion, an antiaircraft battalion, a reconnaissance battalion, a signal battalion, an engineer battalion, a transport battalion, and a medical battalion. The equipment included 10,420 rifles, 1,204 machine pistols, 558 machine guns, 12 152mm howitzers, 20 122mm howitzers, 16 76mm guns, 66 mortars, 16 light tanks, 13 armored cars, 558 motor vehicles, 99 tractors, and 3,000 horses.[8] In January 1939, divisions on the borders averaged 6,959 men, while those in the interior had 5,220 men.[9] The *shtat* of the "12,000" and "6,000" divisions had fewer rifles, trucks, and horses, but had most of the weapons of the wartime division in 1939.[10]

Few if any divisions were at wartime strength when the Germans attacked in June 1941. At the beginning of the Great Patriotic War, the average Russian rifle division had from 8,000 to 12,000 men and 80 to 90 percent of authorized weapons. By July 1941 the official strength of the division decreased to 10,859 men, 171 machine pistols, 270 machine guns, 54 76mm and 45mm guns, and 203 motor vehicles.[11] By mid-July 1941, the average was down to 6,000. The number of guns and mortars had been reduced by over 50 percent and motor vehicles by 64 percent.[12] In mid-September the rifle division lost one of its artillery regiments. The number of 45mm antitank guns had dropped from 36 to 18, 76mm guns from 20 to 12, 122mm howitzers from 30 to 24; and all of the 152mm howitzers had been lost.[13]

During the fall and winter of 1941 the Russians suffered heavy losses during the final German offensives and the winter counteroffensive. In January 1942, the 4th Shock Army divisions began to attack with divisions of 8,000 men each, and after three weeks the divisions averaged only 2,000.[14] By the end of December 1941 the high command had disbanded 124 divisions, but in the same period 308 new divisions formed.[15] The strength of the new divisions was lower, but the supply of technical equipment and weapons improved as evacuated factories resumed production. On December 6, 1941, the *shtat* of the rifle division provided major increases in the number of machine pistols, machine guns, mortars, and antitank rifles.[16] These weapons were comparatively easy to manufacture in small factories. Improvement in the supply of more complex weapons was a longer process. On March 18, 1942, a new *shtat* for the rifle division cut manpower by a further 10 percent but increased the number of mortars, machine pistols, and antitank weapons. Although the number of men in the division declined to 10,566 men, the number of machine guns had increased from 558 to 577. The artillery regiment received two additional batteries of 76mm guns.[17]

The Russians were short of manpower to fill the many new rifle divisions and other units. In July 1942, of the 38 divisions on the Stalingrad Front, half had 6,000 to 8,000 men, but others had fewer, some as few as 1,000 men.[18] In August 1942, divisions in the 64th Army at Stalingrad had the following numbers of men:[19]

138th Rifle Division	4,200 men
29th Rifle Division	11,000 men
157th Rifle Division	1,500 men

The authorized strength of the division declined again in December 1942 to 9,435 men, but the number of automatic weapons and artillery increased. The number of machine guns rose to 605 compared to the 359 authorized in the December 1941 *shtat*. In place of 66 guns, there were 92 artillery pieces including 32 76mm guns. The new 57mm anti-tank gun replaced the 45mm gun as supplies became available. The new Goryunov heavy machine gun was simpler and lighter. The Sudayev, a new machine pistol, replaced some rifles.[20]

There were few full divisions. One-fourth of the divisions had up to 8,000 men; the others had 5,000 to 7,000; and some had from 3,000 to 5,000 men.[21] However, divisions involved in offensive operations were at the higher levels. A German survey based on captured documents showed many divisions in the Don Front in December 1942 near the authorized strength, as follows:[22]

	Men	Machine Guns
1st Rifle Division	9,305	226
153rd Rifle Division	9,804	235
197th Rifle Division	9,177	183
203rd Rifle Division	7,717	139
278th Rifle Division	5,531	51
35th Guards Division	6,051	333
41st Guards Division	5,295	321
195th Rifle Division	9,201	303
8th Guards Division	6,712	323
44th Guards Division	6,364	372
266th Rifle Division	10,163	331

In January 1943, Gehlen made a survey of the changes that had occurred in the organization of the Russian rifle division. The number of men authorized in the division had dropped to 10,800. The actual number in most divisions was even lower. The reduction had resulted from the elimination of the divisional mortar battalion and the 76mm gun batteries in the third battalion of the artillery regiment. A divisional machine gun company was added.

A battery of 120mm mortars was added to each regiment, replacing the regimental mortar battalion equipped with 50mm and 82mm mortars. Each rifle battalion received a new 82mm mortar company. The 50mm mortars went to the rifle companies. The total impact was to increase the number of mortars in the division by 18 120mm mortars. The battalion machine gun companies remained but had fewer heavy machine guns. Fewer of the ineffective antitank rifles were assigned. To reinforce the antitank defense of the division, high-velocity 76mm guns replaced some regimental 76mm guns. The number of machine pistols in the rifle regiment nearly doubled from 188 to 373.

The changes reflected lessons learned during the winter offensive. The new tactics stressed the use of small combat groups with the highest possible firepower. Dispersing the 120mm mortars to the regimental level and the increase in machine pistols were major aspects of the change. Concentrating heavy machine guns at the divisional level gave the commander the ability to concentrate firepower behind individual regiments and battalions. Despite the loss of manpower, the firepower of the division had increased.[23]

The July 1943 division was much the same as December 1942 with a *shtat* of 9,354 officers and men, 1,732 horses, and 125 motor vehicles. The division still had three rifle regiments with three battalions and an antitank battalion with 12 45mm guns. The armament of the artillery regiment increased to 20 76mm guns and 12 122mm howitzers. The division had an engineer battalion, a signal company, a reconnaissance company, and service units. There were 12 76mm regimental guns and 36 45mm antitank guns in the rifle regiments. The division had 605 machine guns and 2,110 machine pistols.

The Russians maintained these divisions at a reduced strength of between 5,000 and 6,000. On August 13, 1943, the 5th Soviet Army had six rifle divisions and all near that strength, as shown:[24]

	Men
312th Rifle Division	4,665
207th Rifle Division	4,989
208th Rifle Division	5,270
352nd Rifle Division	6,215
153rd Rifle Division	5,328
154th Rifle Division	4,719

On August 22, a reduced table of organization was authorized with only 8,000 men and only 228 machine guns, but otherwise about the same armament. Most of the cuts came in the rifle company, reducing the number of riflemen in the group. The rifle regiment consisted of three rifle battalions, a machine-gun battalion, an artillery battalion with twelve 45mm guns and four 76mm guns, a mortar company, a machine pistol company, an engineer company, a signal company, an antitank rifle company, and service units.[25]

The number of men in the rifle divisions fell again in October 1943. A smaller rifle division had an authorized strength of 6,800 men, but the heavy battles of late 1943 had reduced the average actual strength to 3,600. The decline in manpower was reflected in fewer light machine gun fare teams. Only 328 machine guns remained, a serious loss of combat power. There were 656 machine guns in a German division, 636 in a U.S. division, and 1,262 in a British division.[26] The Germans estimated that the combat effectiveness of the Russian rifle divisions declined by 50 percent beginning in 1942.[27] However, the loss of power in the rifle division was offset by increasing the number of armored and artillery units.

The new Soviet rifle division had smaller support and service elements. The gun crews of the 212th Rifle Division lost two of the six men and the extra men went to the rifle companies.[28] Men were combed from service units and women replaced men as signal personnel, telephone operators, laundry workers, ambulance drivers, and military police.[29] Still the reduction in the number of riflemen was serious. A new machine pistol battalion compensated for some of the loss of riflemen. The battalion had two machine pistol companies, an 82mm mortar company, a reconnaissance platoon, a light machine gun platoon, an antiaircraft machine gun platoon, and an antitank rifle platoon. The best men in the division, ages nineteen to thirty years, formed the battalion. The battalion replaced a rifle battalion of one regiment, but was directly responsible to the division commander.[30]

Like many divisions, the 336th Rifle Division was short of infantry in 1943. In December 1943, the division was reinforced to 7,000 men with rifle companies of up to 100 men. Service units in the division were reduced by 40 percent. Limited service men replaced combat-fit men in the service units. Special cadres in each rifle regiment trained the new riflemen.[31] The 212th Rifle Division had only 5,200 men instead of the authorized 8,200 in December 1943.[32] Another division tried to provide the machine-gun battalion with men between ages twenty and twenty-five, while the mortar battalion and the antitank battery received men between ages thirty-five and forty-five.[33]

The rifle division *shtat* was further reduced in 1944. In the summer of 1944 the rifle division *shtat* was still 9,354 men, 44 guns, 48 antitank guns, and 139 mortars. The Guard divisions had 10,585 men and a few more weapons. However, some rifle divisions had been reduced to between 4,000 to 8,000 men. The 8,000-man division had about the same number of guns but only half the mortars.[34] Most of the reductions came in the supporting weapons companies. The rifle company lost 9 percent in the 8,000-man division, 35 percent in the 6,000-man division, and 46 percent in the 4,000-man division.[35] On the Finnish Front, the group had 6 men instead of 12; the platoon, 17 instead of 45; the rifle company, 60 instead of 120; and the rifle battalion 400 instead of 800 men.[36] In the 26th Army fighting against the Finns, the 205th Rifle Division had groups with only four or five men, and platoons with twenty-five.[37] These reductions reflected the Russian policy of concentrating its manpower in the decisive sectors and allowing units in quiet sectors to dwindle. In 1944, one-fourth of the divisions had up to 8,000 men, but the rest had between 5,000 and 7,000 and some had only 3,000 to 5,000 men.[38] By September 1944, most divisions had only two rifle companies in the rifle battalion.[39]

In February 1944, the 93rd Guard Rifle Division, authorized at 8,000 in December 1943, had only 6,000 because of heavy losses. The division's rifle regiments had only two rifle battalions of 424 men each. Rifle companies had 113 men.[40] An example of the losses experienced by Soviet units was in a report concerning a rifle regiment in May 1944. With an authorized strength of 1,000 men, the regiment had suffered 1,638 casualties in twelve weeks, a turnover of 164 percent. Of these, 222 had been killed, 373 missing, 967 wounded, and 71 sick.[41] That the Russians were able to replace such staggering losses was remarkable.

In June 1944, the 112th Rifle Division, during a refit, had increased the rifle companies to 70 men. The rifle regiments had 1,468 men.[42] The table of organization of the I Battalion of the 858th Rifle Regiment, 283rd Rifle Division, authorized only two rifle companies of 87 men each, a machine gun company of 42 men, a mortar company of 43 men, and five administrative platoons with 69 men.[43]

In September 1944, Russian rifle company strength had dropped even lower, as shown here:

Division	Rifle Company Strength	Machine Guns
32nd	40	?
43rd	60	7
70th	50–70	3–6
77th	50	7

Division	Rifle Company Strength	Machine Guns
119th	35	7
145th	35	2
179th	40–75	9
204th	77	2
268th	60	6
306th	60	6
379th	30–40	6

The rifle battalions had been reduced to two rifle companies and a machine gun company, in many instances.[44]

Although the total number of troops on the German Front remained constant, an increasing percentage were nondivisional service and support troops. In 1943, service units were 20 percent of total strength.[45] That percentage increased in 1944. As the Red Army fought westward, the railroads had to be repaired and the track relaid to conform to the wider Russian gauge. By 1945, the number of troops assigned to operation, repair, and building of railroads had risen to 253,000. To help the railroads in carrying supplies, the Red Army employed truck units using the American 2.5-ton trucks provided by lend-lease. By 1945, 165,000 men had been assigned to truck transport duties. The roads needed improvement to carry the heavy traffic. By 1945 250,00 men had been assigned to road construction and repair. In these three categories alone, the Soviets had nearly 670,000 men, about a tenth of the total force on the German Front.[46] Simultaneously the army portion of the total armed service had dropped from 87 percent in July 1943 to 83.4 percent in January 1945. The increase in the service forces and the supporting arms caused in a drop in the strength of the rifle companies.[47]

At the end of the war the official table of organization of a rifle division was three rifle regiments, an artillery brigade (a 76mm gun regiment, a howitzer regiment (152mm and 122mm), and a mortar regiment), a self-propelled artillery battalion (16 SU-76s), a towed tank destroyer battalion (76mm), an antiaircraft battalion, an engineer battalion, and service elements. The division equipment included 3,557 machine pistols, 579 machine guns, 130 guns (including 66 antitank guns and 12 37mm antiaircraft guns), 136 mortars (82mm and 120mm), 16 SU-76s, 445 trucks, and 1,200 horses. Few divisions had a full organization. Most had only a single artillery regiment and few had the self-propelled battalion.[48]

In January 1945, the 9,354 division was still the official *shtat*, but the Germans had found repeated references to the reduced divisions with established tables of organization. In March 1945, the Red Army had three authorized levels for the rifle division: 3,600 men, 4,000 men, and 4,500 men. In the 3,600-man type there were only twelve rifle companies in the division each with 76 men, but with ten machine guns. The rifle battalion had only 241 men and the regiment 774.[49] The decrease in the number of combat troops in the rifle regiments was from 4,500 in the 1943 division to only 1,683 men in the rifle regiments in the 3,600-man type.[50] The 4,000-man division had eighteen rifle companies and the 4,500-man division had twenty-one rifle companies, seven for each regiment.[51]

The strength of the rifle regiments was about 1,000 men. The service units and supporting arms were sharply reduced as well. The number of machine guns was only 110 fewer than in the former division organization. Even the reduced totals were difficult to sustain. The 950th Rifle Regiment of the 262nd Rifle Division in February 1945 had only two battalions and miscellaneous units with a total of only 631 men.[52] In a survey made of fourteen divisions in February, the Germans found the rifle company strength varied from thirty (two examples) to ninety. The average was sixty. The replacement system was working for preferred divisions, however. The 71st Guard Division received 1,000 replacements from the 145th Replacement Regiment on January 24, 1945.[53]

The fierce battles in 1945 eroded the Russian rifle divisions at a rate beyond the availability of replacements. In March 1945, the 91st Guard Rifle Regiment had only one rifle battalion with a total of 161 men, plus antitank, mortar, and cannon batteries, and a company of men with machine pistols, a total of about 400 men.[54] The authorized strength of the regiment was 774 men, so the division must have been below 2,000 men. In March 1945, the eleven divisions of the 5th Army in the Baltic area had an average strength of only 2,625 men. A month earlier, the divisions had 3,000 to 3,200 men, an index of the bitterness of the fighting even in quiet areas.[55]

The authorized strength of a Russian rifle company in March 1945 was down to fifty-three men, a company commander, a first sergeant, two snipers, an observer, an ordnance man, a clerk, and two medical personnel, plus two platoons each with a platoon leader and a rifle adjustor, plus three groups each with a group leader, an assistant group leader, a machine gunner, and four riflemen. The platoon had twenty-three men.[56] In April 1945, the fighting in Berlin reduced rifle companies to twenty or thirty men. Rifle divisions had fewer than 3,000 men in twelve rifle companies. Between April 16 and May 8, 1945, the three Soviet fronts fighting in Berlin suffered 304,000 killed, wounded, and missing.[57]

While the rifle strength declined, the supporting weapons increased. The 45mm antitank guns were being replaced with 57mm and 76mm guns. The artillery regiment received additional 122mm howitzers. Some divisions received SU76s and American .50-caliber antiaircraft machine guns. The 50mm mortars were replaced with 82mm mortars.[58] In February 1945 the Germans found a detailed analysis of the 2nd Platoon, 6th Rifle Company, of the 1050th Rifle Regiment of the 301st Rifle Division in the Fifth Shock Army in February 1945, an example of the status of the rifle platoon in the closing weeks of the war. The 301st was not an exceptional division and could have been considered typical.

The platoon consisted of a lieutenant, a first sergeant, three sergeants, three undersergeants, one corporal, and thirty-two privates—a total of forty-one, unusually high for a platoon then. The age distribution was two at nineteen years, four at twenty years, seven at twenty-one to twenty-seven years, ten at twenty-eight to thirty-eight years, eight at thirty-eight to forty-seven years, four at forty-eight and older, and six unknown. While the average soldier was older compared to an American or British platoon, one-third of the men were in the prime age groups (from nineteen to twenty-seven years of age), and ten more were in the acceptable range (twenty-eight to thirty-eight). The six men of unknown age may have been younger with the result that two-thirds of the platoon (twenty-seven men aged from nineteen to thirty-eight) were in acceptable age groups.

Eleven of the men were Russians, eleven White Russians, five Ukrainians, and fourteen other nationalities. The low ratio of Russians and the high ratio of White Russians resulted from the addition of booty troops during the previous year. The education level was very low—eighteen men had two years or less, fourteen had three to six years, and only six men had seven or more years of education, equal to an elementary school education. Three were unknown. Only two men were Party members and three Komsomols.[59]

The image presented by the platoon was quite different from the more general data. The platoon may have been recently reinforced and not actively engaged for a time. Compared to sixty-man rifle companies, a forty-one-man platoon was remarkably strong. The number of noncommissioned officers was noteworthy—a full complement of the higher grades, but only one corporal. Such a situation often indicated that many replacements had recently been received. Based on all of the factors, it can be assumed that the platoon had been reinforced with twenty or more replacements, one-third new recruits, one-third booty soldiers, and one-third returning wounded. Even though the Russians were experiencing heavy casualties, the replacement system was working.

During the war the rifle division had declined steadily in the number of men but had increased in the number of weapons. In the final months, there were not enough men to serve the light machine guns and even that number dropped. Given the intense feeling for division tradition, it is not surprising that the Russians had refused to disband divisions in 1944 when men were no longer available to provide new units and replace losses. Within the division regiments and battalions were abolished. The Russians adopted a new attitude toward divisional strength and adjusted their tactics to a division of 5,000 or fewer. The field army was increased from six rifle divisions to nine and given more tanks and artillery.

Although the Russian rifle divisions became smaller after 1943, the total number of troops on the Eastern Front had not declined by 1945. The shortage of riflemen was the result of a decision to create more artillery and tank units at the expense of the infantry. Considering the situation and the outcome, the decision was a good one.

CHAPTER 6

The Replacement System

Maintaining the strength and, more important, the effectiveness of a military unit once it entered combat was crucial in World War II. Short campaigns had been fought with little concern for rotation or replacements; however, long wars had demanded a well-organized system for replacing losses and relieving the survivors.[1] A human being could withstand a limited amount of stress from combat. However, there was a point beyond which an individual could no longer act positively. Stress was cumulative, each individual having an "account" from which withdrawals were made every time the person faced danger. The size of individual "accounts" and what each person perceived as danger varied widely. Few could endure the stress of continuous front-line combat for more than a year, and the duration of intense combat was much lower.

The emotional and physical condition of the individual combatant had to be considered. Exhaustion resulting from prolonged combat or difficult assignments affected both the emotional and the physical condition of the individual and therefore his chance of survival. Exposure to disease, injury, or death had to be reduced to the lowest possible level. An atmosphere that encouraged the hope of survival had to be created. The Russian soldier, like the soldier of any other nation, could not endure a year of continuous front-line duty, even if he were able to survive enemy action.

To relieve the stress on a unit, an informal truce often developed in the quiet sectors: we won't shoot if you don't shoot. This arrangement made it possible for divisions to hold quiet sectors for many months. Operations on the Eastern Front followed the pattern of a few days of intense combat to break through the defense followed by a period of exploitation with a lower danger level. Then another stalemate developed as the attack weakened from extended supply lines and wear and tear on men and vehicles. The turnover in the rifle companies was high from death or wounds inflicted by enemy action, sickness, or transfer to the rear for other duties.

There were several approaches to maintaining the combat effectiveness and integrity of a unit. One was to rotate the entire regiment, battalion, or company, sending all of the survivors of the old unit to the rear. In
earlier wars regiments had been disbanded and the men sent to other
duties or discharged. In 1941 the Russians disbanded many divisions
depleted beyond rebuilding. They created entirely new divisions using
the same division number but few, if any, of the men from the previous
unit. One drawback was the loss of accumulated experience of the officers and noncommissioned officers that had given the unit a tradition
and integrity. Most of the disbanded divisions were probably beyond
redemption. The men had been killed or captured, leaving only a few
stragglers. The Russians made every effort to rebuild divisions because a
disbanded unit had to be replaced. Some units could be rebuilt from a
handful of highly motivated individuals with a high level of unit pride.
Others were difficult to restore even after light losses.

Another approach to maintaining unit effectiveness was to feed individuals into the units to replace losses. However, the replacements had to
learn their roles before combat, making it preferable to withdraw the division from the front line. The more aggressive veterans tended to have
higher casualties after prolonged service on the front and needed rest periods. Unless the unit was rested, it faced a steady deterioration of quality.

Rotation was a compromise between discarding the unit when
fatigued or maintaining its strength through continual replacement. The
Russians rotated units out of the line after they had been reduced to a
low level of effectiveness. While the division was behind the line, replacements arrived and were trained. A refreshed division returned to the line
to replace another division that went through the same process. This
replacement method required extra units or courage by the commander
to reduce his front-line strength. The advantages of rotation were mani-
fold: new men had time to assimilate and train; veterans had a welcome
relief from combat; and the army commander had a reserve in time
of severe crisis. Stalin's order of March 16, 1942, required divisions to
receive replacements while in reserve behind the lines; a division could
not receive replacements during combat. Stalin repeated his admonition
in an order on May 1, 1942.[2]

Rotation required the formation of extra divisions. However, forming
too many units had the disadvantage that the demand for equipment
and service units increased. There was a temptation to create more units
during a period of few losses and an excess of replacements. When the
fighting intensified, a nation might be unable to provide the necessary
replacements, as the Germans learned in 1941.

Replacements came from two sources: returning wounded and newly trained men. Returning the wounded man to his own unit created a problem if too many wounded returned directly to their units regardless of need. One unit that had suffered many casualties that had been replaced with new men would be over strength if all of the wounded were returned later while other units were short of men. The Russians tried to return men to their previous units if at all possible, and because of the heavy turnover in the rifle companies, the problem in overstrength that plagued the U.S. army seldom occurred.

The newly trained men preferably should come from the identical geographical area as the unit in order to fit quickly. An alternate approach drew men for the original unit and replacements from the nation at large. If the regional basis was retained, how restricted should that basis be? State or province, region, county, or even town? Regionally oriented units had better cohesion because the men shared the same language and customs. Because of the uneven casualty rates, it was difficult to obtain the right proportion of replacements from each region. In the end the Soviets used any replacements that were available to fill the gaps in the rifle companies.

Combat effectiveness demanded that men, weapons, and supplies be maintained at a workable level, not necessarily the official table of organization. The workable number might have been below the authorized strength, but at a level considered combat effective—for example, rifle companies with about 100 men. Eventually the authorized tables would be changed to reflect a more efficient or more attainable situation, as the Russians did after 1942.

The Soviet mobilization system had excelled in the task of creating new units. The plan to create these units had a vital impact on the replacement system. The methods of providing replacements, returning wounded to combat, and reconstructing worn divisions were all related to the mobilization process. The Russians had increased the number of divisions rapidly during the late 1930s and in 1940 and 1941. The territorial divisions, composed mostly of part-time soldiers, had drawn their men from a restricted geographical area. The territorial divisions had been eliminated in the late 1930s, technically ending the relationship of divisions to regions. The philosophy was the "All-Union" army, with units drawing men from all areas of the Soviet Union. The Soviet reason for abandonment of the regional affiliation was the difficulty in training nationality units to fight in a variety of climates. Because of the wide range of nationalities in the Red Army, one should be wary of the "Russian" ability to withstand cold.[3]

Regional affiliation was an especially thorny problem for the Soviets. In the first instance, the Red Army had over 100 nationalities with significant numbers. The largest were the Russians, Ukrainians, White Russians, Tartars, Jews, Kazakhs, Armenians, Georgians, Uzbeks, Mordavinians, Chuvashes, Azerbaijanians, Bashkirs, and Ossetians.[4] The requirement that nationality units be trained in two languages was difficult because all the manuals were in Russian.[5] The problem of training a platoon of men who not only did not understand Russian but did not even have a common second language seemed insurmountable.

The problem was not only language but also questionable loyalty to the Soviet Union. The czarist regime had exempted some Caucasian nationalities from military service because of questionable loyalty. Even the Communists considered some nationalities untrustworthy or otherwise unsuitable for military service. Before the Law of Universal Military Training in 1938, some nationalities had been exempt from military service: the Lapps from the north, some Caucasian nationalities, and others from less developed regions. The Germans were able to recruit thousands of prisoners from Azerbaijan, Georgia, and Turkestan to fight for Germany in the Ost battalions. The Germans formed the 162nd Infantry Division on May 21, 1943, from Ost battalions and the staff of the former German division.[6] Even late in the war the Soviets were distrustful of certain nationalities. In November 1944 the 2nd Guard Army ordered all Kalmyks, Chechen-Ingush, Ossetians, and Crimean Tartars along with the nationals of enemy countries to be relieved from duty and sent to the rear.[7]

Added to these difficulties were cultural and religious differences and historical racial conflicts. For these reasons and because of the size of the Soviet Union with its limited transportation system, in practice, divisions formed before the war drew their men from a single district.[8] Even after the war had begun new divisions drew their men from a single district. In the fall of 1942 the Panfilov Division, named for a Kazakh hero, was formed from men from the Kazakh Republic.[9]

Most units had a mixture of Russians, Ukrainians, and White Russians with a few other nationalities. An artillery battery of the 233rd Rifle Division in December 1944 was 45 percent Russian, 45 percent Ukrainian, and 10 percent other nationalities.[10] The 101st Rifle Brigade enlisted men in 1943 were from Kazahkstan, but the officers were Russians.[11] Although the official policy after 1938 had been not to create regionally oriented units, necessity produced not only divisions but entire armies that drew their men from a single military district or from two adjoining districts. However, the Soviets did not maintain the nationality orientation of units through selective replacements. Replacements came from any available source. Problems of language and assimilation continued throughout the war.

To maintain a ground army of more than 6 million men on the German Front, the Red Army needed masses of replacements. The Red Army outnumbered the Germans about two-to-one and suffered casualties at the same rate. Available men were needed for new artillery and armored units, reducing the number of replacements. In the late fall of 1942 the average rifle company had only 145 men and the rifle battalion 609. In 1943 the rifle company was down to 120 and the battalion 513. In 1944 the rifle company was at 90 men with the battalion at 405.[12] Although Soviet tactics had improved as the war progressed, breaking through the well-prepared German defenses was costly in men.[13] In March 1943, the Soviets launched ten attacks of more than a thousand men and six minor attacks on the German 260th Division. The Germans counted over 1,500 dead, compared to their own losses of 150 killed, 27 missing, and 539 wounded. Including wounded and captured, the Russians had lost over 5,000 men in these attacks.

Another Red Army rifle regiment had 1,638 casualties in twelve weeks from December 1, 1943, to February 24, 1944, including 227 killed, 373 missing, 967 wounded, and 71 sick. On April 2, 1944, the regiment had only 600 men. During the winter months, other armies had far higher rates of sickness, suggesting that the regiment had evacuated only the most seriously ill. The missing 373 were usually prisoners. Although some wounded returned, permanent losses of over 1,000 men in three months represented 50 percent of the authorized strength.[14] In August 1944 the First Ukrainian Front lost 122,000 men killed and wounded.[15] In February 1945 the 287th Rifle Division had 10,000 men, but lost 80 percent of its men in attacks, according to a prisoner.[16] Losses of this magnitude required an efficient replacement system.

Before the war, privates had served two years and NCOs three years training in territorial divisions. In September 1939, when the draft age had been lowered from twenty-one to nineteen, the army absorbed many more recruits and training became a serious undertaking. Each year in October and November about 1.5 million men were added, so that by June 1941 four classes were in the army instead of two. Not all had been trained when war began. In June 1941 reservists from fourteen classes were called up, creating a monstrous administrative problem absorbing the men and creating new units.[17]

The reserves reported to a reception center where they were checked in and assigned to a company according to mobilization plans. The reception center conducted medical examinations and reassigned men as necessary. At the reception center each company received the proper allotment of military specialties. Men shipped personal property home and received uniforms and equipment. After the first wave of divisions had left for the front, the reception centers transferred their duties to replacement regiments. As each division went to the front, it left behind a replacement regiment located in its home station. The training battalion of the 95th Guard Rifle Division was located near Staszow. It consisted of two rifle companies, a heavy-machine-gun company, a light-machine-gun company, and a rocket-launcher company. Training in this battalion lasted only three weeks and was probably advanced training for men who had received prior training in other units.[18]

Most new recruits had received prior training either at school, in the Komsomois, or in the Ossoawiachim, a paramilitary organization. Older men had received training in sports organizations where they had learned marksmanship and individual combat skills. After June 1941 induction and training of recruits shifted to replacement training regiments that fulfilled the duties of the reception center.[19] The regiments trained recruits, formed the trained men into march companies, and sent them to army replacement regiments.

The period of training varied with the arm. Each arm had its replacement regiments, infantry, armored, artillery, and others. The better educated recruits went to the technical arms and services. Because the Revolution of 1917 had eliminated the upper class and reduced the middle class, there were not enough educated men available for the army in 1941. Less than 12 percent of the Soviet soldiers had a high school education or higher, and more than 60 percent had completed only elementary school.[20]

The infantry training depended on the situation at the front. Normally training lasted two to four months and sometimes more. Tank crews trained from eight to twelve months. Stalin's order of March 16, 1942, stressed improved training for the recruits. Stalin repeated his admonition to intensify training in an order on May 1, 1942.[21] Training was hard and emphasized endurance, close combat, night fighting, combat in forests and marshes, camouflage, deception, field fortifications, and discipline.[22]

By February 1944 the Germans had identified over 300 replacement regiments. Another 500 had been identified in the past but were either abolished or redesignated. Each replacement regiment normally had 3,000 men in training, although some prisoners had reported as many as 4,000 to 6,000 in some regiments and one regiment held 10,000 men.[23] Some regiments specialized in training heavy machine gunners, riflemen, snipers, submachine gunners, and antitank riflemen. Each regiment normally had three battalions with 150 to 250 cadre in each. Some training camps were huge. The camp near Kostroma had five regiments, each with four battalions, organized in two brigades.

Fremde Heer Ost compared the information on the Russian system to the Germany Replacement Army in 1943 and again in 1944. In 1943 the Germans had 1,021 battalions with 206,900 cadre and the Soviet system had 1,866 battalions (622 regiments) with 280,000 cadre. In 1944 the German system had only 560 battalions with 133,200 cadre while the Soviet system had 1,815 battalions (605 regiments) plus 336 school battalions (84 regiments) for NCOs for a total of 2,151 battalions with 407,000 cadre.[24]

In September 1942 a training brigade at Kostroma had received 11,000 men of the class of 1924 and trained them until March and April 1943, over six months. At the end of training in March, the replacements formed into march companies and battalions and went to the front. By mid-May only the cadre remained.[25] In the Moscow Military District there were sixty units training replacements. In May 1944 the reserve and training brigades formed eight training divisions. During 1944 and 1945 1,020,000 officers and men had trained in the Moscow Military District and went to the front.[26]

Men were drafted according to their date of birth and those sharing a common birth date formed a class. The class of 1923 consisted of men born in 1923 drafted in the winter of 1941–42 as eighteen-year-olds. The drafting of the class of 1924 began in May 1942. Later young men were drafted and began training at age seventeen. The Red Army called up the seventeen-year-olds early to allow more time for training and withheld them from combat until they reached eighteen.[27] The younger men often went to new units where they received additional training as the unit organized.

In August 1942 the Russians called up 1.4 million 17-year-olds from the class of 1925. The young recruits were used to fill new formations and therefore had more training.[28] The men of the class of 1925 arrived in divisions as replacements in August, September, and November 1943, more than a year after they had been drafted when most of them were eighteen.[29] While the class of 1925 was still training, the Russians began to call up the class of 1926 (seventeen-year-olds) in January 1943, six months earlier than the previous class. Combined with the men from the class of 1925 and other sources, Gehlen assumed that in 1943 the Russians would have enough men to replace their losses plus an additional million to form new units.[30] In a study prepared in 1943, the Germans estimated that 2.6 million Russians would be drafted in 1943; 1.3 million would be used to replace losses; 400,000 would reinforce worn-down units; and 900,000 would go to new units.[31] Members of the class of 1927, drafted in 1944, were not used in combat until 1945. In February 1945 the Germans estimated that only 400,000 of the class of 1927 were in units and that 1.3 million were still training.[32]

Replacements normally flowed in march companies or battalions from training units in the rear to field replacement regiments assigned to each front and field army. These regiments also served as a processing center for returning wounded, conscripted civilians, and stragglers.[33] The number of men processed by a field replacement regiment in a month was often over a thousand.[34] Men went from the regiments to the divisional replacement battalions.

Each division incorporated a replacement battalion, also called a school battalion, for training newly arrived replacements and to hold recuperating sick and wounded. The division made every effort to ease the entry of the new men. The new troops received additional training in group, platoon, company, and battalion tactics, as well as individual training. At times the situation at the front and the shortage of training cadre limited the training to the latter.[35] During the buildup for the winter offensive of 1942–43, commissars met new soldiers coming to the 65th Army at the rail unloading point and sent them to a rifle division or other unit. There the commander and the unit commissar indoctrinated the new recruits on unit traditions and spoke with each man. The men received their weapons and an experienced soldier was made responsible for each new man. The army made a special effort to provide commissars who spoke additional languages, as one-third of the men in the Stalingrad Front did not speak Russian.[36]

The 271st Rifle Division had a school battalion with three rifle companies and a machine-gun company with up to 130 men in each company. The 30th Rifle Division had a similar battalion.[37] New recruits received six to eight weeks' training in the school battalion before joining a rifle company.[38] The school battalion also held lightly wounded men, sick, and stragglers. In addition the school battalion trained new platoon leaders and gave additional training to inadequately trained replacement officers.[39] Training continued in the front line for some recruits who had not trained well enough during the process from the interior to the rifle company. If the situation permitted, the training took place immediately behind the front. Techniques taught included sniping, reconnaissance, and unit training.[40]

The Soviet system trained and sent to the field army a prodigious number of replacements and quality sometimes suffered. The quality of replacements for the rifle companies had been poor in the early years of the war. In March 1942 the replacements sent to the front were over-age and untrained. Some were less than eighteen years old and others were over forty. The 1st Shock Army received men forty-six and forty-seven years old.[41] In June 1942 Timoshenko complained that the replacements scarcely knew the rudiments. They were peasants, office workers, shopkeepers, and schoolboys who could not fire an antitank rifle or a 50mm mortar.[42]

During the Battle of Stalingrad the Russians continually fed thousands of replacements to the divisions in combat. Faced with the crisis, the quality of replacements had deteriorated. Some of the replacements were criminals who had volunteered to fight in return for their freedom. Entire battalions were formed of released prisoners.[43] On September 21, 1942, 8,000 replacements were sent across the Volga. On September 23, the 13th Guards Division received 2,000 men, although some were boys from Stalingrad ages seventeen to nineteen presumably with very little training.[44]

The problem of quality extended to new units sent into combat before they were ready in 1942. Yeremenko, a front commander at Stalingrad, complained in August 1942 that the new reserve armies lacked equipment and included poorly trained old reservists hastily formed into divisions.[45] As late as 1943 the 226th Rifle Division commander had complained that replacements arrived badly trained and some with no uniforms.[46] Conditions were improving, though. Pavel Baranov was a Russian born in 1925 and inducted on August 8, 1943, at age eighteen. He trained in the 72nd Replacement Regiment for four months before going to the Machine Pistol Company of the 508th Rifle Regiment, 174th Rifle Division.[47] The machine pistol company usually had the best men in the regiment.

As the Soviets prepared in 1943 for the Battle of Kursk, they desperately sought replacements. Although July 1943 may have marked the high point in the rifle strength of the Red Army, serious weaknesses in quality were evident. The Red Army had conscripted men with prior military service in newly reoccupied territory and thrust them directly into rifle companies. Untrained men were sent back to receive training. In October 1943 young men drafted in the reoccupied territory returned to the replacement training regiments.[48]

The service units and hospitals surrendered combat-fit men to reinforce the rifle divisions. In September 1943 gun crews had been reduced from nine men to six; the surplus men went to the rifle companies.[49] Even with these emergency measures, a rifle division averaged between 5,000 and 6,000 men with only a few Guard divisions at 7,000. The strength of the rifle division continued to decline to provide men for more supporting arms units. The army needed more service units as it moved away from the production areas and depots near Moscow.

In the fall of 1943, Gehlen, head of Fremde Heer Ost, had requested details concerning replacements provided to Red Army units from all of the German army intelligence officers. The reports, based on prisoner interrogations, gave Gehlen enough documentation to make an informed guess. In the six months ending in December 1943, the Germans estimated that the Red Army had received 3.4 million replacements including 896,000 from the replacement training regiments, plus returning wounded and booty troops.[50] Individual divisions had received from 300 to 1,000 replacements each month. Some had received many more; the 71st Guard Rifle Division received 3,500 in November 1943.[51]

An analysis of the reports gave information on 513,000 replacements and the following breakdown:

New recruits from training centers	92.3%
Returning wounded	6.5%
Men combed from the rear and service units	1.2%

The percentage of returning wounded was very low, but may reflect the ability of the prisoners to distinguish the source of the replacements. The breakdown on training is very surprising:

Untrained	40.9%
Short training period (less than 1 month)	26.7%
1 to 12 months' training	32.4%

The breakdown by age reinforced the thesis that the untrained men were booty troops.

Under 18 years of age	13.3%
18 to 25 years of age	32.3%
25 to 35 years of age	21.9%
35 to 40 years of age	22.5%
Over 40 years of age	10.0%

The percentage of untrained men and men with scant training and the age groups reflected the inclusion of booty troops as replacements. These men were better trained than the report suggested, as most had prior military service either before the war or in the partisans. Young men drafted in the reoccupied area went back to the training regiments. The 54.4 percent over twenty-five represented most of the 70.6 percent of untrained and short-training-period men. The 32.4 percent that had one to twelve months' training correlated with the 45.6 percent under twenty-five.

Russians made up 75 percent of the half-million, and all other nationalities 25 percent.[52] From July to October 1943, replacements included in the various reports had totaled 1,173,283. Covering only four months, this information was the basis for the estimate of 3.4 million provided in the year. Most of the replacements were from the class of 1925 (eighteen-year-olds) or civilians from the liberated territories. Still in training in the rear were recruits from the classes of 1924, 1925, 1926, and 1927.[53] A study of the reports of eight Soviet armies in the center showed that 28 percent of the replacements had been from the class of 1925.[54] In October 1944 another study showed that the replacements received by ten divisions and four other units were mostly Ukrainians and in the older age groups, probably booty troops. Other nationalities included Azerbaijanians, Uzbeks, Tartars, Poles, and White Russians. Returning wounded formed a small percentage. The booty soldiers were often in the forty- to fifty-year-old bracket.[55]

Throughout the war, the civilian population had been a ready source of replacements. Belov with the 2nd Guard Cavalry Corps was surrounded near Viasma in February 1942. He inducted former Red Army men from partisan units and other civilians to the age of forty-five. In one month, he recruited 2,436 men for his corps.[56] At Stalingrad, Eremenko had mobilized every man in the city between eighteen and fifty. Initially, they formed in detachments with work clothes. Later they received uniforms and some training. These men had provided the Soviet divisions with tens of thousands of replacements.[57]

As the Red Army liberated Soviet territory, more men became available from civilian sources, partisans, and soldiers who had remained behind in 1941. In March and April 1944, the 6th Army had mobilized every man in the reoccupied area with the objective of raising the strength of its rifle divisions to 6,000 men.[58] From March 1944 to May 1944 the 2nd Ukrainian Front took in 265,000 men from the formerly occupied territory. In the same period the 3rd Ukrainian Front took in 79,000 men. In some units more than half the men were booty troops. The newly acquired soldiers received ten days' training before assignment to units.[59] Two weeks after an area was reoccupied, the Russians drafted all men between sixteen and fifty, leaving the women to do the farm work.[60] Two other sources of manpower in the reconquered territory were the partisans, used immediately as replacements, and liberated "Ost workers" (men forced to work for the Germans), who after receiving a short training course went to the front. In February 1945 six divisions had received nearly 5,000 replacements, 60 percent of whom were former Ost workers.[61]

Women also replaced men in the rifle divisions and in the supporting units. As in no other army in World War II, the Soviets made extensive use of women in both combat and noncombat roles. Women fought as pilots and as snipers, but more frequently acted as military police and communications personnel. Over 2 million women served in the Soviet armed forces during the Great Patriotic War.[62]

Another shortage was noncommissioned officers. Future NCOs trained in army and front replacement regiments or in the school battalions of the rifle divisions. The course lasted three or four months.[63] Some NCOs trained at the rear in special schools. The 2nd Guard Cavalry Corps received a large contingent of young, tough, well-trained NCOs to replace heavy losses in December 1941.[64] Good NCOs were usually scarce. In November 1942, the 51st Mechanized Brigade had only 841 NCOs instead of the authorized 1,156. Most were graduates of an NCO course and under twenty-five years of age, but 195 had received no special training; only 222 had prior command experience; and only 164 had prior combat experience.[65]

Officers came from two sources: battlefield commissions and officer training schools. The Red Army had begun the war woefully short of senior grade officers because of the purge of the late 1930s. The Russians revamped the entire system of training officers and established military schools offering two- and three-year programs. By 1939 there were 14 military academies and 109 military schools.[66] With the outbreak of war, new measures provided thousands of officers for the new divisions. In 1941 the Red Army had increased the number of academies to 19 and maintained 203 military schools training 240,000 students. By 1943 there were 310 officer training schools.

Infantry schools trained machine-gun and mortar officers. Artillery schools trained heavy mortar officers. Men with secondary school education were given preference. The courses lasted from three to seven months.[67]

In October 1941 each field army had formed a school for junior officers to be trained in special three-month-long courses. Similar schools were created in the fronts and military districts.[68] As an example, in November 1942, a Lieutenant Sobolev was drafted at age nineteen. He attended an NCO school for one month, and after some combat attended an officer training school for three months beginning in February 1944.[69] Front-line training was part of the curriculum of all of the officer schools.

The Voroshilov Academy trained commanders of divisions and larger units, chiefs of staff, and chiefs of operation sections. The course lasted four to six months. The general staff officers trained at the Frunze Academy. Regimental commanders and staff officers also trained at front and army schools.[70] Lack of academy training was no block to higher ranks. By 1945, 120 former enlisted men were commanding regiments, and others had obtained higher ranks and served on staffs.[71] Battlefield commissions went to those who displayed heroism and to NCOs who had demonstrated exceptional ability. The dearth of professionally trained officers was shown by the 51st Mechanized Brigade formed in October 1942. In November, the brigade had 358 officers of which only one had academy training. Of the rest, 257 had been to officer training school and 80 had attended short courses. They were young: 150 were under twenty-five; and 148 were between twenty-five and thirty-five. Only 148 had been in combat before, suggesting that over 200 were either recent graduates of schools or had transferred from rear area units to form the new unit.[72] By late 1942, the supply of officers was greater than needed. The length of courses increased to nearly a year for infantry officers and up to eighteen months for other branches, providing better training in the schools and academies. In late 1943, some surplus officers had returned to civilian positions, especially engineers.[73]

When an officer had completed his training or left a hospital, he went to an officer replacement regiment. The Germans identified forty-two officer replacement regiments by 1944. Each front had at least one regiment; most fronts had two; and one had three regiments. The strength varied from 200 to 4,000 officer replacements, and in one instance there were 7,000. The reserves of officers were highest in 1943 and declined in 1944 when each replacement regiment had from 500 to 1,000 officers. Returning wounded officers rejoined their previous regiments.[74] In 1943, 250,000 wounded officers had returned to duty. With the shortage over, training schools lengthened their courses and the academy training increased from one to two years.[75] The abolition of the position of deputy commander for political affairs (commissars) in May 1943 had made 122,000 officers available. The commissars were eliminated first in the rifle company and then in the staffs of the corps, division, brigade, fortified sector, and other units.[76]

In early 1943, with a pause in operations, the Soviets had turned their attention from forming new armies to rebuilding reduced formations. After Stalingrad, the Russians did not lose entire armies to German encirclements; the problem became one of replacing the heavy losses. Attention turned to improving individual battlefield competence. Thousands of men went to schools and received additional training. These men returned to their units and created the strong divisions that defeated the Germans at Kursk.[77]

Once the operations had begun in July, losses escalated, and the quality of the rifle replacements declined. In November 1943 the 226th Rifle Division received 200 badly trained replacements with no uniforms.[78] Even then the supply was not sufficient to meet the demand. In the face of heavy losses, the high command abolished rifle brigades to provide replacements or form new divisions. The 4th and 125th Rifle Brigades reconstructed the 212th Rifle Division in 1943.[79]

Service units were combed for combat-fit men. In December 1943, the 336th Rifle Division had reduced its service units by 40 percent to provide riflemen, while additional combat-fit men were replaced by limited service men. The service personnel trained as riflemen in a special school unit. The target was to increase the rifle companies to 100 men.[80] In June 1944 the 2nd Guards Army ordered a comb-out of its service units for men under forty, or if good soldiers, under forty-five. Each division had to produce at least 400 men from its service units to replace men over forty-five in the rifle companies.[81]

Returning the wounded provided high-quality replacements. After recovery the wounded wanted to return to their original units. Official policy did not automatically allow men to return to their units, but in practice the wounded went to the replacement regiment of the army from which they had come to complete their convalescence.[82] In 1941 Belov, in command of the 2nd Guards Cavalry Corps, complained that wounded men had not been allowed to return to their original units. Wounded soldiers deserted to get back to the 2nd Guards Cavalry Corps, so Belov established a reserve regiment stationed at the rear of his corps to accept the wounded.[83] The returning wounded were a significant factor. In February 1944, the 176th Guard Rifle Regiment of the 59th Guard Rifle Division reconstituted its third battalion, which had been abolished in November 1943 because of a temporary manpower shortage. Most of the men were returning wounded along with some booty troops.[84]

At the end of 1944 the quality of the replacements was better than in 1942. One Russian unit had received replacements in October 1944 to increase the strength of the rifle companies from 50 men to 110. Most of the replacements were eighteen- and nineteen-year-olds, with a few seventeen-year-olds, from Central Russia and the Urals. A few were from White Russia and some were older men. The recruits had received six months' training in the replacement regiments.[85]

The most effective element of the Soviet process of maintaining combat strength was its rotation of divisions. Having created over 500 rifle divisions, the Red Army was able to take worn-out units behind the lines for refitting to a far greater extent than any other major power. Divisions were allowed to dwindle to a few thousand men and then were sent to the rear for rebuilding.[86] In the first twelve months of the war, burned-out divisions had reformed with new conscripts and returned to the front, although the men were not completely trained or equipped.[87] On March 16, 1942, Stalin's Order #1457 had prohibited the addition of replacements to divisions in combat. New replacements were to be added only to divisions behind the lines for rehabilitation. Therefore the commander was forced to withdraw divisions from time to time from the front line.[88]

Some units were repeatedly refitted. In August 1941, the 3rd Airborne Corps had escaped from the Kiev pocket with severe losses. It was refilled with replacements and reappeared as the 87th Rifle Division in December 1941, taking part in the winter offensive. Again depleted, it was pulled out, rebuilt, and took part in the Kharkov offensive as the 13th Guards Division. By July 1942 it was down to 666 men who swam across the Don River after acting as a rear guard. In September 1942 it was rebuilt again and entered the battle for Stalingrad at full strength.[89]

Later in the war, units that had sustained losses were withdrawn to the rear, rebuilt with replacements, and held as part of the Stavka reserve.[90] This process plus the formation of new units provided the Soviet high command with a strategic reserve that could be employed decisively. In the winter of 1942–43, 108 rifle divisions were sent to the front from the Stavka reserve along with many other units. In the summer and fall of 1943 more than 200 rifle divisions were provided from the reserve.[91] The classic example is the creation of the Steppe Front behind Kursk in the summer of 1943. When the Germans finally penetrated the Russian defenses in July 1943, armies from the Steppe Front were sent forward to drive back the advancing Germans and initiate a counteroffensive.

As the number of units increased, the limited number of infantry replacements had to be shared with new units and divisions receiving replacements while still on the front line. As a result, the rebuilding behind the lines was not as thorough. In October 1943, the 71st Rifle Division was withdrawn from the line and received 100 officers, 450 NCOs, and 3,950 men in two weeks. The division also received 1,800 rifles, 120 light machine guns, 47 heavy machine guns, and 430 machine pistols. Even with these additions, the division had only 7,200 men and was short of weapons.[92]

In view of the heavy losses and the limited number of replacements, the Russians could not maintain the rifle elements of the divisions at the same strength. The authorized strength of the rifle division had dropped from 10,566 in July 1942 to 8,000 in the summer of 1943, and then to 6,800 in October 1943. In 1943 and during the first half of 1944 the bulk of the armies seldom had been involved in active operations simultaneously. The replacement system was able to maintain the rifle companies at about 100 men. However, in 1944 practically all of the armies were engaged and the bonus of the booty troops had been exhausted. The artillery and armored units had first call on the available recruits both as replacements and to create additional units. The inevitable result was the shrinkage of the rifle units. In March 1944, the rifle division was down to

5,400 men with only 2,200 riflemen.[93] Actual strength was even lower. The 212th Rifle Division had only 5,200 men in December 1944.[94] In September 1944 the 242nd Rifle Division was placed in reserve to absorb replacements. The Second Battalion of the 897th Rifle Regiment received 90 men, 13 new Ukrainian recruits, and 77 returning wounded. The service units were combed out and the men sent to the rifle companies. As a result rifle company strength rose to 70 or 80 men.[95]

In the last six months of the war, there were not enough to maintain the strength of the rifle divisions and create new units. The Soviets were forced to reduce the size of the divisions. In February 1945 there were three authorized levels of rifle divisions: 4,500 men, 4,000 men, and 3,600 men. The last had only twelve rifle companies with seventy-six men and nine light machine guns each.[96] In February 1945, the 950th Rifle Regiment of the 262nd Rifle Division had reduced its 3rd Battalion to a cadre of six officers. The remaining two battalions, antitank company, 76mm gun battery, and 120mm mortar company had only 109 officers, 141 NCOs, and 381 men, a total of 631 men. On February 15, the regiment received 15 officers and 137 men from the 231st Replacement Regiment, increasing the strength of the regiment to 783. With only three rifle companies in each of two battalions, the rifle company strength was about 100.[97]

At the end of the war the average rifle division had only 4,000 men.[98] Divisions became the equivalent of regiments in their rifle strength, but had the support of a divisional artillery regiment—not a bad situation. The Soviets strove to give the rifleman maximum support. When a division withdrew to refit, the artillery regiment remained at the front to provide extra support to other divisions.[99] The Russians did not maintain large rifle companies in 1945, but relied heavily on artillery and tanks for firepower. The rifle units were given lavish numbers of submachine guns and light machine guns, and as long as there were enough men to fire the automatic weapons, the combat value of the company was not depleted seriously. The rigid discipline, the commissars, and the NKVD reinforced the motivation of the troops.

The use of tactics costing heavily in Russian lives needed a system that provided large numbers of replacements and organizations that could continue to function with a low level of manpower. Therefore, divisions were refilled with whatever men were available and withdrawn for refit when their numbers dwindled. Considering the material available and the task of defeating the German Army in the field, it was probably the only system that would work.

Millions of Russians with previous military service in World War I and the Civil War that followed were quickly assembled in 1941 into hundreds of new divisions.

The Red Army suffered heavy casualties in urban warfare which destroyed many Russian, Polish, and German cities.

Russian infantry were heavily armed with machine pistols
which gave them heavy fire power in comparison to the
bolt-action rifles of the Germans in the early years of
the war.

In 1943, the SU-85 self-propelled 85mm gun was produced in large numbers. It countered the German Tiger tank and provided close support and antitank defense to the infantry, which rode on the guns until contact was made with the Germans.

Russian T-34 tanks supported infantry attacks in 1941. Few of the men wore steel helmets.

In the rugged terrain of the Balkans, Soviet cavalry advanced in areas where mechanized forces could not.

Russian infantry advancing in Bulgaria as the Red Army defeated the German forces in the Balkans.

Heavily armed Soviet marines patrolled the coastline of the Baltic Sea as the Red
Army advanced.

The Red Army held a line extending from the Black Sea in the south to the Arctic Ocean in the north. There was little opportunity to enjoy the reindeer in the north.

The most hazardous type of combat was street fighting. The Germans made determined stands in most cities as the Red Army advanced after defeating the Germans at Stalingrad. Hostile fire could come at any moment as the infantry rooted out the German defenders.

Cutting through barbed-wire entanglements was the first task confronting attacking infantry. Artillery barrages often targeted the barbed wire to partially destroy the fences.

In 1945, the Red Army drove through Hungary and liberated Austria. Infantry was carried on SU-76 self-propelled guns that formed the spearhead of many attacks.

The Russian T-34/85 tank was widely used in the attacks in 1944. The Russian 85mm gun was the answer to the 88mm guns on the German Tiger tank, which had dominated the battles in 1943.

Masses of Katyusha rockets mounted on American trucks were able to launch an instant barrage that often caught the German defenders before they could retreat into their bomb-proof shelters.

Russian artillery regiments relied on American jeeps and trucks that could traverse rugged terrain with four-wheel and six-wheel drive. Two-wheel-drive Soviet trucks were road-bound.

Soviet airborne troops dropped behind German lines, hindering enemy efforts to reinforce areas being attacked by the Russians.

The IL-4 Sturmovick was a ground-support aircraft that dropped bombs accurately from low altitudes on German positions. The airplane was comparatively slow and needed a rear gunner to withstand attacks by German fighter planes.

The entry of Soviet T-34/85 tanks into liberated towns brought out cheering crowds.

Each Soviet tank brigade had a battalion of infantry specially trained to ride the tanks into battle. When enemy resistance was encountered, the infantry jumped off the tanks to defend the vehicles from attacks by Germans armed with short-range *Panzerfaust* antitank rockets.

The Soviet SU-76 was the most common armored vehicle in the Red Army. It was relatively inexpensive to manufacture and had a reliable engine and track mechanism. Infantry rode into battle on the guns and jumped off to engage the enemy.

Thousands of Germans surrendered in the closing days of the war, in marked contrast to the many who fought desperately in Berlin and other cities.

The end of the war was marked by many informal ceremonies. The joy was clearly visible on the faces of the survivors.

The Red Army met the American 69th Division on the Elbe River, marking the end of German resistance.

CHAPTER 7

Formation of the Tank Force

Theory and doctrine concerning the use of tanks determined the organization of armored units and the design of tanks. In 1929, W. K. Triandafilov had published his work *Character of Operation of the Modern Army* expressing Soviet tank theory. The Field Regulations of 1929 and 1936 reflected Triandafilov's doctrine: "The enemy must be attacked in a resolute and courageous manner wherever he is found. . . . Tanks which support combat teams are used . . . for penetrating the enemy line, with the goal of destroying his reserves, artillery, headquarters, and storage areas."[1] The Field Regulations stated that in offense the tanks were needed to break through the enemy defenses. The defenses were stronger in the 1930s because there were more machine guns and defensive technique had improved. The role of tanks in defense was to lead the counterattack if the enemy penetrated the Russian position.[2]

In 1941 Soviet forces had been deployed in depth with additional divisions in reserve to reconstruct a line if the front-line troops were encircled. However, the poor state of readiness of the Soviet armored forces had deprived the Red Army of an effective counterattack force. Although Russian resistance in the pockets slowed the German advance, eventually the Russians were captured.[3]

German theory in 1941 was practically identical with Russian doctrine. German defensive theory centered on how to prevent enemy tanks from dislodging the infantry. The Germans had developed the elastic defense that included a line of antitank guns at the rear of the main line of resistance. Enemy tanks were permitted to penetrate the defensive zone, while the accompanying infantry was driven back by machine guns. Once through the zone, the isolated attacking tanks would be destroyed by the antitank gun line.

The Germans believed that tanks, the most potent offensive weapon, should be concentrated in the breakthrough areas. The tanks were to be used in large groups, not parceled out to the infantry. The minimum unit to be used in an attack was a tank battalion, about fifty tanks. The attack was to be concentrated in a front of one kilometer or less. Tanks were not to be used in small numbers because antitank guns would pick them off one by one. With large numbers, the tanks would be on the antitank guns before many tanks could be destroyed.

Once the tanks broke the main line of resistance, the blitzkrieg theory called for a deep thrust with unprotected flanks. There was little danger as long as the tanks kept moving. In France the technique worked well when the French panicked and there was a good road network enabling the tanks to keep moving. The objective was to disrupt enemy communications. The enemy troops would be rounded up only at the conclusion of a drive.[4] In contrast, the wedge-and-pocket doctrine called for the tanks to turn in and form pockets that would be held and eventually reduced by the infantry. The objective of the wedge-and-pocket strategy was the destruction of the front-line enemy troops, whereas the blitzkrieg destroyed communications and the will to fight.

The defense used machine guns to separate the infantry from the tanks, and antitank guns to destroy the isolated tanks. The machine guns would stop the infantry and force them to take cover while the tanks kept moving. Without infantry to protect them, the tanks could be destroyed by grenades, rocket launchers, and antitank rifles. Without the infantry the breakthrough was worthless. If the infantry fell more than 500 meters behind the tanks, the attack lost its impact.[5] To enable the infantry to stay with the tanks, the riflemen would have to be carried in tracked personnel carriers. Western armies and the Germans used half-tracks. The Russians used light tanks with handles welded to the hull to carry riflemen, but they had to dismount when the tanks encountered machine-gun fire. The lack of communication between the riding infantry and the tank commander and the exposure to snipers were drawbacks to the Russian technique.[6]

In 1941 the Russians did not have a good infantry support tank to destroy machine-gun positions and chase the enemy from their trenches and bunkers. This mission required a machine gun and a gun that could fire a high-explosive round. The 45mm gun on Russian light tanks could not fire high-explosive shells and the armor was too thin. The Russian light tanks were vulnerable to German antitank guns. To counter the German antitank gun line, the Russians relied on direct fire from the 76mm guns in the divisional artillery. Russian theory stressed that the divisional artillery be used both in the traditional indirect fire role and in direct fire against visible targets. Although the artillery could reduce the antitank gun line, a well-armored tank was needed to eliminate it.

A few medium tanks were available in 1941 to support the infantry, the old T-28 mediums and a limited number of new T-34s. The T-34 had a large enough gun to fire high-explosive shells and sufficient armor to withstand the German 37mm antitank guns, although it was vulnerable to long-range fire from the 88mm gun. The heavy KV had enough armor to close and destroy the German antitank guns with relative impunity, but few were available in 1941. For the rest of the war the equation of gun versus armor changed constantly. How to break through the main line of resistance with minimum loss was the fundamental objective of Soviet tank doctrine and organization.

The organization of the Red Army tank force began with a few tanks left over from the czarist army and foreign purchases. At first the Soviets had no doctrine for using tanks.[7] In the 1920s the Germans were developing their tank doctrine under the Weimar Republic. The chief of the German General Staff, General Hans von Seeckt, saw the need for a partnership of the Soviet Union and Germany to provide facilities to develop tank and aircraft doctrine. The creation of a strong Poland allied to France gave the Soviet Union and Germany a common enemy. In 1920 members of the General Michael Tukhachevskii's staff and the German General Staff began conversations. In April 1920 war broke out between Russia and Poland. The Poles had defeated the Russians by July 1920 and the Treaty of Riga on March 18, 1921, ended the war.

The defeat led Lenin to accept German overtures and approve a commercial treaty signed on May 6, 1921.[8] Closer political and commercial cooperation followed the signing of the Treaty of Rapallo on April 16, 1922. Military cooperation formed part of the pact signed on April 4, 1926. The treaties created a secret military understanding in violation of the Versailles Treaty, giving the Germans the opportunity to train officers and men in prohibited weapons and to establish factories in Russia to manufacture them. In return the Germans trained officers of the Red Army, in both Germany and Russia.[9] The Germans set up the Company for the Promotion of Industrial Enterprises in Moscow under the direction of Major Fritz Tschunke, a former army officer. This company arranged for a Junkers aircraft factory near Moscow and other joint firms for the manufacture of military equipment. Simultaneously German flying and tank schools were created in Russia.[10]

The aviation school was established at Lipezk. The tank school established at Kazan on the Kama River in 1926 became the testing ground for early German tank designs and a place for the exchange of German and Russian ideas on tank developments.[11] Russian officers attended the classes along with German officers. The program included tactical training with a tank company and battalion. Students learned all of the skills: driver, gunner, loader, radio man, and tank commander. Russian tank units took part after the first year. Usually there were about ten German students.[12] Russian officers trained in Germany while future famous German panzer commanders gained experience at Kazan. Many officers who led German tank units in World War II had attended the tank school.[13]

At first there were no tanks at Kama. In the early 1920s the Russians had experimented at Kama with the MS-I, a light tank based on the Renault FT, and a later version, the MS-II. In the fall of 1928 the Germans brought in three Leichter Traktors built by Rheinmetall in 1926, copying the British Vickers Mk II Medium Tank. The Leichter Traktor weighed 12 tons and had a 37mm gun. In 1929 the Germans brought in six Gross Traktors, a forerunner of the Panzer IV, for testing. The Gross Traktor weighed 23 tons and carried a 75mm gun.[14] In the fall of 1931 Krupp made a modified Kleiner Traktor based on two Carden Lloyd light tanks that the Russians had shipped from Kama to Germany.[15]

The Germans also helped in the development of tank production at the Bolshevik Factory in Leningrad and the Kharkov Locomotive Factory.[16] However, cooperation ended on November 1, 1933, after Hitler came to power. The last class at Kama ended in the fall of 1933. The Germans had some difficulty in retrieving the equipment from Kama, but Tukhachevskii helped the Germans retrieve all the equipment in August 1933. The Russians had learned a great deal from the Germans while the Germans gained valuable practical experience. The cadres for the first three German panzer divisions formed in 1934 and 1935 had trained at Kama.[17]

Russian tank production had a slow start, beginning with copies of the French Renault tank. In July 1927 the government approved the design of the MS-I or T-16, later modified as the T-18. The Bolshevik Factory in Leningrad began production in 1928 and had made 960 T-18s by 1931.[18] The Russians also purchased foreign tanks, tested them, and incorporated ideas in their own design. Among the imports were the Vickers-Armstrong Mk VI tankettes, the Vickers-Armstrong E Tank, the Vickers Mk II Medium Tank, and the Christie M1930 convertible tank.[19]

The T-27 was a copy of the Vickers-Armstrong Mk VI tankette with some modifications. The T-27 was manufactured at the Zavod Number 37 factory in Moscow and later at the Bolshevik plant in Leningrad. The T-27 was a 1.7 tontankette with a two-man crew. The Mark VI model provided to Russia had a Ford Model T four-cylinder 22.5 horsepower engine.[20] The Russian version used a GAZ truck engine, a Russian copy of the same Ford engine. In 1938, ninety copies the three-ton British Model A4E 11 amphibious tank, designated the T-37, were made at the Lenin Machine Works in Omsk.[21]

The Russians manufactured copies of the Vickers-Armstrong E light tank with modifications in 1930 as the T-26 at the Bolshevik Factory in Leningrad.[22] Later the Ordzhonikidze Tractor Plant at Kharkov made T-26s, which remained a standard-type until 1941.[23] The T-26B was armed with a 45mm gun, weighed nine tons, and had a speed of thirty kilometers per hour.[24]

The BT tanks were light tanks based on the design of the American inventor Walter Christie. He sent engineering drawings and several models to the Soviet Union disguised as agricultural tractors. Soviet engineers came to the Christie plant to study manufacturing techniques.[25] The tracks could be removed on the original design and the tank ran on its road wheels over paved surfaces at high speed. Although the Soviets abandoned this feature in later models, the large road wheels remained. The Christie tank was modified to become the BT tank in 1931 manufactured at the Kharkov Locomotive Works. In 1938 production began at the Chelyabinsk Tractor Plant. The BTs had a crew of three and were armed with a 45mm gun.[26] The most common tanks in the mechanized corps were the BT-7 armed with a 45mm gun, weighing 13.8 tons and with a speed of fifty-three kilometers per hour. Tank units usually had a mixture of tanks. The 48th Tank Battalion in June 1941 had BT-5s, BT-7s, and T-28s. The best light tanks were the BT-7M produced in 1938 and the T-26.[27]

Medium and heavy tanks were built in smaller quantities in the 1930s. The T-28 medium tank, built at Chelyabinsk, had three turrets and a crew of six, and resembled the British A6 medium tank. The short-barreled 76mm gun and machine guns were designed to break through fortified lines. The T-32 was a 34-ton medium based on the Christie chassis built in small numbers at the Kirov Works in Leningrad, the Stalin Works at Kramatorsk, and Uralmash.[28] The heavy T-35 weighed 50 tons, had five turrets, and was armed with a 76mm gun, a 45mm gun, and five machine guns. The crew was two officers and nine men! The T-35 was based on the Vickers A1 and probably built at Uralmash.[29]

Forming the new tanks into units began in 1929 when the Soviets formed a mechanized research and experimental unit at Naro Fominsk with a tank battalion, an artillery battery, an armored car battalion, and a motorized infantry battalion.[30] In 1930 a mechanized brigade was formed, and later there were three motorized infantry brigades. The mechanized brigade had two tank battalions, two rifle battalions, a reconnaissance battalion, an artillery battalion, and service units.[31]

A massive production program began to equip the new tank units. By 1932 the Soviet Union had 3,000 tanks—more than any other country in the world. From 1930 to 1934, 11,000 tanks were manufactured. On January 1, 1934, the Red Army had 6,632 tanks and 326 armored cars in service.[32] From 1935 to 1937, 3,000 more tanks were made each year. By the end of the second five-year plan the army had more than 15,000 tanks, mostly light T-26s and BTs.[33]

The 1st Mechanized Brigade and two rifle divisions provided the cadre in 1932 for two mechanized corps (the 11th and 45th) consisting of two mechanized brigades, a rifle-machine gun brigade, and an antiaircraft battalion. Each corps had 500 BT-2 and T-26 light tanks and 200 T-27 tankettes. The 11th Corps was located in the Leningrad District and the 45th in the Kiev District.[34] The 11th Rifle Division provided the cadre for the 11th Mechanized Corps containing the 31st and 32nd Mechanized Brigades and the 33rd Rifle Brigade. The brigades took the numbers of the rifle regiments in the 11th Rifle Division. The 45th Rifle Division formed the 45th Mechanized Corps with the 133rd and 134th Mechanized Brigades and the 135th Rifle Brigade, again using the regimental numbers. The mechanized brigades had three tank battalions with T-26 tanks, an artillery battalion, an engineer battalion, an antiaircraft company, and some additional BT tanks. The rifle-machine gun brigade had three rifle battalions, an engineer battalion, and an antiaircraft battalion.[35]

Five additional independent mechanized brigades were formed in the next few years—the 2nd in the Ukraine, the 3rd, 4th, and 5th in White Russia, and the 6th in the Far East. There were plans to form fifteen tank battalions and sixty-five tankette battalions to support the rifle divisions.[36] Two additional mechanized corps were formed in 1934, the 7th in Leningrad and the 5th Corps (from the 1st and 5th Mechanized Brigades). The 11th Corps transferred from Leningrad to Transbaikal.[37] In January 1935 the Red Army had four mechanized corps (5th, 7th, 11th, and 45th), 6 mechanized brigades (including the 2nd, 3th, 4th, and 6th), six tank regiments, eight independent tank battalions, fifteen mechanized regiments assigned to cavalry divisions, and eighty-three tank battalions in rifle divisions.[38]

In 1935 all of the tank regiments reformed as brigades. The medium brigades had four battalions with eighty T-28 medium tanks and thirty-seven T-26 or BT light tanks. The heavy brigades had four battalions with sixty T-35 heavy tanks and thirty-four light tanks.[39] The independent brigades had 145 T-26 tanks, 56 artillery-observation and flamethrower tanks, and 28 armored cars.[40] In 1938 the 5th Heavy Tank Brigade had a table of organization of three battalions with a total of ninety-four T-35s, forty-four BTs, and ten flamethrower tanks. T-28s substituted for T-35s.[41]

The tank brigades were designed for infantry support and were distributed among the rifle formations. In 1935 the Kiev Military District had 12 rifle divisions, a cavalry corps, and two tank brigades, the 17th and 34th.[42] In November 1937, besides the four mechanized corps (5th, 7th, 11th and 45th), the Red Army had twenty-one independent tank brigades, three independent armored car brigades, and eleven tank regiments. The heavy tank brigades had 183 tanks (136 T-28s, 37 BTs, and 10 flamethrower tanks). The T-35 brigade had 94 T-35s, 44 BTs, and 10 flamethrower tanks. The light tank brigades had 278 BTs or 267 T-26s. The tank regiments had from 190 to 267 tanks. Each rifle division had a battalion of BT, T-26, and/or T-38 tanks.[43]

The change in doctrine in 1938 called for employing tanks concentrated in large tank corps as opposed to mechanized corps. In August 1938 all tank units received new designations. Four new tank corps had two light tank brigades and a rifle-machine gun brigade, 12,364 men, 660 tanks, and 118 guns. The tank corps were located in Leningrad (10th), White Russia (15th), Kiev (25th), and Transbaikal (20th).[44] Other units included six independent tank brigades, six tank regiments, fourteen mechanized regiments in the cavalry divisions, and thirty-seven tank companies and twenty-three tankette battalions assigned to rifle divisions. The light tank brigades had four tank battalions and a reconnaissance battalion with a total of 295 BT and T-26 tanks. The heavy tank brigades had four tank battalions with 139 T-28 and T-35 tanks.[45] In September 1938 the Vinnitsa Army Group included the 25th Tank Corps with the 4th Tank Brigade, the 5th Tank Brigade, and the 1st Motorized Brigade. The independent 23rd and 26th Tank Brigades were also in the army group.[46] Additional tank brigades formed during 1938 and 1939. By January 1939 there were four tank corps (10th, 15th, 20th, and 25th), twenty-four independent light tank brigades, four heavy tank brigades, and tank battalions assigned to rifle and cavalry divisions.[47]

General D. G. Pavlov had returned from the Spanish Civil War and in July 1939 convinced Stalin that the experience there proved that large tank units could not operate successfully.[48] Added to the upheaval in the Red Army command created by the purges of 1937 and 1938, Stalin altered the tank philosophy and disbanded the tank corps on November 21, 1939. In December 1939 the Soviet high command developed a new plan for the armored force. Most tanks were assigned to independent heavy and medium brigades to support the infantry.[49] The medium brigade had four battalions with 258 T-28s, T-26s, and BTs. The T-28s were to be replaced by the T-34 when it became available. The heavy tank brigades had three battalions equipped with 117 T-28 medium tanks and

T-35 heavy tanks plus 39 BTs.[50] Motorized divisions (as opposed to motor-ized rifle divisions that had three motorized rifle regiments) were to be formed with a tank regiment, two rifle regiments, an artillery regiment, and service units. These divisions had 257 tanks and 73 armored cars. The plan included the formation of 15 motorized divisions, 8 in 1940 and 7 later. The first four formed in early 1940 were the 1st, 15th, 81st, and 109th. The motorized divisions were to act as highly mobile reserves for the field armies and to work with horse-mechanized groups.[51]

The "Spanish" doctrine lasted only eight months. The success of the German panzer divisions and panzer corps in September 1939 and in May 1940 influenced Stalin to reestablish the mechanized corps on June 9, 1940.[52] On July 15, 1940, the General Staff authorized eight mecha-nized corps plus two tank divisions. Nine corps were assembled from existing tank brigades and the eight motorized divisions formed under the December 1939 plan. Individual tank brigades formed tank divisions. In addition the new plan included 32 independent brigades and 10 regi-ments. The light brigades would have 258 BT and T-26 tanks, the heavy brigades 156 T-28 and T-35 tanks.[53] In July 1940 General Eremenko, com-mander of the 6th Cavalry Corps, was ordered to Minsk where he was to form the 3rd Mechanized Corps.[54] The first five corps formed were the 1st, 4th, 5th, 6th, and 8th.[55]

The distribution of the first nine corps was probably as follows:

Mechanized Corps	Military District
1st	Leningrad
2nd	Odessa
3rd	Baltic
4th	Kiev
5th	West
6th	West
7th	Moscow
8th	Kiev
9th	Kiev

In December 1940 and January 1941, war games tested the new for-mations. G. I. Kulik, the deputy commissar for defense, defended the large 18,000-man rifle division with horse-drawn transport and opposed any further mechanization. Kulik referred to the experience in Spain where tanks were used only in small formations, and opposed any addi-tional tank formations. Stalin asked the military district commanders for their opinions. They favored the mechanized corps and requested one to three corps for each district. Stalin agreed and ordered the formation of additional corps.[56]

The revised plan in February 1941 called for an additional twenty corps to be formed in February and March of 1941.[57] The new mechanized corps had two tank divisions and one motorized division. The tank division had two tank regiments, one motorized rifle regiment, and an artillery regiment, with a total of 375 tanks and 11,343 men. The tanks authorized were 63 KVs, 210 T-34s, and 102 T-26s and BTs. The motorized division had one tank regiment, two motorized rifle regiments, and an artillery regiment with 11,000 men, 275 light tanks, and 158 guns and mortars. The mechanized corps had a total of 1,031 tanks (including 420 T-34s and 126 KVs) and 36,000 men. Besides the mechanized corps, there were three independent tank divisions and two independent motorized divisions.[58]

The military districts formed thirteen mechanized corps in February and March 1941, as follows:[59]

Military District	Mechanized Corps
Leningrad	10th
Baltic	12th
Western	11th, 13th, 14th, 17th, 20th
Kiev	15th, 16th, 19th, 17th, 24th
Odessa	18th

In April 1941 the 4th Army created the 14th Mechanized Corps using the 29th Tank Brigade at Brest to form the 22nd Tank Division and the 32nd Tank Brigade at Prugan to form the 30th Tank Division. The existing 205th Motorized Division was at Bereza-Kartuzskaia. Additional troops to fill the larger table of organization came from the 42nd Rifle Division. The corps had T-26 and T-38 tanks previously assigned to the two tank brigades.[60]

Additional mechanized corps were formed later in the following districts:

Moscow	21st
Orel	23rd
Kharkov	25th
North Caucasus	26th
Central Asia	27th
Transcaucasus	28th
Far East	30th

The revised plan called for 30,000 tanks including 16,600 T-34s and KVs and 7,000 armored cars. The General Staff anticipated that the organization would be completed in four or five years and that in the interval older tanks would be used for training.[61]

However, Hitler did not give Stalin time to create an armored juggernaut armed with powerful tanks. In June 1941 the Soviet Union had a large number of obsolete and obsolescent tanks built over the previous decades. Technical difficulties had delayed production of the KVs and T-34s. Only 256 KVs and 117 T-34s were built in 1940.[62] In March 1941, 508 KVs and 967 T-34s were available and by June 1, 225 T-34s and 639 KVs had been manufactured.[63] The T-28 medium tanks and T-35 heavy tanks substituted for the missing T-34s and KVs.

A new light tank, the T-60, was scheduled to replace the BTs and T-26s and 2,421 were built in 1940.[64] About 3,500 T-26, BT, and T-60 tanks were produced during 1941. However, 50 percent of the light tanks (manufactured between 1931 and 1935) were worn out in 1941.[65] In June 1941, 29 percent of the tanks needed overhaul and 44 percent needed major repairs. There were no reserves of spare parts and few repair facilities.[66] In June 1941 only 27 percent of the tanks were in working order.[67]

The process of expansion and reorganization that had begun in July 1940 and enlarged in February 1941 was barely under way by June 1941. The motorized divisions had only half their transport and 40 percent of their artillery in June 1941.[68] However, some motorized divisions were well equipped with artillery. Six of the mechanized corps, including four with no KV or T-34 tanks, had nearly the authorized number of guns and mortars. Of the 2,148 guns and mortars authorized to the six corps, 1,874 were available. The major shortage was antitank guns.[69] Despite shortages of transport many of the motorized divisions were functional in June 1941, having been formed in late 1939.

The tank divisions were not as functional. The types of tanks in the tank divisions were mostly T-28s, BTs, and T-26s as follows:[70]

Type	8th Tank Division	10th Tank Division	7th Tank Division
KV	50	63	51
T-34	150	38	150
T-28	68	61	
BT-7	31	181	125
T-26	36	22	42
TOTAL	335	365	368

The actual number of tanks in the mechanized corps in June 1941 varied from corps to corps.[71] Where data refers to two corps, the total was divided. In the West the total includes the 5th corps plus two tank divisions not formed into a corps. In the Far East the total includes two tank divisions and one motorized division not in a corps. The delayed production of the KV and T-34 meant that only four corps had significant numbers of modern tanks, three in the Kiev District and one in the Western District.

		Total Tanks	**KV & T-34**	**KV**	**T-34**	**BT**	**T-26**
1st	Leningrad	753	8				
2nd	Odessa	489	60	10	46	215	87
3rd	Baltic	692	55				
4th	Kiev	892	414				
5th	Western	2,602					
6th	Western	1,021	352	114	420	416	126
7th	Moscow	567	5				
8th	Kiev	858	171				
9th	Kiev	285					
10th	Leningrad	753	7				
11th	Western	237	31	3	28	44	162
12th	Baltic	691	54				
13th	Western	294				15	263
14th	Western	520				6	504
15th	Kiev	733	131				
16th	Kiev	608					
17th	Western	36				24	1
18th	Odessa	280					
19th	Kiev	280	11				
20th	Western	93				13	80
21st	Moscow	567	4				
22nd	Kiev	647	31				
23rd	Orel	413	21				
24th	Kiev	222					
25th	Kharkov	300	20				
26th	North Caucasus	184					
27th	Central Asia	356					
28th	Transcaucasus	869					
30th	Far East	2,969					
TOTAL		19,211	1,375				

In June 1941, the Germans had 5,262 tanks. Of these 877 were obsolete Mk I light tanks and 187 T-35 Czech tanks that were not assigned to combat units. In addition, there were 377 self-propelled 75mm guns.[72]

Tank	Main Gun	Total Number
Mk I	machine gun	877
Mk II	20mm	1.072
Flamethrower	flamethrower	85
T-35	37mm	187
T-38	37mm	754
Mk III	37mm	1,440
Mk IV	75mm L24	517
TOTAL	5,262	
TOTAL excluding obsolete tanks	4,198	

The 5,262 German tanks compared to about 15,000 Soviet tanks in mechanized corps in the Western military districts. Over 4,000 Soviet tanks were in the Far East, Central Asia, and the Caucasus.

Not a single German tank was in the same class as the 1,861 T-34s and KVs, of which 1,375 had been assigned to the mechanized corps. The Mk IV had a short-barreled, low-velocity gun with little antitank capability. The 10,000 or more T-26s and BTs had a better gun than the 1,440 German Mk III panzer that still made up much of the strength of the German panzer divisions. The BTs and T-26s were still in use in the Red Army tank brigades and regiments used to support the infantry in February 1943.[73]

Although the Red Army had over 22,000 tanks in June 1941, only 15,000 were in the western districts and only a quarter of those were operational. In terms of operational tanks the Germans outnumbered the Soviets. The Germans destroyed or captured over 20,000 tanks in the West in 1941.[74] The remarkable German victory can be attributed to the training and experience of the German units and the high level of maintenance, not the quality or quantity of their tanks. The Germans had launched the surprise attack during a period when the Soviet tank brigades were being reorganized into divisions short of modern tanks. Six months later, the Germans would have found the Russian mechanized force a far more proficient antagonist.

Many Russian tanks had been lost because of mechanical problems, not German action. Poor training and incomplete units were manifested in a variety of ways. Many tanks were not ready for action because they were old and there were too few service units. Some tanks lacked routine maintenance and many needed major overhaul. The 16th Mechanized Corps had 16 percent of its tanks in repair; the 3rd Mechanized Corps had 45 percent of its tanks in repair.[75] Poor supply arrangements resulted in many tanks running out of fuel and being captured intact by the Germans. Lack of experienced commanders led to long road marches, resulting in excessive wear on the tracks and mechanical breakdowns. Poor tactics had exposed the tanks to German antitank guns. By July 15, 1941, only 1,500 tanks were operational against the Germans.[76]

The mechanized corps were disbanded by the end of 1941 and the remaining tanks used to form brigades. The motorized divisions were converted to rifle divisions if they had survived. Most of the motorized divisions were disbanded and new rifle divisions formed with the same number.

The large-scale production of tanks by the Soviet Union in the 1930s had left the army with large numbers of obsolete tanks. However, the Germans were also using the Mk II and Mk III in June 1941. The Soviet problem was not due to the quality of the tanks but to the superior German ability to maintain and use its tanks. Only after the Red Army had acquired experience in handling tanks and the tank schools had turned out trained crews to man the new tanks would the Soviet Union be able to reap the benefits of its tank quality.

By December 1941 the Soviet armored forces were in disarray. Large-scale tank production was still in the future and the crews that survived the destruction of the mechanized corps had few tanks. Beginning in 1942 the tank force would be resurrected based on prewar tank men and new production from factories in the east.

CHAPTER 8

Organization of the Tank Forces

The German invasion had caught the Soviet tank arm in the midst of expansion. The result was incredible losses of tanks, many through lack of fuel or mechanical breakdown because of the shortage of trained service units.[1] A similar problem had crippled the French armored divisions in 1940. Like the French, the Russians had not developed large self-sufficient tank formations. Without the necessary supply and repair units, the organizations were unable to maintain their tanks in operating condition.

The priority in 1941 was to replace the thousands of tanks lost in the first months of the war. Given the disruption of Soviet tank production in 1941 and the need for great numbers of tanks, the Russians concentrated on building four types: the T-34, the KV, the T-60, and the T-70. To increase production using unskilled labor, the Soviets simplified the design of tanks and prohibited any unnecessary variations or improvements. Changes were made to reduce the cost of manufacture, either in man-hours or in material, or to make major essential improvements in the gun, armor, or engine. Soviet tanks appeared rough and poorly made, but their important parts were finished to a high standard. The ideal design was one that was just good enough: anything better was wasted effort. The outstanding characteristic of Soviet tanks was simplicity, making them easy to manufacture, operate, and maintain.[2]

Russia entered the war with a large stock of obsolescent tanks, mostly light tanks including 11,000 BTs and 6,000 T-26s. The 1,861 T-34s and KVs were better than any German tank. The remaining 5,000 were of little value.[3] Production since early 1941 had concentrated on the T-34 and the KV to the exclusion of other mediums and heavies. New production concentrated on the T-60, the T-70, the T-34, and the KV. Production of the T-60 light tank began in July 1941. The two light tanks manufactured in 1941 and 1942 were the T-60 and T-70. The T-60 weighed 6.4 tons, had a crew of two, carried 20mm gun, 15 to 35 millimeterse of armor, and a speed of 45 kilometers per hour.[4] The T-70 was an improved T-60 with a 45mm gun, armor of 15 to 45 millimeters, and weighed 9.8 tons. The dis-

119

ruption caused by the German advance reduced the monthly output
from 2,000 in June 1941 to 1,400 in September 1941 from factories in
Gorki and Kirov.[5] The Soviets stopped production of light tanks in 1943
and turned the manufacturing facilities to the production of SU-76s.

The Russians used the T-34 medium tank with improvements
throughout the war. It weighed 30.9 tons, carried a 76mm gun, had a
crew of four, a speed of 55 kph, and armor from 45 to 52mm. The M1939
76mm gun was a high-velocity piece, with a 30.5 caliber barrel, compared
to the short 24 caliber 75mm gun on the German Panzer IV in 1941.[6]
The bad points of the early T-34 were the two-man turret requiring the
tank commander to be the gunner, discomfort for the crew, poor vision
for the commander, problems with the transmission, and short track life.[7]
Later models of the T-34 had the M1940 76mm gun with a 41.5 caliber
barrel, giving it higher velocity, and a larger turret. In 1943 the Russians
modified the T-34, replacing the 76mm gun with the M1939 85mm antiaircraft gun. The modified tank was called the T-34/85. The weight
increased to 32 tons, the crew to five, and the armor to 90mm, but the
speed remained at 55 kilometers per hour.[8] The Russians stressed the
heavy projectile approach instead of high velocity. The 85mm gun had a
heavier projectile than the 75mm gun used on the German Panther, but
the latter was able to penetrate thicker armor at longer ranges.[9]

The heavy tank in July 1941 was the KV-1 weighing 47.5 tons, with a
crew of five, an M1940 41.5 caliber 76mm gun, 75 to 100mm of armor,
and a speed of 35 kph. The KV-2 had a 152mm howitzer for use in
destroying bunkers. The Russians made only a few of the KV-2s because
of manufacturing problems and limited need for the heavy projectile.[10]
There was a need for a lighter version of the KV to attain a better balance
between engine power and weight that would give greater speed. The KV-
1S entered production in August 1942, and by April 1943, 1,370 had
been built. They were assigned to heavy tank regiments.[11]

In October 1943 a further development of the KV was the KV-85
equipped with the 85mm antiaircraft gun. Production of the JS-1 heavy
tank armed with a 122mm gun to replace the KVs began in December
1943. The JS-2 weighed 46 tons, had a crew of four, a 122mm gun,
90–120 millimeters of armor, and a speed of 37 kilometers per hour. In
1945 the JS-3 appeared weighing 47 tons with a speed of 40 kilometers
per hour. The Guard heavy tank units received JS tanks in early 1944.
The purpose of the heavy tank was to destroy German tanks and antitank
guns at long range from positions behind the T-34s. At Korsun the 11th
Guard Heavy Tank Brigade successfully engaged the German 503rd
Heavy Panzer Battalion equipped with Tigers. The 122mm guns on the

JS tanks outranged the German 88mm guns.[12] The Russians fought the entire war with three basic tank chassis: the T-60/T-70, the T-34, and the KV/JS. This limited inventory greatly simplified maintenance and repair.

In July 1941 the plentiful supply of tanks was still far in the future and new units were needed to make use of what was available. Faced with the heavy losses of tanks in the first weeks of the war, on July 15, 1941, the Stavka had dissolved the mechanized corps. The remaining tank divisions reorganized with a revised table of organization. The new tank division had two tank regiments, a motorized regiment, an antitank regiment, an antiaircraft battalion, and other units.[13] Ten new tank divisions had formed in July and August 1941, each with 217 tanks, but the new formations still were not functional, lacking service units.

Two of the new divisions soon reformed as motorized divisions and one disbanded. The 10th Tank Division reformed in September 1941 as the 1 st Motorized Rifle Division with two motorized rifle regiments, an artillery regiment, and a tank regiment. The motorized divisions converted later to regular three-regiment rifle divisions.[14] Seven tank divisions were still active in December 1941, including four in the Far East. The three remaining in Europe disbanded in 1942.[15]

Tank brigades with a limited number of service units had replaced the disbanded tank divisions. The tank brigades cooperated with the infantry and received logistical support from the field army to which they had been assigned. On August 23, 1941, the tank brigade included a tank regiment with three battalions with ninety-three tanks, twenty-two T-34s, seven KVs, and sixty-four light tanks. One tank battalion had a KV company and two T-34 companies. The other two battalions had light tanks. The brigade also had a rifle battalion, an antiaircraft battalion, and other units.[16] However, the medium and heavy tanks were not available and the brigades consisted mostly of light tanks. In August 1941 the 48th Tank Battalion had received ten T-34s but lost them in combat soon thereafter.[17]

The shortage of medium and heavy tanks led to a further reduction in the brigade three weeks later on September 13, 1941. The new tank brigade had only two tank battalions with a total of seven KVs and sixty other tanks. There was no tank regimental headquarters in the brigade. Even then most brigades had fewer than the authorized number of tanks.[18] In September independent tank battalions worked with rifle and cavalry divisions. The battalions consisted of a medium company of seven T-34s and two light tank companies (each ten tanks), with 130 men and twenty-nine tanks.[19] In November 1941 a heavy tank company reinforced the independent heavy battalion. The battalion had five KVs, eleven T-34s, and twenty light tanks.[20] Few tank battalions had this full complement.

On December 9, 1941, the tank brigade was changed in response to new tactics and an increasing supply of T-34s and KVs. The two tank battalions in the brigade each had a company of five KVs, a company of seven T-34s, and a company of T40s or T-60s.[21] Each brigade was authorized three additional KVs and 14 T-34s in place of 20 light tanks compared to the previous organization. By December 1941 the Red Army had 7 tank divisions (four in the Far East), 76 tank brigades, and 100 independent tank battalions.[22] The new units formed with men from training and replacement units and new and repaired tanks.[23] In December 1941 the 48th Tank Battalion had 12 light T-26s and 6 BT-7s. The replacements suggest that light tanks were still in depots from the prewar inventory as late as December.[24] In the Moscow parade in November 1941, the 31st Tank Brigade had four KVs, seven BT-7s, and ten T-26s. The brigade also had 8 25mm antiaircraft guns and 30 trucks.[25]

In the winter offensive, the Russians lost many more tanks because of poor tactics.[26] Mixing the heavy KVs and other types of tanks in the same tactical units did not work and the battalions could not stay together. The T-34 was fast and traveled well over most types of terrain, but the light tanks could not cope with difficult terrain. The slow KVs stopped at the first stream and searched for bridges able to bear their heavy weight.[27]

In January 1942 the strength of the brigade had dropped again.[28] Special tank brigades were formed to work with cavalry formations (twenty T-34s and twenty-six light tanks). Brigades working with the infantry had KVs in place of some of the light tanks (ten KVs, sixteen T-34s, and twenty light tanks). A month later the authorized strength dropped again. In February 1942 tank brigades attached to rifle divisions had only twenty-seven tanks, equal to a weak battalion.[29] The cavalry brigades remained at forty-six. On the other hand, new brigades were being formed. In February 1942 the 79th and 80th Tank Brigades formed at Gorki with twenty T-34s and twenty T-60s followed by two tank brigades each month after that.[30] The rapid expansion of the tank force spread the tanks among many brigades giving company, battalion, and brigades commanders an opportunity to learn their craft during the lull in operations. On February 16, 1942, there were 120 independent tank brigades.[31]

The reduction of the authorized strength was part of a plan to form many tank brigades each with a few tanks using officers from the abolished mechanized corps. The abolition of sixty tank divisions each with two tank regiments made available many field grade officers with tank experience. Using these officers to form new brigades had created the structures required when more tanks and crews became available in the spring of 1942. The Russians continued to form new tank brigades instead of replacing losses in existing ones. The new brigades had only three companies—one heavy, one medium, and one light. The 28th Tank Brigade formed on March 10, 1942, in Moscow with tanks made at Nishnij-Tagil and other factories had only five KVs, ten T-34s, and eight T-60s—equal to one battalion.[32] The organization was ideal to provide training and experience to brigade and company commanders. These skeleton brigades could be reinforced as more tanks rolled off the assembly lines and crews came from the training schools.[33]

In March 1942 the move to fill the skeleton units had begun. On March 10, 1942, a new organization authorized the tank brigade at two battalions each with a company of five KVs, a company of ten T-34s, and a company of eight light tanks—double the numbers given to the 28th Tank Brigade that same day. The new organization eliminated the reconnaissance company; reduced the antiaircraft battalion to a battery; joined all the service units into one company; and reinforced the motorized rifle battalion. The new battalion had a rifle company, an antitank company, and an antitank rifle company. Manpower decreased from 1,800 men to 1,152, but the forty-six tanks now included ten KVs, twenty-four T-34s, and twelve light tanks, replacing four light tanks with T-34s. Another indication that the Russians had formed the January and February brigades as training units was that there were fewer men in the new brigades while the number of tanks increased.[34]

In April 1942 the expanded tank production and available tank brigades had reached a point that an improved command structure was necessary. At Kerch in March 1942 there were four tank brigades and three tank regiments with no coordinating headquarters other than the army commander.[35] With increasing Soviet offensive capability, large tank formations became necessary to provide administrative and tactical control. Therefore, the tank corps was established on March 31, 1942, with two tank brigades each with fifty tanks (ten KVs, twenty T-34s, and twenty T-60s). Some tank corps had a third tank brigade with 168 tanks (30 KVs, 60 T-34s, 60 T-60s, and 18 other tanks). The number of tank corps increased steadily. New corps formed each month, bringing together existing tank brigades.[36] Four corps (1st, 2nd, 3rd, and 4th) were raised in early April and others followed. By the end of 1942 there were twenty-nine tank corps.[37]

On May 29, 1942, the tank corps was changed to include one heavy tank brigade and two medium brigades. This change alleviated the problem of mixing types of tanks in tactical formations. The corps also had a rifle brigade or battalion, a motorcycle battalion, an antiaircraft battalion, and a battalion of rocket launchers.[38] The 13th Tank Corps had the new table of organization and included the 13th and 88th Tank Brigades plus the 65th Heavy Tank Brigade. The 13th Tank Brigade, formed at Stalingrad on April 24, 1942, had the 85th and 88th Tank Battalions equipped with T-34s and T-70s. The 65th Heavy Tank Brigade had KVs. The corps also included the 20th Motorized Rifle Brigade, the 34th Engineer Company, and other units.[39] The new corps signaled a change in tank tactics from being parceled out to the infantry in small numbers to use in larger numbers.

By May 1942, 172 tank brigades were in existence and the supply of tanks was increasing. In the winter of 1941–42 the Russians had produced 4,500 tanks and in the first six months of 1942, 11,000.[40] Large-scale production of medium tanks in the factories in the east began in the spring. Light tanks were being produced in converted automotive factories around Moscow and lend-lease provided British and U.S. tanks.

The main armored strength was in the south. The Russians planned to launch a preemptive strike against the German forces gathering for the summer 1942 offensive south of Kharkov. The Pushkin Tank Group had four tank corps—the 4th, 13th, 23rd, and 24th. The group included the following tanks

T-34	127
KV	82
T-60	206
T-70	14
Valentine, Mk III	30
Stuart, M3	76
Grant, M3	33
TOTAL	568 tanks in 12 brigades

Each brigade averaged forty-nine tanks compared to the authorized fifty. The brigades had one-third of the authorized heavy tanks and one-third of the medium tanks (substituting the Grants for T-34s). In place of the missing mediums and heavies were light tanks, Valentines, and Stuarts. Nearly one-fourth of the tanks were imports and 40 percent were light tanks.[41] The Red Army commanders lacked the experience and skill to use the new tank corps. The Germans destroyed the Pushkin Tank Group in the encirclement at Izyum in May.

The Russians were still suffering from many problems in the employment of tanks that led to the heavy losses. Mixing heavy, medium, and light tanks in tactical units caused the units to splinter as the slower tanks could not keep up with the faster ones. The more agile T-34s arrived in range of the German antitank guns before the slow heavily armored KVs needed to break through the defensive lines. The difference in weight often left the KV behind, waiting for a bridge to be repaired or built. Poor crew and unit training continued to be a problem. The lack of radios in each tank complicated command. The two-man turret on Russian tanks forced the tank commander to act as gunner and made command more difficult. All of these factors contributed to poor tactics.[42]

Crew and unit training was still unsatisfactory. The 13th Tank Brigade, an element of the 13th Tank Corps, arrived at the front only thirty-nine days after being formed, making a 600 kilometers journey by rail from Stalingrad to the Kharkov area ending on June 2, 1942, and then a further move of 100 kilometers on June 4, 1942. Loading and unloading the tanks on and off flat cars and reassembling crews and tanks must have caused some confusion.[43] The brigade fought in pitched battles from June 10, 1942, to July 5, 1942. The other brigades of the 13th Corps, the 65th and the 88th Tank Brigades, were so badly mauled that they were disbanded and replaced in the 13th Corps by the 158th and 167th Tank Brigades.[44] This was very rough duty for a tank corps that had been in existence less than two months. The replacement brigades had less training.

Not only was training deficient, but the command structure was incomplete. The Pushkin Tank Group was an ad hoc formation to control four tank corps. A permanent organization was needed to control the tank forces and take full advantage of their power. In May 1942 the formation of tank armies began. The purpose of the tank army was to penetrate the German defenses and to exploit the breakthrough.[45] Infantry supported by tanks had been unable to sustain the momentum of the attack after the breakthrough because of lack of mobility. The first tank armies formed in 1942 also lacked mobile infantry, using regular rifle divisions instead of motorized infantry. As a result, the infantry could not keep up with the tanks. The problem was not solved until late 1942, with the formation of mechanized corps for the tank armies.[46]

The Stavka directive of May 25, 1942, had ordered the activation of the 3rd and 5th Tank Armies using the headquarters of field armies in the Moscow Military District. The 3rd Tank Army, formed at Kharkov, consisted of the 12th and 15th Tank Corps, the 154th and 264th Rifle Divisions, the 179th Tank Brigade, the 8th Motorcycle Regiment, the 1172nd Tank Destroyer Regiment, the 62nd Guards Mortar Regiment, the 226th Antiaircraft Regiment, the 54th Motorcycle Battalion, the 182nd Engineer Battalion, the 470th Antiaircraft Battalion, and other units.[47] The army fought for two weeks on the Western Front, from August 22 until September 9, taking part in the Kozelsk offensive. The

3rd Tank Corps and the 3rd Guards Mechanized Division were added to the army and in September 1942 the army transferred to the Stavka reserve where it remained until January 1943.[48] This powerful army remained in reserve, protecting Moscow during the fierce battles in the south and the Stalingrad counteroffensive. Such misappropriation of resources weakened the Soviet potential.

The 5th Tank Army had formed in June 1942 near Elista south of Stalingrad with the 2nd and 11th Tank Corps, the 340th Rifle Division, the 19th Tank Brigade, five artillery regiments, and other units.[49] In July 1942 the 7th Tank Corps joined the army, which moved to the Don River and entered combat. In less than two weeks the tank army had suffered heavy losses and was withdrawn from the front in mid-July. The army disbanded and the remaining units transferred to the Bryansk and Voronezh fronts.[50]

To replace the 5th Tank Army, on July 22, 1942, the Stavka ordered the formation of the 1st and 4th Tank Armies from four tank corps stationed at Stalingrad and the headquarters of the 38th and 28th Field Armies. The tank armies consisted of two or three tanks corps, one tank brigade, one or two rifle divisions, a light artillery regiment, a Guard mortar regiment (rocket launchers), an antiaircraft battalion, and a mortar battalion.[51]

The 1st Tank Army included the 13th and 28th Tank Corps, the 131st and 399th Rifle Divisions, the 158th Tank Brigade, and other artillery, engineer, and service units. The 1st Tank Army went to the front at the end of July on the Don north of Kalach, but disbanded when it suffered heavy losses in August. The army headquarters formed the headquarters of the new Southeastern Front.[52]

The 4th Tank Army had not received all of its equipment in August and the men lacked training. The army, consisting of the 22nd and 23rd Tank Corps, the 18th Rifle Division, the 133rd Tank Brigade, a tank destroyer brigade, and other units, entered combat in September on the Don Front. On October 22, 1942, the army, having lost most of its tanks, became the 65th Field Army.[53]

On August 30, 1942, a second formation of the 5th Tank Army had formed at Voronezh and on September 22, 1942, it moved to the Bryansk Front. In November the 5th Tank Army took part in the Stalingrad offensive. It consisted of the 1st and 26th Tank Corps; the 8th Cavalry Corps; the 14th Guard, 47th Guard, 119th, 124th, 159th, and 346th Rifle Divisions; the 8th Tank Brigade; a motorcycle regiment; and 26 artillery and mortar regiments.[54] In April 1943 the 5th Tank Army was again disbanded and its units formed a new 12th Field Army.[55]

During the summer of 1942 the Russians had launched attacks in many places with very little success. The attacks in the north and center may have held German divisions that otherwise would have gone south to help in the drive toward Stalingrad. The attacks did give the Russian commanders experience in breakthrough operations with tanks, as opposed to the winter of 1941–42 attacks which had limited tank support.[56]

Four independent tank corps (1st, 3rd, 4th, and 16th), each with twenty-four KVs, eighty-eight T-34s, and sixty-nine light tanks, were assigned to the Bryansk Front and two more to the Western Front, forming a powerful tank strike force in reserve near Moscow.[57] The number of tanks was significantly higher than the March 1942 organization. Although the KV was scarce, there were ample quantities of T-34s.

Reinforcing the tank forces in the summer of 1942 was part of the general rebuilding program. The mainstays of the Red Army tank forces were the T-60 light tank, the T-34 medium, and the heavy KV. Tank production had increased much more quickly than the Germans had anticipated. Heavy tank production at Chelyabinsk was probably the slowest to pick up speed. In July the Russians took the heavy KVs out of the brigades and formed separate heavy-tank regiments. The T-34s, light tanks, and imported tanks made up the tank brigades. The new organization for tank brigades in July 1942 called for fifty-three tanks: thirty-two T-34s and twenty-one T-60s or T-70s, a major increase in the proportion of T-34s. In essence the change from the March 1942 organization consisted of replacing the two small companies of KVs with an additional company of T-34s. The brigade consisted of two battalions. The 1st battalion had two companies of T-34s and the 2nd battalion had one company of T-34s and two companies of T-70s. The brigade also had an antitank battery and a motorized rifle battalion.[58]

After the severe losses in the south in the summer of 1942, the tank corps were rebuilt. On July 19, 1942, the remnant of the 13th Tank Corps went to Saratov to refit. The 158th Tank Brigade, presumably with all the remaining tanks of the tank corps, had transferred to the 23rd Tank Corps on July 5, 1942, leaving only remnants of the 85th and 167th Tank Brigades with the 13th Corps.[59] Evidence of the improving tank supply was the receipt on July 24, 1942, of seventy-four T-34s and forty-nine light tanks.[60] During this period, German panzer divisions had about 100 tanks.

The 13th Tank Corps transferred its three tank brigades and received three new tank brigades (6th Guard, 13th and 254th) on August 4, 1942. Two of the new brigades had two tank battalions each of three companies of seven T-34s, for a total of forty-two T-34s per brigade. The third brigade had fewer T-34s, but two additional light-tank companies, eighteen light tanks. Each brigade had a motorized rifle battalion, a 76mm antitank gun battery, and service elements. The motorized brigade in the corps had three motorized rifle battalions, an antiaircraft battalion, an artillery battalion, and a tank regiment with three companies totaling twenty-three T-34s and sixteen T-70s.[61]

The 13th Corps had 137 T-34s and 34 light tanks, a far more potent force than in July.[62] The corps returned to battle in the Don Basin for the third time on August 7, 1942, supporting the 64th Army. Each of its tank brigades supported a rifle division instead of remaining together as a striking force. Despite heavy fighting, the corps had thirty-four to fifty-six tanks on September 2, 1942.[63] The experience of the 13th Tank Corps revealed continued lack of skill in using tanks. The tank corps were used for antitank defense instead of being held back as a powerful counterattack force. The steady supply of new tanks and new tank brigades available in 1942 did little to stop the Germans because of poor tactics.

The inclusion of rifle divisions in the tank armies had not been productive. The foot soldiers were unable to keep up with the tanks. The lack of infantry and antitank guns close behind the tank spearheads made it difficult to withstand the inevitable German panzer supported counterattacks after a Russian breakthrough. A conference held in late 1942 recommended major changes in the organization of the tank forces. The rifle division was to be removed from the tank armies and replaced by the new mechanized corps. The new tank armies had two tank corps, a mechanized corps, a guard mortar regiment, a howitzer regiment, a tank destroyer regiment, a motorcycle regiment, an engineer battalion, an aviation regiment, a truck regiment, and two repair battalions.

In September 1942 the mechanized corps had been authorized to replace the rifle divisions in the tank armies. As part of the buildup for the operation to surround the 6th German Army, the Russians formed eleven mechanized corps consisting of three mechanized brigades, each with three motorized rifle battalions, a tank regiment, a mortar battalion, and an artillery regiment. The mechanized brigades had 3,500 men and thirty-nine tanks fitted with handles to enable a battalion of riflemen to ride into battle on the tanks. The other two battalions had to dismount from their trucks and walk during operations. In addition the mechanized corps had two additional tank regiments or a tank brigade, a light artillery regiment, an antiaircraft regiment, an antitank regiment, and a guard mortar battalion armed with rocket launchers, an engineer mine company, a repair battalion, and other units.[64]

The 1st and 2nd Mechanized Corps, formed on September 8, 1942, each had a single tank brigade and 175 tanks. The 3rd and 5th Mechanized Corps had two tank brigades with a total of 224 tanks. The 4th and 6th Mechanized Corps had no tank brigade, but two tank regiments with a total of 204 tanks. Five mechanized corps formed using a tank corps as cadre: the 27th (1st Mechanized Corps), 8th (3rd), 28th (4th), 22nd (5th), and 14th (6th) Tank Corps were redesignated.[65] Other corps were reformed Guard mechanized rifle divisions.

The 6th Mechanized Corps formed on October 26, 1942, from the 14th Tank Corps. The commander had led the 30th Tank Division in June 1941 and fought in the Battle of Moscow in September and October 1941. The corps had the 51st, 54th, and 55th Mechanized Brigades; the 76th, 77th, 78th, 79th, and 80th Tank Regiments; the 41st Armored Car Battalion; the 80th Engineer Battalion; the 417th Tank Destroyer Regiment; the 409th Guards Mortar Battalion; the 56th Engineer Mine Company; the 36th Repair Battalion; the 46th Medical Battalion; and other units. The 51st Mechanized Brigade formed on September 16, 1942, at Gorki, the 54th in September in the Urals, and the 55th in the Chelyabinsk Oblast. The tank regiments formed at tank training centers.[66] On December 4, 1942, less than six weeks after being authorized, the 6th Corps had 13,340 men including 1,751 officers, 4,213 NCOs, and 7,376 men. Equipment included 117 T-34 tanks and 78 T-70 tanks, a total of 195, a few less than the table of organization.[67] On January 6, 1943 (ten weeks after formation), the corps was in combat against the German SS Viking Division.[68]

Additional mechanized corps formed at the end of 1942 and early in 1943. In November 1942 the 13th Mechanized Corps had 205 medium and light tanks, 9 rifle battalions, 92 guns, and 90 mortars.[69] This unit was more powerful than the tank corps, and equal to two German panzer divisions of the time. The organization changed little until the end of the war, acquiring one or two selfpropelled artillery regiments in late 1943, and T-34s replaced the light tanks. By 1944 the mechanized corps had 191 T-34s, 16 SU-85s, 12 SU-152s, and 20 SU-76s.[70]

The mechanized brigade under the October 1942 table of organization had a tank regiment with thirty-nine tanks, three motorized rifle battalions, an artillery battalion with twelve 76mm guns, a mortar battalion with twelve 82mm mortars and six 120mm mortars, a reconnaissance company with armored cars or scout cars, a company of men armed with machine pistols, an antiaircraft battery with eight 37mm antiaircraft guns and twelve 12.7mm machine guns, an antitank rifle company with thirty-six antitank rifles, and service elements. On September 17, 1942, a motorcycle battalion was added and on November 26, 1942, a medical battalion.[71]

The motorized rifle battalion in the mechanized brigade usually consisted of three rifle companies with about 100 men each, a heavy machine company with nine to twelve heavy machine guns; a mortar company with six 82mm mortars; an antitank battery with four 45mm guns; an antitank rifle company with sixteen antitank rifles; a truck company with forty trucks; and medical, supply, and signal platoons.[72]

The motorized brigades, later redesignated as mechanized brigades, were authorized in September 1942. All but two of these brigades were assigned to tank corps. They were similar in organization to the mechanized brigades, having three motorized battalions, a tank battalion (instead of a tank regiment), an artillery battalion, a mortar battalion, and an antitank company. The motorized brigade had 3,000 men, twenty-four guns, and thirty-four mortars.[73]

The mechanized brigades had elite soldiers. The 51st Mechanized Brigade formed on September 15, 1942, in the Gorki area. Most of the officers had attended officer training schools, although eighty had only a short course. They were in their twenties and thirties. Only sixty of the officers were over thirty-five. There were only 841 of the authorized 1,159 noncommissioned officers. Most were under thirty; only forty were over thirty-five. Most had received special training. There were 2,016 men compared to the authorized 1,840 to make up for the shortage of noncommissioned officers. The total brigade had 3,215 officers and men compared to the authorized 3,369. Most of the men were in their twenties and thirties. Only 113 were over thirty-five. All had received some training. The number of Communists and Komsomols was nearly 300, almost 10 percent of the total.[74]

By November 1942 the 51st Mechanized Brigade had received its equipment. There was a full allotment of uniforms and personal equipment. The brigade had the authorized number of weapons with the exception of the eight antiaircraft guns. The brigade had only 50 instead of the authorized 235 1.5-ton trucks and 45 instead of the authorized 73 2.5-ton trucks. It was also short about half of the munitions allotted. The status of the brigade suggested that the Russians had ample quantities of men and equipment for their newly formed units except for trucks. That shortage would be eased in the following year by American vehicles.[75]

In the second half of 1942, four types of tank units supported the infantry: the independent tank brigade with 53 tanks, the independent tank regiment, the heavy breakthrough tank regiment, and the tank battalion. In September 1942 the 5th Guards Army had three tank brigades with 135 KVs, T-26s, T-34s, T-70s, and English Matildas. The tank brigades were parceled out to the infantry. The 69th Tank Brigade was attached to the 120th Rifle Division.[76] In September 1942, the 124th Tank Brigade was attached to the 80th Rifle Division of the 54th Army. In August 1942, the 212th Tank Brigade was attached to the 88th Division of the 31st Army.[77] One positive factor in Soviet tactics was the employment of tank regiments and brigades as complete units instead of being distributed in platoons to smaller rifle units.[78]

The independent tank battalions varied from fifteen to forty-six tanks. The average in early 1942 was five KVs, sixteen T-34s, and ten T-60s. Some battalions had fifteen KVs and others thirty T-60s. The battalions were usually assigned to armies and attached to divisions as needed.[79] Independent tank regiments were formed in September 1942 with twenty to forty tanks to work in close cooperation with the infantry. The tank regiments replaced the independent tank battalions. The authorized strength of the new regiments was two companies of T-34s and one company of T-70s, with a total of 339 men, twenty-three T-34s, and sixteen T-70s.[80] At first these regiments had received tanks considered unsuitable for the tank corps—older light tanks and imported tanks, Valentines, Matildas, and Grants. The lend-lease tanks were arriving at the rate of 200 or more per month. The British Matildas and Valentines were slow, heavily armored infantry tanks. The American Grati medium tank was not as well armored, but had a 75mm gun and a 37mm gun, making it desirable for infantry support. The 75mm fired high-explosive shell against enemy infantry and artillery and the 37mm gun was useful at short range against German tanks. The Grant used gasoline instead of diesel fuel. The gasoline was more likely to explode than the oil and therefore the Grant was not popular with the tank crews. The American Lee light tanks were used in the tank brigades.[81] In November 1942 the Germans estimated that twenty tank brigades had American and British tanks and thirty-three were partially equipped. As Soviet tank supplies increased, the number of front-line tank brigades with Western tanks dropped to thirteen plus twenty-one brigades with some imported tanks.[82]

By December 1942, seventy-four independent tank regiments had been organized.[83] Five tank regiments went to each new mechanized corps. Other tank regiments went to the tank and cavalry corps, and there was a substantial surplus available for infantry support. In October 1942 the KVs formed heavy Guard tank regiments to work with the infantry. The authorized strength was four companies with a total of twenty-one tanks and a service company.[84] By September 1942, heavy tank production was in full swing at Chelyabinsk, estimated at 100 tanks per month and probably more. The 4th, 5th, 6th, 9th, and 10th Guard Heavy Tank Regiments formed in September 1942 at Chelyabinsk, taking KVs directly from the production line. Each regiment had four companies of six KV-1Ss. The KV-1S was an improved KV that weighed forty-six tons, had 180mm of armor on the turret, and was armed with an improved 76mm gun.[85] The KV-1S had a better balance between engine power and weight and greater speed. The KV-1S entered production in August 1942 and by April 1943, 1,370 had been built in eight months.[86] The fact that five regiments formed in one month at Chelyabinsk, and that an average of 171 tanks per month were built from August 1942 to April 1943, reinforced the belief that production exceeded 100 tanks per month. The total production of KVs in 1942 was 2,553, or an average of more than 200 per month.[87]

The number of tank brigades in January 1943 increased to 202, and 81 tank regiments had been formed.[88] The production of T-34s and KV1Ss increased sharply in the second half of 1942, providing an ample supply of tanks for units. While some tank brigades were not refitted, those that remained received more T-34s and KV1Ss. New Soviet tanks went to the tank brigades in the corps, while the older light tanks, British Valentines, and American Grants went to training units and independent tank brigades and regiments supporting the infantry.

Compared to later years only a limited number of tanks were supporting the attacking armies. The average in 1942 and 1943 was 80 to 110 tanks per army with 10 to 15 tanks per kilometer of front being attacked. In December 1942 the Don Front had fewer than 300 tanks assigned to the seven armies and the reserve. The units included five tank brigades and sixteen regiments. The quantity was lower because the tank units had been in action for a month. The total of tanks employed was only a feeble shadow compared to the numbers of tanks available in the last two years of the war.

Even after the initial Russian victories in November and December 1942, the tank force was in disarray. All of the tank armies were either disbanded or in the Stavka reserve near Moscow. In January 1943 Stalin authorized the formation (or rebuilding) of five tank armies with a total of 8,500 tanks at the front, 400 in the Stavka reserve, and 4,300 in nonoperational commands and districts.[89] By January 1943 there were two tank armies (plus two forming), twenty-four tank corps (plus two forming), and eight mechanized corps (plus two forming).[90] The tank armies were Stavka reserve units moved to strategic areas to give the Red Army overwhelming superiority.

By early 1943 the tank units had evolved into a well-balanced offensive force capable of striking the Germans on any front. In the final two years of the war the number of tank units remained relatively constant, although they gained in strength with additional self-propelled regiments and other supporting troops. Tank losses were more than compensated by new production. Tank units often had more than the authorized number of tanks to replace losses. The Germans estimated that by June 1943 the Red Army had 8,500 tanks at the front in located units and 4,000 in unlocated units, a total of 12,500 tanks in Europe. The Red Army had, in fact, over 20,000 tanks and SUs in January 1943 and added over 2,000 per month during 1943.[91] By the spring of 1943 the Soviet tank forces had matured and were ready to seize the initiative. The Soviet high command chose to await the German attack at Kursk, where the Russian tanks played an appropriate role in counterattacking at the end of the battle. In mid-July the tank forces led the offensives that would slowly drive the Germans back to Berlin.

CHAPTER 9

Refining the Tank Formations

By the summer of 1943, the Red Army had a new doctrine for the employment of tanks. The tank armies and the tank and mechanized corps became the main striking force. A participant in the battle at Kursk had noted that by July 1943, "We had to all practical purposes solved the question of organized armour concentration."[1] After July 1943, the Red Army was able to defeat the German Army on any front. The Russian superiority was such that political objectives motivated offensives and campaigns instead of military considerations.

The Soviet armored forces had made major strides in the first half of 1943 to reach that level of confidence. The number of tanks provided to support an offensive increased dramatically from an average of ten to fifteen tanks per kilometer in 1942 to more than thirty tanks per kilometer in 1943. The change was apparent in February 1943 in the Soviet attacks around Leningrad. The 67th Army, the 2nd Shock Army, and the 8th Army had a total of 494 tanks in support, mostly T-60s, BT-5s, and T-26s.[2] In July 1943 the 29th Guard Tank Brigade and the 1453rd SU Regiment with eighty-five tanks and SUs supported the 31st Guard Rifle Division. There were thirty-two armored vehicles per kilometer of front.[3] By 1945 the density of tanks doubled again. In the attack on Berlin in 1945 from 210 to 230 tanks supported a field army with 50 to 60 tanks per kilometer of front.[4]

During 1943 3 tank armies, 5 tank corps, and 4 mechanized corps were reformed, increasing the totals to 5 tank armies, 37 tank and mechanized corps, 80 independent tank brigades, and 149 tank and mechanized artillery regiments. Although the number of tank brigades had dropped to 166 (including the brigades in the corps), 89 more tank regiments had formed.[5] The 1st Tank Army reformed on January 30, 1943, using the headquarters of the 29th Army plus the 6th and 31st Tank Corps, and the 3rd Mechanized Corps. The new 1st Tank Army moved to the northwest near Ostashkovo to help break the blockade of Leningrad. On February 23 the 1st Tank Army had in addition to the mechanized and tank corps the 112th Tank Brigade, the 7th, 62nd, 63rd, and 64th

Tank Regiments; the 6th and 9th Airborne Divisions; the 14th, 15th, 20th, 21st, 22nd, and 23rd Light Rifle Brigades; the 79th and 316th Guard Mortar Regiments; the 989th Howitzer Regiment; the 552nd, 1008th, and 1186th Tank Destroyer Regiments; the 11th Antiaircraft Division; the 59th Engineer Brigade; the 71st and 267th Engineer Battalions; and the 83rd Signal Regiment.[6] This was a much bigger organization than the tank armies of 1942. The massive infantry component and the tank brigade and regiments made the new organization nearly three times as strong as the previous armies. After breaking the Leningrad blockade, the 1st Tank Army moved to the Kharkov area in the Voronezh Front from March until April 4, 1943.[7] Subsequently the army moved to the Kursk area.

The 2nd Tank Army reformed on January 10 with the headquarters of the 3rd Reserve Army of the Bryansk Front and the 3rd and 16th Tank Corps. Instead of a mechanized corps the army had the 60th, 112th, and 194th Rifle Divisions and the 115th Rifle Brigade. The 28th Light Tank Brigade and the 11th Guard Tank Brigade were also assigned. The Lack of mechanized infantry limited its mobility, but the two extra tank brigades and rifle units gave the army shock power. In February the army transferred to the Central Front.[8] The army remained in the Central Front north of Kursk until June. In June the army had in addition the 51st Motorcycle Regiment, the 37th Guard Mortar Regiment, the 1st Antiaircraft Division, the 357th Engineer Battalion, the 9th Signal Regiment, and the 54th Aviation Regiment.[9]

The 3rd Tank Army had been in the Stavka reserve in January 1943. Later in the month it went to the Voronezh Front with the 12th and 15th Tank Corps; the 2nd Mechanized Corps; 7th Cavalry Corps; the 48th Guard; 111th, 180th, and 184th Rifle Divisions; the 37th Rifle Brigade; and the 173rd, 179th, and 201st Tank Brigades. Again this army had been heavily reinforced. The cavalry and extra tank brigades doubled the mobile content and five rifle units were equal to a field army. The army was equal to a small mechanized "front" with the equivalent of two tank armies and a field army. The army took part in the Ostrogohsk-Rossosh operation and then went to Kharkov in March.[10] On April 26, 1943, the 3rd Tank Army was abolished. The headquarters and most of the rifle divisions and tank brigades formed the 57th Army.[11] The tank corps went to the 3rd Guard Tank Army formed on May 14 with some of the old 3rd Tank Army. On June 5 the army had the 12th and 15th Tank Corps, the 91st Tank Brigade, the 50th Motorcycle Regiment, the 138th Signal Regiment, the 372nd Aviation Regiment, and the 182nd Engineer Battalion. On July 14, 1943, the 2nd Mechanized Corps was added to the army.[12]

The 4th Guard Tank Army formed in the Stavka reserve on February 22, 1943, with the 2nd Guard and 23rd Tank Corps and the 1st Guard Mechanized Corps. The army fought at Kupyansk and Krasni Liman in April 1943, but then disbanded.[13] A new 4th Tank Army formed on June 26 with the 11th and 30th Tank Corps and the 6th Guard Mechanized Corps, the 1545th Tank Destroyer Regiment, the 51st Motorcycle Regiment, the 51st Armored Car Battalion, the 88th Engineer Battalion, the 118th Signal Regiment, and the 593 Aviation Regiment. The second 4th Tank Army did not receive guard designation until March 17, 1945.[14]

The 5th Guard Tank Army had reformed with the headquarters of the 3rd Guard Tank Corps on February 10 plus the 18th and 29th Tank Corps and the 5th Guard Mechanized Corps. The army was placed in reserve at Rostov. In March the army moved from Millerovo to the Steppe Front behind Kursk.[15] On July 6 the army had in addition the 53rd Guard Tank Regiment, the 1st Guard Motorcycle Regiment, the 678th Howitzer Regiment, the 689th Tank Destroyer Regiment, the 76th Guard Mortar Regiment, the 6th Antiaircraft Division, the 4th Signal Regiment, the 999th Aviation Regiment, and the 377th Motorcycle Battalion.[16]

The optimum organization of a tank army included two tank corps, a mechanized corps, an antiaircraft division, a tank destroyer brigade, a howitzer regiment, a guard mortar regiment, and service units with a total of 46,000 men and 648 tanks. Service units included a signal regiment, an aviation regiment, a transport regiment, a repair battalion, and medical units. None of the tank armies had this exact complement of units.[17] In the early months of 1943 the Russians continued to assigned large numbers of rifle divisions and brigades with horse-drawn equipment to the tank armies. The rifle formations enabled the tank army to hold a sector of the front in defense and to consolidate gains in attack, but still the slow-moving infantry prevented the rapid exploitation that was the purpose of the tank army.

On April 10, 1943, the Soviets authorized a new organization for the tank army with two tank corps, one mechanized corps, two tank destroyer regiments (each twenty 76mm guns), two mortar regiments (each thirty-six 120mm mortars), two antiaircraft regiments (each sixteen 37mm guns), two self-propelled artillery regiments (each nine SU-76s and twelve SU-122s), a Guard mortar regiment (twenty-four M13 launchers), and possibly some howitzer regiments. The tank army then had a substantial artillery component with 700 guns and mortars.[18] The tank army also received a motorcycle regiment and either an armored car battalion or an additional motorcycle battalion for reconnaissance.[19]

The tank corps and the tank brigade also were reorganized in January 1943. The tank corps previously had three tank brigades, one motorized brigade, an armored car battalion, a guard mortar battalion, and engineer mine company, a truck company, and two repair units. The corps had 7,800 men, 168 tanks (98 T-34s and 70 T-70s), 108 guns and mortars, 8 M13 rocket launchers, and 871 motor vehicles. On January 10 the tank corps was reinforced with a mortar regiment (36 120mm mortars), a self-propelled artillery regiment (17 SU-76s and 8 SU-122s), 40 reserve tanks (33 T-34s and 7 T-70s), and reserve crews, including 100 tank drivers.[20]

More units continued to be added to the tank corps in the next four months, an engineer mine company and an engineer battalion in February, an antiaircraft regiment (seventeen 37mm guns) and a signal battalion (in place of a company) in March; a towed tank destroyer regiment (twenty 45mm guns), an antiaircraft battalion (twelve 85mm guns), and aviation and medical units in April; and a heavy tank destroyer battalion (twelve 85mm guns) in May. Also in May the self-propelled artillery regiment received four more SU-122s.[21] The tank corps was a powerful, well-balanced force by May 1943 with ample artillery resources to break through defenses and more than 200 tanks including the reserves—far stronger than the German panzer division of the time, which had only two fifty-tank battalions in the panzer regiment compared to four fifty-three-tank battalions in the Russian tank corps. The panzer division had four motorized infantry battalions—one less than the Soviet tank corps.

The Soviet tank brigade had been strengthened in January. The brigade then had two tank battalions with fifty-three tanks (thirty-two T-34s and twenty-one T-70s), a motorized rifle battalion, an antitank battery (four 76mm guns), an antiaircraft battery (four 37mm guns), a service company, and a medical unit. The motorized rifle battalion had a mortar company with six 82mm mortars. The brigade had 1,058 men.[22] In January 1943 a company with antitank rifles was added to the tank brigade and in March 1943 an antiaircraft machine gun company with nine machine guns substituted for the previous unit.[23] In November 1943 the light tanks were eliminated from the tank brigades, which then had three battalions of T-34s and a motorized battalion armed with machine pistols. The brigade had 1,354 men, sixty-five T-34s, four 45mm antitank guns, six 82mm mortars, nine antiaircraft machine guns, and a company of antitank rifles. That organization remained until the end of the war.[24]

The mechanized corps had been strengthened in early 1943. The corps had three mechanized brigades, a tank brigade (or two tank regiments), an artillery regiment, an antitank regiment, and a Guard mortar battalion. Added in January were a self-propelled artillery regiment (seventeen SU-76s and eight SU-122s), a mortar regiment (thirty-six 120mm mortars), an antiaircraft regiment (sixteen 37mm guns), a tank reserve of forty tanks, and a reserve of 147 tank crewmen and 100 drivers. A towed tank destroyer regiment (twenty 45mm guns) replaced the anti-tank regiment in April and in May the corps received an antiaircraft battalion with 85mm guns. Included in the corps were 16,369 men, 246 tanks and SUs (176 T-34s, 21 T-70s, and 49 SUs), 252 guns and mortars, and 1,800 motor vehicles.[25]

The mechanized brigades in the corps were reinforced in January. The brigade had three motorized rifle battalions, a tank regiment, a mortar battalion, an artillery battalion, and an antiaircraft battalion. The tank regiment received thirty-two T-34s and seven T-70s instead of twenty-three and sixteen. The brigade had 3,491 men, thirty-nine tanks, twenty-four 76mm guns, twelve 37mm antiaircraft guns, thirty 82mm mortars, and four 120mm mortars.[26] More riflemen rode into battle on the tanks. A T-34 carried five men, while a T-70 carried only three. The changes in early 1943 increased the riding capacity from 163 to 181.[27] Despite the intensive level in operations the mechanized rifle units were in good condition. The 3rd Guard Mechanized Brigade in December 1942 had 3,333 men (345 officers, 337 NCOs, and 2,651 privates), 231 trucks, twenty-two T-34s, nine T-70s, four 76mm guns, twelve 45mm guns, six 120mm mortars, and thirty-six 82mm mortars.[28]

In January 1943 the motorized brigade, an element of the tank corps, had three motorized rifle battalions, a company of men with machine pistols, an antitank company (twelve 45mm guns), a mortar battalion (120mm and 82mm mortars), an artillery battalion (twelve 76mm guns), and an antiaircraft battalion. The brigade was authorized at 3,162 men.[29] In February 1943 both the motorized and mechanized brigades received an antiaircraft machine gun company in place of the 37mm gun battalion, and added an engineer mine company.[30] In March 1943, the mechanized brigade with the tank corps (formerly called motorized brigades) had 3,500 men, ten tanks, thirty-three guns, thirty-six mortars, 254 1.5-ton trucks, and 79 2.5-ton trucks.[31] By July 1943, the mechanized brigades with the mechanized corps had forty-one tanks (instead of ten), twelve 76mm guns, twelve 45mm antitank guns, thirty 82mm mortars, six 120mm mortars, 338 trucks, and 3,800 men.[32] The mechanized rifle units were continually reinforced in 1943 to provide the tanks with better support.

The mechanized brigades suffered heavy casualties because of the tactics used. Riding into a heavily defended area on top of a tank was extremely hazardous. When the enemy fired, the riflemen were supposed to jump off and seek cover. However, the Germans often withheld their fire until they could hit many riflemen with the first volley. After refitting in Ordzhonikidze in June 1943, the 58th Mechanized Brigade had a full complement of guns and mortars and 120 men in its rifle companies by July 5. The total brigade had 3,400 men. The offensives that followed the Battle of Kursk quickly wore down the brigade. On August 21, 1943, after less than two months of heavy fighting, there were only 600 men left in the brigade.[33]

The motorized rifle battalion in the tank and mechanized brigades usually consisted of three rifle companies (each with 100 men, two heavy machine guns, four to twelve light machine guns, forty or more machine pistols), a heavy machine gun company (nine to twelve heavy machine guns), a mortar company (six 82mm mortars), an antitank battery (four 45mm antitank guns), an antitank rifle company (sixteen rifles), a truck company with forty trucks, a medical platoon, a supply platoon, and a signal platoon.[34] These battalions were the elite of the infantry, but they took heavy losses in helping the tanks break through the German lines.

The 34th Guard Mechanized Brigade was hit severely at Orel. The brigade had formed in Moscow in July 1942, trained at Smolensk, and entered combat at Veliki Luki. From there it went to Orel and by the end of July after heavy fighting, the brigade had only 150 riflemen, less than two companies. The brigade went to Derjupino for refit. Rifle-company strength increased to 100 men each and the 12th Tank Regiment received thirty-three T-34 tanks plus a company of T-70 light tanks. All weapons were at authorized levels, but trucks were scarce. With only 4 trucks per battalion instead of 40, the troops had to march. Lend-lease was making an impact as the reconnaissance company had eight American scout cars.[35] The 3rd Guard Motorized Brigade, refitted in August 1943, had 3,200 men and 245 trucks, many of them American, enough to allow all the riflemen to ride.[36]

After the Casablanca Conference in January 1943, Hitler had assumed, or may have known positively, that there would be no second front in 1943. The Germans stripped their armies in France to the bone. Hitler had reinforced the 5th Panzer Army in Tunisia in late 1942 to delay the Western power's efforts in the Mediterranean, but in May 1943 he abandoned Sicily, leaving only a few German divisions newly formed from replacement battalions. Italy eventually received training divisions bearing the numbers of divisions that had been destroyed at Stalingrad. France had only occupation divisions armed with captured weapons and little transport and reserve divisions made up of replacement training battalions. Practically all of the German combat-worthy divisions moved to the Eastern Front in early 1943.

The major infusion of divisions from the West had provided Manstein with the resources to halt the Red Army offensive in the spring and retake Kharkov. The Soviet tank forces suffered heavy losses in the reverse. The spring thaw turned the Ukraine into a sea of mud and halted operations. The Russians had lost many tanks—about 1,000 per month—but the factories replaced them quickly. During the lull the Soviets lost fewer than 250 tanks per month from April to June.

Stalin had learned from spies that the Germans would attack at Kursk and began to match the buildup. He was dissuaded from launching a preemptive attack, which had led to disaster in May 1942. Instead the Red Army concentrated on creating a massive defensive system to destroy the German tank forces, holding their tanks in reserve to mount a counteroffensive. The forces that opposed the German Army at Kursk were formidable. The Central. Voronezh, and Steppe fronts had 5,000 tanks in formations plus reserves compared to only 2,700 tanks and assault guns in the attacking German units with no reserves. The Russians had an additional 2,500 tanks in the Bryansk Front, the Western Front, and in reserve. Although a higher percentage of Russian tanks were light (almost one-third of those on the Central and Voronezh fronts), they still had a substantial margin of superiority. A serious weakness was that the tank army headquarters formed since January lacked experience in handling large numbers of tanks. The 4th Tank Army was not even completely organized.[37] The inability to use tanks properly had been a fatal flaw in 1942, but the Soviet leaders learned much since then.

The Russian tank strength was overwhelming on the front in the Kursk area with 3,300 tanks. In the Central Front were the 2nd Tank Army, the 9th and 19th Tank Corps, two tank brigades, fifteen tank regiments, and six SU regiments. The Voronezh Front had the 1st Tank Army, the 2nd Guard and 5th Guard Tank Corps, six tank brigades, eight tank regiments, and three SU regiments. In reserve, the Steppe Front had 1,630 tanks in the 3rd and 4th Tank Armies; the 10th Tank Corps; and the 1st, 2nd, and 3rd Guard Mechanized Corps.[38] The Soviet tanks outnumbered the Germans three-to-one, and the defenses would take a heavy toll of the German tanks before the Russians tanks were deployed.

The Soviet defenses at Kursk had great depth. The first echelon included separate tank brigades, tank regiments, and self-propelled artillery regiments deployed in the army defensive zones for local counterattacks. The armored vehicles formed a major part of the reserves of the armies. Nearly half the tanks on the Central and Voronezh fronts were in the first echelon. The second echelon and the reserves included tank armies and tank corps about thirty to fifty kilometers behind the front.[39]

The Russian defenses stopped the German offensive on the north side of the Kursk bulge, but on the south side the German tanks penetrated the deep antitank defenses. The Germans had penetrated the first echelon of defenses on the first day, but on the second day the Russian tank armies and corps joined in the battle. On July 12 tank units of the Steppe Front moved in to stop the Germans. A battle resulted as two large tank forces met at Prokhorovka with over 1,200 tanks involved. Each side lost about 300 tanks.[40] Failing to penetrate the Soviet defenses, the Germans withdrew.

The Red Army launched counteroffensives at Orel and Belgorod. At Orel three tank armies were unable to break through the defenses and exploit. At Belgorod careful preparation enabled the tank brigades and regiments to help the infantry break through the defenses. The tank armies and tank and mechanized corps then exploited the breach. For the first time in the war the Russian tank forces did not expend their strength in penetrating the defenses and were able to advance rapidly with strong forces after the breakthrough.[41] The Russians advanced quickly against sporadic resistance that gradually wore down the tank units. Extended supply lines delayed the arrival of replacements. On August 25, 1943, the strongest Soviet tank army (the 2nd) had only 265 tanks and self-propelled guns. Two other tanks armies had 162 and 153 tanks and self-propelled guns, respectively.[42] Reduced to less than a corps, the tank armies finally halted.

The Soviets quickly rebuilt their mechanized units when communications were restored. In September 1943 the 15th Mechanized Brigade had 100-man rifle companies. In October the 56th and 26th Mechanized Brigades were at full strength.[43] In December 1943 the 1st Mechanized Brigade had 253 officers (short 46) and 740 NCOs (short 263), but a full complement of 1,925 men. The brigade had 219 trucks (short 43, but an additional 55 trucks were being repaired). The brigade was also short two 76mm guns, two 45mm antitank guns, and eleven 82mm mortars. Supplies were short with only 1.2 units of fire, one-fifth of a fill of fuel, and two days' rations.[44] In January 1944, the 67th Mechanized Brigade was short about sixty artillerymen and fifty-six tank crew members. It was short twelve T-34 tanks and twelve light tanks in its tank regiment and had only 92 trucks instead of 300.[45] On the other hand, the brigade authorized strength had increased to twenty T-34 tanks and thirty-two T-70 light tanks over the 1943 strength of only forty-one tanks.[46]

These examples provided concrete evidence that although the Red Army had suffered serious losses at the Battle of Kursk and in the following offensives, there were good reserves of weapons to replace losses and a functioning replacement system for men. Soviet production was increasing rapidly in the summer of 1943. Not only were the losses at Kursk quickly replaced, but the armored formations became stronger. The German panzer forces never regained the level of July 1943, but Soviet tank production replaced losses and built reserves.

In August 1943 the mechanized corps received more armor with two additional self-propelled artillery regiments, one with SU-76s, the other with SU-85s, giving the corps a total of three regiments with sixty-three SUs.[47] The tank corps in August had one light SU regiment with twenty-one SU-76s and a medium SU regiment with sixteen SU-122s. The 85mm antitank battalion was eliminated, probably because the gun was too clumsy for an antitank gun. Later in the year an SU regiment with twelve SU-152s was added to the tank corps.[48] The strength of each brigade increased to sixty-three tanks in October 1943. The armored-car reconnaissance unit reorganized in November 1943 as a motorcycle battalion with two motorcycle companies, a tank company, a rifle company in armored personnel carriers, and a tank destroyer battery.[49]

In November the tank brigade had three tank battalions each having two companies with a total of sixty-five T-34s or T-34/85s. There were no light tanks in the brigade. The brigade had a motorized battalion with 1,354 men armed with machine pistols, four 45mm guns (or 76mm), six 82mm mortars, four 37mm antiaircraft guns, and nine antiaircraft machine guns.[50] At the end of 1943 engineer tank regiments were formed with twenty-two T-34s and eighteen PT-3 mine-clearing tanks.[51]

The Soviets created ad hoc mechanized units when needed. In December 1943, the 59th Army formed a unit with the 16th Tank Brigade, a self-propelled artillery regiment, a rifle regiment, an artillery battalion, and an engineer company. In the same month, the 2nd Shock Army formed a similar unit based on the 152nd Tank Brigade.[52]

By the end of 1943 there were 5 tank army headquarters, 24 tank corps, 13 mechanized corps, 80 independent tank brigades, 106 independent tank regiments, 43 independent SU regiments, and additional independent tank battalions.[53] In 1944 and 1945 the Russians formed only a few new mechanized units for the strategic reserve. Instead they concentrated on maintaining existing units. Worn units were withdrawn from combat and rebuilt.[54] On January 20, 1944, the Stavka ordered the formation of the 6th Tank Army to consist of the 5th Guard Tank Corps, the 5th Mechanized Corps, the 57th Guard Mortar Regiment, the 181st Engineer Battalion, the 76st Signal Regiment, and the 387th Aviation Regiment.[55] The components were existing units that joined to form an additional tank army.

The tank armies had received additional artillery in 1944, a light self-propelled artillery brigade, and a towed light artillery brigade. The light self-propelled brigades had sixty SU-76s and five T-70s, but some continued to use SU-57s, American T48 half-tracks with 57mm guns. The light artillery brigade combined the existing artillery regiments and added some. The light artillery brigade had two regiments of 76mm guns (each twenty-four guns) and a regiment of twenty of the new 100mm antitank guns. Late in the year, the army received an engineer brigade with two motorized engineer battalions and a pontoon battalion.[56] Tank armies in 1944 had from eight to ten self-propelled artillery regiments.[57] The number of tanks in the tank army decreased in 1944 from 654 to 620, but the number of self-propelled guns increased.[58]

The tank corps also had been reinforced in 1944. At the end of February the three SU regiments were increased to twenty-one SUs each (SU-76s, SU-122s, and SU-152s), giving the corps sixty-three instead of forty-nine. In May the medical units combined to form a battalion. At the end of August the corps received a light artillery regiment with 24 76mm guns, and in November more tank and automotive repair units. In addition the tank corps had a motorized rifle battalion, an antiaircraft regiment, a mortar regiment, a Guard mortar battalion, a tank destroyer battalion, a reconnaissance battalion, and a motorcycle battalion. The corps had 198 tanks, 63 SUs, 20 armored cars, 42 120mm mortars, 48 82mm mortars, 16 37mm antiaircraft guns, 44 76mm guns, 24 45mm antitank guns, and about 900 trucks. By the end of 1944 tank strength had increased to 207, all T-34s, simplifying maintenance. Previously the corps had T-34s, T-60s, T-70s, and foreign tanks. In April 1944 the T-34/85 with an 85mm gun replaced the T-34 in the tank corps.[59]

The independent tank units received better tanks as they became available. In February 1944 the breakthrough tank regiments were redesignated Guard heavy tank regiments and equipped with twenty-one JS-2 tanks.[60] In December 1944 the heavy Guard tank brigade had three heavy tank regiments each with twenty-one JS-2 tanks. The brigade had 1,666 men, sixty-five JS-2 tanks, three armored cars, nineteen armored personnel carriers, and three SU-76s.[61] The independent tank brigades were still using light tanks and imported tanks. In July 1944 the 29th Tank Brigade had one battalion of T-34s (twenty tanks) and two battalions of T-70s (each twenty tanks). In addition a regiment of JSU-152s (fifteen vehicles) was attached to the brigade.[62]

The mechanized corps had received additional weapons in 1944. The 5th Mechanized Corps in April 1944 had 200 tanks and SUs, 74 guns, 39 armored cars, and 8,000 men.[63] The mechanized brigades had a good supply of weapons but were short of men. In February 1944 the new organization for the tank regiment called for thirty-five T-34s, replacing all of the light tanks.[64] In August 1944 the 20th Guard Mechanized Brigade had three motorized battalions with only 400 men each, a tank regiment with 30 T-34s, and an artillery battalion with 10 76mm guns, and a truck company with 120 trucks, sufficient to move the entire brigade. The brigade including an engineer company, a reconnaissance company, and a signal platoon had from 1,500 to 1,700 men compared to an authorized strength of over 3,000.[65]

By January 1945 two additional mechanized corps had been formed, eleven more tank brigades, and fifty-two more tank regiments, many with heavier tanks. Light tanks were phased out except for special purposes. Sherman tanks with 77mm guns were arriving to supplement Soviet production.[66] Tank units received more tanks in their table of organization and were maintained closer to full table-of-organization strength with an efficient replacement system. A common practice was for a tank unit to give to a nearby tank unit all remaining tanks and crews as needed. The remaining headquarters and troops went to a tank park located near a tank factory and obtained a new stock of tanks and fresh crews from the tank schools.

At the end of the war a tank army had 50,000 men, 850 to 920 tanks and SUs, 800 guns and mortars, and 5,000 trucks.[67] The army included two tank corps, a mechanized corps, a motorcycle regiment, a light artillery brigade (with two regiments of 76mm guns and one regiment of 100mm guns), two mortar regiments, two antiaircraft regiments, a light self-propelled artillery brigade, a Guards mortar regiment, an engineer brigade, a signal regiment, an aviation communications regiment, a truck regiment, and two repair battalions.[68]

The 3rd Guard Tank Army on January 1, 1945, was very close to authorized strength. The army had 701 tanks, 60 SU-57s, 63 SU-76s, 63 SU-85s, 63 SU-122s, 220 76mm guns, 20 100mm guns, 222 82mm mortars, 138 120mm mortars, 48 M13 rocket launchers, 98 57mm guns, and 80 37mm antiaircraft guns.[69]

The 1945 tank corps had three tank brigades, a motorized rifle brigade, two SU regiments, a mortar regiment, an antiaircraft regiment, a light artillery regiment, a heavy tank regiment, a Guards mortar battalion, a motorcycle battalion, and a truck company. The corps had 212 T-34s, 25 armored cars, 8 M13 rocket launchers, 21 SU-76s, 16 SU-85s, 12 SU-152s, 12 122mm guns, 12 76mm guns, 12 45mm guns, 16 37mm antiaircraft guns, 42 120mm mortars, and 52 82mm mortars.[70]

The 5th Guard Mechanized Corps in April 1945 had 12,135 men, 64 T-34 tanks, 51 armored personnel carriers, 35 armored cars, 22 SU122s, 30 SU76s, 32 76mm guns, 27 57mm guns, 51 120mm mortars, and 69 82mm mortars. The corps included the 24th Guard Tank Brigade; the 10th, 11th, and 12th Guard Mechanized Brigades; the 379th Heavy SU Regiment; the 1447th Medium SU Regiment; the 104th Guard Light SU Regiment; the 285th Mortar Regiment; the 763rd Antiaircraft Regiment; the 11th Guards Mortar Battalion; the 2nd Guard Motorcycle Battalion; the 68th Guard Engineer Battalion; and the 388th Reconnaissance Battalion[71] Even after the strenuous fighting of the final weeks of the war, the Russians maintained the strength of the corps. The weapons total equaled and sometimes exceeded the authorized numbers.[72]

In the final months of the war, the tank armies had more infantry to cope with the stiff German defenses. The support would often take the form of a rifle corps or several rifle divisions attached for a specific operation. In the Korsun operation the 47th Rifle Corps supported the 6th Guard Tank Army. At Debrecen the 33rd Rifle Corps reinforced the same army. In Berlin the 61st Guard Rifle Division, the 48th Guard Rifle Division, and the 20th Rifle Division supported the 3rd Guard Tank Army.[73] The added riflemen eliminated pockets of resistance bypassed by the tanks before the Germans had the time to reform a defensive line.

In 1945 there were six tank armies, fourteen independent tank corps, seven independent mechanized corps, twenty-seven independent tank brigades, seven self-propelled artillery brigades, and many tank and self-propelled artillery regiments. There were 12,900 tanks and SUs in units at the front.[74] The self-propelled artillery brigades were of three types. The light brigades now had SU-76s, the medium brigades SU-100s (replacing the SU-85), and the heavy brigade had JSU-152s and JSU-122s.[75]

By the end of 1943 the tank force of the Red Army had refined its organizational structure that would remain until the end of the war. More units would be formed in the following years, but the essential force was in being by early 1943. With the six tank armies and additional tank and mechanized corps, the Red Army had a powerful offensive capability that the Germans could not stop after the spring of 1943. The major task in the final years of the war was replacing losses and maintaining the existing units at strength. The tank armies and tank and mechanized corps were competently led and superbly equipped. There were enough replacements to maintain the rifle companies at 100 and to provide tank crews for new tanks. The tank armies could break through the German defenses at will.

CHAPTER 10

Tank and Crew Replacements and Training

The Red Army lost over 96,500 tanks and SUs with crews during World War II. All of these men and machines had to be replaced and additional men trained to form new units in the expanding armored force. The annual rate of Soviet tank losses was nearly equal to the total number assigned to combat units, and during active operations was nearly twice the average number. The life expectancy of a tank and crew in combat was about six months.

In the early years of the war the Russians had lost more tanks than the Germans, a testimonial to the effectiveness of German antitank defenses and the need for more Soviet antitank weapons to destroy German tanks. After losing over 10,000 tanks in the first month of the war, the Soviets were reduced to about 1,500 tanks in combat units in the fall of 1941. The number in units had increased to 6,900 by November 1942 and there were 20,000 on hand by January 1943. The Russians had built about 28,000 tanks in 1942 and lost 15,000. The Germans estimated Russian losses for nine months in 1942 at 12,660, an average of 1,330 per month. Many tanks were in depots and in training units. With losses at about 1,250 per month and production at 2,300 per month, the number of tanks on hand and the number of tank units increased by from 7,700 in January to 20,000 by the end of 1942.[1]

The heavy Russian losses in 1942 resulted from the overwhelming defeat of the Red Army tank forces at Izyum and in the Don Basin battles. The heavy Soviet losses included not only tanks destroyed by German fire but also tanks that had run out of fuel. The Germans lost fewer tanks in the same period because the Germans retained control of the battlefields. The Russians lost tanks that were immobilized by light damage or lack of fuel while the Germans were able to recover and repair even heavily damaged tanks. The Germans began with 4,362 in January 1942, produced 6,189 during the year, and ended the year with 3,383 with an apparent loss of 7,446, although the published figure was 7,168.[2] The average number of German losses was about 600 per month. According to one report, in the months March through October 1942 the Germans lost only 1,693 tanks to enemy action.[3] During this period the Germans controlled the battlefields and lost about 200 tanks per month. In early months of the year and in the final months, the Russians controlled the battlefields after the actions. The Germans losses were much greater and they apparently lost over 1,400 tanks per month.

The greatest tragedy in the loss of a tank was that 75 percent of the crew were killed or so seriously injured that they never returned to duty.[4] Therefore, replacement tanks had to arrive with crews. To provide crews for the new tanks, the Red Army developed an enormous training program. The magnitude of the program can be gauged when one considers that about 24,000 tanks and SUs were produced annually and each needed a crew of four or five men. Allowing for some survivors of lost tanks, the training program had to produce roughly 100,000 tank crew members per year. The actual number of tank specialists trained exceeded 400,000 providing some indication of the extent of the losses among tank crews as follows:[5]

	1941	1942	1943	1944	1945	Total
Tank Crews	5,152	34,664	28,618	21,795	16,920	107,149
SU Crews			4,355	13,032	10,115	27,502
Repair Crews		6,529	5,431	9,991	2,992	24,943
TOTAL CREWS	5,152	41,193	38,404	44,818	30,027	159,594
TOTAL MEN	15,749	83,205	96,877	126,004	81,437	403,272

The appalling significance of the table was that few men survived the destruction or even damage to a tank. The Soviets trained almost as many tank crews as the combined number of new tanks and imported tanks. The war began with 22,000 prewar tanks supplemented by wartime production of 109,000 tanks and SUs and imports of 14,000 for a total of 145,000. The total crews were 22,000 prewar plus 134,600 trained during the war for a total of 156,600. More than 35,000 tanks were on hand at the end of the war. The Red Army mechanized force lost over 310,000 men killed, captured, or wounded seriously enough to prevent their return to duty.[6]

Comparing the training totals to the number of tanks produced, the Russians trained fewer crews in 1941 than tanks produced (5,152 crews trained, 6,300 tanks produced). There were enough survivors from the prewar tank crews to man the extra tanks and also staff the growing training establishment. In 1942 more crews were trained than tanks produced and imported (34,664 vs. 29,190). The Soviet training program probably built up a reserve of about 5,000 crews in 1942 and maintained that number until 1944. In 1943 about equal numbers were trained and tanks produced (28,618 vs. 27,656). In 1944 fewer crews were trained than tanks produced and imported (21,795 vs. 34,000) and in 1945 the number of crews trained was far less than new tanks (16,920 vs. 28,000). In 1944 and 1945 very few crews were captured and the practical elimination of light tanks from the combat forces would have resulted in more survivors of destroyed or damaged tanks. The far higher proportion of two-man crews trained in 1942 and 1943 than in 1944 and 1945 supports that theory.

Despite the disparity of losses in 1942 between the Germans and Russians, the Soviet Union was winning the production race and had 8,500 tanks at the front in January 1943 compared to a total of 6,643 Germans tanks.[7] Despite the possession of the productive capacity of all of Western Europe, the Germans were unable to match the production of Soviet tank factories. The Russians continued to lose heavily in the winter of 1942–43. The Russian offensives from November 1942 to March 1943 were very costly. The Popov Tank Group that broke through German lines was reduced to a skeleton by February 1943 with only 137 tanks remaining. The supply, replacement, and maintenance systems had not functioned adequately.[8] However, rapidly expanding production quickly replaced the losses in the following months. The Soviet tank force was in excellent condition in June 1943.

In September 1943 the Fremde Heer Ost received claims of 20,434 Russian tanks destroyed from July 5, 1943, to September 30, 1943, the period covering the Battle of Kursk and the Soviet counteroffensive that followed. The FHO reduced this figure by 50 percent to 10,217. The Soviets lost 11,703 tanks in eight operations during that period.[9] Despite the heavy losses at Kursk in July 1943 and in the offensive that followed in August 1943, Soviet tank strength continued to grow. Production and lend-lease imports more than replaced the losses. German tank strength did not increase correspondingly. Although the German tank and assault guns production increased, the total on hand increased only from 6,643 in January 1943 to 7,233 in January 1944 and not all were on the Eastern Front. After Kursk the Germans were never able to recapture the initiative.[10]

In January 1944 German intelligence reached the conclusion that despite heavy losses, the Russian tank strength was growing. Analyzing the available data on the tanks facing Army Group South from July 1, 1943, to December 31, 1943, the Germans estimated that the Russians had 7,180 tanks on July 1 and 9,320 on December 31, an increase of 2,140. Reducing the claims of tanks destroyed by the army and air force by 50 percent (to eliminate duplicate claims), the German intelligence officers estimated that Army Group South had destroyed 9,000 Russian tanks in the six months. Therefore, the Germans believed that the Russians must have added 11,140 tanks to the fronts in the south. The Germans divided the total into 2,200 tanks added as new units, 640 in units transferred from other fronts, and 8,300 from replacement centers, presumably new and repaired tanks. An average of 1,380 new and repaired tanks went forward as replacements each month. The Red Army actually had a total of 21,100 tanks and 3,300 SUs in January 1944.[11]

The Germans studied the serial numbers of destroyed Russian tanks to learn the date and place of manufacture. Destroyed tanks usually had been manufactured less than six months before their loss.[12] The length of time between production of a tank and entry into combat was very short. Sixty T-34/85s produced at Omsk and Nishnij-Tagil in early January 1945 were damaged and captured by the Germans by January 25, 1945.[13] Heavy JS-122s produced in August and September 1944 at Chelyabinsk were at the front in the 78th Guard Breakthrough Tank Battalion in October and destroyed by the Germans in January 1945.[14] Sixty T-34/85s made at Gorki and Nishnij-Tagil and sent to the 135th Tank Brigade of the 23rd Tank Corps in December 1944 were destroyed by the Germans in January 1945.[15] The average life of a tank sent into combat was probably less than six months.

Although Soviet production of tanks was sufficient to replace losses, the production of SUs exceeded losses and made possible the rapid expansion of the number of mechanized or self-propelled artillery units.[16] A German study in July 1944 revealed that of 360 tanks and SUs destroyed in that month, 73 percent were T-34s and KV-1s, and only 6 percent were SUs. Of the remaining, 15 percent were obsolete tanks and 6 percent were miscellaneous types. The destruction ratio was at least twelve tanks to one SU, whereas production in 1944 was only four tanks to three SUs.[17]

Of the tanks damaged by enemy action, the Russians sent 10 percent to army or front workshops for repair and 15 percent to the rear for rebuilding in factories.[18] Losses could come at an alarming rate to individual units. The 23rd Tank Corps began an attack on January 27, 1945, with 270 tanks. By February 8, 1945, German ground fire and air attack had destroyed or damaged 266 tanks.[19] Another tank brigade with sixty-three tanks lost thirty to German fire and fifteen from mechanical breakdown in six weeks[20] Despite the severity of the losses, the tanks were replaced with new or repaired ones complete with crews and stocked with shells.

About two-thirds of Soviet tank losses came from German fire, but the other 25 to 30 percent of losses came from mechanical problems.

Long-distance movement of a tank under its own power was very wearing on its tracks and engine. One tank regiment claimed that it had made a 300-kilometer road march under its own power from Tarnopol to Saratov without losing a single tank, although 10 percent of the tanks had over 200 hours of running time. This was an exceptionally good performance but wasteful.[21] The road life of a Soviet tank varied from 1,000 to 1,500 kilometeres.[22] Using one-fourth of the track life of a tank regiment on a road movement to a rear area instead of waiting for rail transportation was incredible.

The method of replacing tanks and crews was as complex as that of replacing riflemen. The choice was between sending replacements to units at the front or withdrawing units from the front and rebuilding them in the rear. To rotate tank units away from the front required extra tank brigades and later tank corps. Beginning in late 1941 over a hundred new brigades were created. Trained cadres for the formation of the tank brigades and for the tank corps in 1942 came from the survivors of the 1941 mechanized corps. With the availability of the new brigades, the Russians could withdraw a reduced unit and replace it with a new unit.

An example of how the rotation and replacement program made possible keeping a tank corps in action despite punishing losses was the experience of the 13th Tank Corps in the summer of 1942. In June and July 1942 the 13th Tank Corps was heavily engaged in the battles in the south. Beginning the battles with the 65th, 85th, and 88th Tank Brigades, the corps took heavy losses. The 65th Brigade was relieved by June 6 and the 88th Brigade by June 16 after suffering heavy losses. The 158th and 167th Tank Brigades replaced the two brigades. On June 20 the corps had 180 T-34s and T-60s, near authorized strength.[23] By July 19, 1942, after more heavy combat, the remnants of the 85th and 167th Tank Brigades went to Saratov for new tanks and crews. The 158th Tank Brigade went to the 23rd Tank Corps. On July 21 the 13th Tank Corps received three new tank brigades—the 163rd, the 166th, and the 169th. The corps was close to full strength with 123 tanks: 74 T-34s and 49 light tanks.[24]

The new independent tank brigades and regiments organized near the tank factories. The 237th Tank Brigade was formed at the Kaganovitsch factory in Nishnij-Tagil in November 1943, receiving 40 T-34s directly from the factory.[25] The 27th Tank Regiment formed in November and December 1943 in Naro Fominsk near Moscow. The cadre came from tank units worn down in combat. The tank crews were twenty- and twenty-one-year-olds direct from the tank schools[26]

The 230th Tank Regiment was formed in February 1944 at Tschuguyev with men from the 27th and 28th Training Regiments in

Baku and the tank school in Kazan. The crews had trained from four to nine months with British tanks. The regiment received lend-lease tanks at Baku—ten M4A2 Shermans and ten Valentines, along with three armored cars and ten trucks. The regiment entered combat in March 1944.[27] The 223rd Tank Regiment formed in Gorki in December 1943. The crews came from the tank school in Kazan. The regiment also received lend-lease tanks, eleven M4A2 Shermans and nine Valentines, an armored car, and thirty trucks.[28]

The cadres for the new units had come from recovering wounded and others with combat experience. Before the war, the Russians had a large tank training program. Tank officers trained at schools in Orel, Kharkov, Saratov, Kiev, Pushkin, Gorki, Poltava, and in the Urals. New schools opened in the east between February and April 1941 as the Soviet tank force expanded. On August 12, 1941, three large tank schools opened at Chelyabinsk, Stalingrad, and Kharkov. In 1942 the school curriculum was revised with a more practical course.[29] By 1943 the tank training schools were in full operation supplying crews for the new and repaired tanks. In 1944 three Guard tank schools were opened, presumably to train crews for heavy tanks.[30]

In 1942 tank crew training was not satisfactory. Training as many as 34,000 crews in a new program was certain to produce faults. Mellenthin, a German panzer commander, had commented that in 1942, tank crews especially in the mechanized corps had hardly any training.[31] The tank corps sent into battle in 1942 had insufficient time to complete their organization and unit training. The Russians had curtailed individual training with the expectation that the individuals would gain experience as the new units trained in the rear. That scenario did not develop as the Germans drove through the Don Basin in late 1942, forcing the Russians to use all available units in the attempt to halt the offensive.

The basic training of tank crewmen took place in schools. There were fifty or more such schools in 1943.[32] The crews trained in twelve tank school regiments plus a school for self-propelled artillery. Each regiment had about 2,000 men. Some regiments were located near tank factories at Sverdlovsk (12th regiment), Nishnij-Tagil (2nd and 19th Regiments), Bogorodsk (near Moscow), Chelyabinsk (7th Regiment), and Stalinogorsk (near Moscow, the 6th Regiment).[33] There was a school brigade at Baku to train crews for Shermans and Valentines imported by way of the Persian Gulf.[34] The 231st Tank Replacement Regiment at Kurgan had 4,000 men in the school regiment.[35]

The length of training varied. In early 1943, the 6th Tank School Regiment at Stalinogorsk had four battalions. The first battalion trained crews to operate KVs; the second battalion trained T-34 crews; and the third battalion trained crews for the T-60, the T-70, the Valentine, and the Matilda. The cadre formed the fourth battalion. The student battalions had six companies with sixty to seventy men. Two companies trained driver-mechanics; two companies trained turret gunners; one company trained radio operators; and one company provided a two- or three-month short course for men going to new units where they would complete their training[36] The length of training depended on the specialty. A gunner trained for four months, loaders for only two months, and driver-mechanics for nine months.[37]

Some training regiments were larger than the 6th. The 12th Tank School Regiment at Sverdlovsk trained men exclusively on T-34s. The regiment had four battalions with four companies in each battalion. The companies had 160 to 200 men.[38] The 29th Tank School Regiment at Chelyabinsk had only nine companies, but had 3,000 men training as gunner-tank commander, loader-mechanic-assistant driver, and radio operator.[39]

The 333rd Tank Replacement Regiment at Savitaia (100 kilometers south of Chaborovsk) had four companies, each with 150 men. The first company trained tank commanders who also served as gunners. The second company trained loaders; the third, drivers; and the fourth, radio operators. Training normally lasted eight months. The regiment had seventy BT-5s and T-26s for training. From Savitaia, radio operators went to the 7th Tank Replacement Regiment at Chelyabinsk for five additional months of training. At Chelyabinsk crews assembled, worked up new T-34s from the factory, and went to the front.[40]

The 25th Tank School Regiment at Kurgan in the Urals gave three months' training to tank gun loaders. Training for the tank commanders, drivers, and radio operators lasted from three to four months. The school regiment had about 4,000 men and sent some of them directly to the front without tanks. Others went to the 2nd Tank Replacement Regiment at Nishnij-Tagil. There in one week they formed into crews, received new tanks from the factory, became familiar with the tank, prepared it for combat, and loaded on trains for the front.[41]

Special schools trained tank officers and sergeants. The Kamyshin Tank Officer Training School at Omsk had 1,600 men in four battalions each with four companies. The students came from tank units. Training concentrated on the T-34 and lasted twelve months. In the T-34, the tank commander was also the loader, so the course included gunnery training, radio operation, map reading, gas defense, and tank tactics. The instructors had combat experience and 60 to 70 percent were either old or seriously wounded, some having lost an arm or an eye, for example.[42] An officer from the training school at Kamyshin described his experience in the tank force in detail. Born in 1922, he had been a tractor driver in civilian life. Drafted in August 1942 at the age of twenty, he had trained for two months as a rifleman before assignment to the motorized rifle battalion of the 90th Tank Brigade refitting at Saratov. In November 1942 the brigade went into combat south of Stalingrad. Shortly after, the prisoner went to the tank officer training school. Although training usually took twelve months, this officer had become ill and did not complete his training until February 1944.[43]

The students were of high quality. At Stalinogorsk no new draftees were in the school. Many were recovered wounded men and all had experience at the front, mostly as truck drivers or riflemen. They were twenty to twenty-five years old, although a few were older. Most of the men were Russians.[44] The school at Baku had returning wounded plus some new recruits and men previously considered unfit for military service. Many were Ukrainians and Volga Tartars.[45] The men in the 29th Tank Replacement Regiment at Chelyabinsk were mostly from Siberia and Kazakhstan.[46] The 12th School Regiment at Sverdlovsk had men from tank units that had suffered heavy losses, probably survivors of crews of destroyed tanks and recruits from Central Asia.[47]

When the tank crew men had completed their individual training, they went to a tank replacement regiment at a tank factory. The officer described above was sent to the 2nd Replacement Regiment at Nishnij-Tagil in March 1944 and was assigned a tank and crew. The tanks were newly completed from the factory and the crews were from training schools. In five to ten days the new crews installed radios and machine guns, loaded ammunition, and prepared the tank for combat. On April 5, 1944, forty new T-34s with 40 officers and 120 men boarded trains and traveled to Dubossary, arriving on April 25, 1944. Twenty of the tanks went to the 41st Tank Brigade.[48] The officer was captured within a few days.

The state of training of Soviet tank units in 1942 can be seen by examining a study of the 51st Mechanized Brigade in November 1942. The document had been captured by the Germans and translated. The brigade had 358 officers and warrant officers, 841 NCOs (compared to the authorized 1,159), and 2,016 men (authorized 1,840). The were 3,215 officers and men, short 124 of the authorized strength of 3,369. The shortage was in NCOs as could be expected in a newly formed unit.

Of the 358 officers, 136 had combat experience against the German Army and 12 against other forces. Only one officer had advanced military schooling, 257 had military school training, 80 had only short-course training, and 20 had no officer school training. The officers were quite young: only 60 were over the age of thirty-five and most were under thirty. The NCOs were also young: 495 were twenty-five or under, 307 from twenty-six to thirty-five, and only 40 over thirty-five. Most had specialized training (646) and 164 had combat experience. The men were also young—only 276 between the age of thirty-one and thirty-five and 113 over thirty-five. Practically all were well trained, 1,339 had a full training course, 290 had three months' training, and 387 had six months' training. Many were Communist Party members as might have been expected. Nearly half the officers (156 of 358) were Party affiliated, nearly a third of the NCOs (275 of 841); and 296 of the men had Party affiliation, mostly Komsomols (267).[49]

The equipment of the brigade was very near authorized levels except in the number of trucks. The brigade had an authorized strength of 308 1.5-ton and 2.5-ton trucks but had only 125. That shortage was serious as capacity to carry the men and equipment was too limited. Without trucks the men had to walk.[50] Shortage of equipment was a universal problem in training units in most armies. Troops in combat received the best equipment; those in training received what remained. Units often picked up needed equipment on the way to the front.

As the war progressed training improved and the supply of replacement crews exceeded the demand. A substantial reserve of possibly 5,000 crews was built up in 1943 ready to take over tanks as they were produced. Tank losses had to be replaced as well as men. Imported tanks were especially significant in the early years of the war. Tanks provided by Great Britain and the United States were used in the training program after Soviet production reached a level to supply the combat needs. The British and Americans sent 14,430 tanks to the Soviet Union, making up a considerable portion of Soviet tank strength, about 14 percent.[51] The Americans sent 1,676 light tanks, 1,386 Grants, 2,007 Shermans with the 75mm gun, and 2,095 with the 76mm gun to the Russians. The British sent 3,782 Valentines and 1,084 Matildas. The Canadians also sent 1,400 Valentines.[52] The rate of delivery varied. In 1942 4,500 tanks were delivered—2,000 U.S. and 2,500 British. In 1943 the total dropped to 3,650.[53] The remaining 6,000 were delivered in 1944 and 1945.

The British Mk II Matilda was a slow, heavily armored infantry tank with a two-pounder gun. The two-pounder could not fire an effective high-explosive round essential for a good infantry support tank so the Soviets rearmed some Matildas with 76mm guns. Although the tank engine was highly regarded, the narrow tracks did not work well in snow or mud.[54] The Valentine, from Britain and Canada, came in three models:

the Mk III with a two-pounder, and Mk IX and X with a 75mm gun. The Russians replaced the two-pounder on some Mark III Valentines with a 76mm gun, making them more suitable for the infantry support role. The later models of the Valentine worked well in infantry support, but its tracks were too narrow to work well in mud or snow.[55] The Russians referred to the Matilda as the "Mk II" and the Valentine as the "Mk III." The British tanks were mixed with Russian tanks in units to surmount the shortcomings. In February 1942 the 4th Shock Army had the 141st Tank Battalion with four KVs, seven T-34s, and twenty T-60s; and the 171st Tank Battalion with twelve Matildas, nine Valentines, and ten T-60s.[56]

The Russians preferred the Valentine to other British models. Instead of complicating their inventory with a variety of types, the Russians in 1942 requested that the British send only Valentines.[57] In response to the Soviet demands, the British continued to produce the Valentine. In a twelve-month period, 1,000 Valentines were manufactured and all went to the Soviet Union.[58] Practically the entire Canadian output of Valentines went to the Soviet Union. Late in the war a few Churchill Mk IVs were sent and used by heavy tank regiments for infantry support, but they were not comparable to Soviet tanks in bad weather.[59] Some Churchills were shipped in parts and assembled at Gorki.

Russian tank crews disliked the American light tank, the Stuart, "M3L" and the medium Grant, "M3S" because they used gasoline (instead of diesel fuel) and caught fire easily. One Russian said that sitting in a Stuart or a Grant was like being in a coffin. The Grant with its crew of seven was known as "a coffin for seven comrades."[60] The Sherman was first shipped to the Soviet Union in June 1943. The Sherman had an improved 75mm gun mounted in the turret rather than on the hull, as on the Grant. The Russians were given the version of the Sherman with a diesel engine that reduced the fire hazard. The 75mm gun on the 1943 Sherman was inferior to the 76mm on the T-34. The comparative muzzle velocities were 662 meters per second for the T-34 versus 385 meters per second for the Sherman.[61] A good antitank gun usually had a muzzle velocity of about 700 meters per second. Therefore, the early Shermans were used primarily as infantry support tanks with the gun firing high explosive.

Later Shermans, M4A4s, mounted the British 17-pounder gun (76mm) equal to the German Panther tank gun. The performance of the 76mm gun on the M4A4 Sherman was substantially better than the 85mm gun on the T-34/85. The 76mm penetrated up to 212mm of armor at 500 meters, compared to 138mm by the Russian 85mm. At 1,000 meters the comparison was 179mm versus 100mm. Another advantage was that the Sherman carried seventy-one 76mm rounds, while the T-34/85 carried only fifty-six.[62] In December 1943, 85 percent of the U.S. tanks sent to Russia were Shermans.[63]

In 1941 and early 1942, lend-lease tanks came via Murmansk, the most dangerous route, threatened by Nazi sea and air attack. The Germans cut the Murmansk route in the summer of 1942 and only a few convoys arrived during winter months until late 1944. In March 1944 six U.S. ships were unloaded at Archangel. Included in the cargo were 100 medium tanks.[64] Most deliveries came by way of Iran in 1943 and 1944 and many tanks may have come from stocks in North Africa. Delivery by way of the Persian Gulf was slow at first because of poor port management and inefficient operation of the railroad lines to Russia. However, once the Americans had brought in service troops to improve and manage the facilities, deliveries increased sharply. In January 1944 there were 475 British and American tanks in Tbilisi in the Caucasus and an additional 260 had been unloaded in Iran, including Valentines, Churchills, Lees, and Shermans.[65] Delivery via Vladivostok was limited to nonmilitary supplies and required a long rail journey over the Trans-Siberian Railway.

As early as January 1942, the Russians were using British tanks in combat units. The 117th Tank Battalion had twelve Matildas and nine Valentines, plus ten Russian T-60s.[66] In November 1942, fifty-three tank brigades were equipped entirely or partially with lend-lease tanks.[67] By March 1943 of 108 tank brigades whose armament was known to the Germans, 13 were equipped entirely with British and U.S. tanks and 21 were partially equipped.[68] By June 1943, of the 256 Soviet tank brigades, 61 were either entirely or partially equipped with lend-lease tanks.[69] By the end of the year, 1,250 lend-lease tanks were included in twenty-six brigades and nineteen regiments.[70] As more Russian tanks became available, the need for lend-lease tanks decreased, but significant numbers continued to arrive. By October 1944, nineteen brigades and nineteen regiments were using British and U.S. tanks.[71]

Foreign tanks were used in many types of units. Despite their poor quality, the tanks delivered in 1942 went to combat units because of the shortage of Soviet tanks. In 1943 more Russian tanks were available and the foreign tanks began to be phased out of elite combat units and used for infantry support and training although in August 1943 the 5th Mechanized Corps was using British tanks.[72] The better quality tanks delivered in late 1943 and 1944 (the Sherman M4A4 and the Churchill) were assigned to combat units. In December 1943 a tank breakthrough regiment in the Ukraine had 21 Churchill tanks.[73] In March 1944 the 223rd Tank Regiment had eleven M4A2 Shermans and seven Valentines. In

February 1944 the 212th Tank Regiment used British Centaurs and the 35th Tank Regiment used Valentine Mk IXs. Both regiments were elements of the 4th Guards Mechanized Corps.[74]

In March 1944 newly formed tank regiments were receiving ten Shermans and ten Valentines recently delivered via the Persian Gulf.[75] From the details concerning the formation of these regiments, the quantity of foreign tanks probably exceeded need, as the plentiful supply of Russian tanks was sufficient to maintain the tank corps and brigades. Therefore, the lend-lease tanks were given to newly trained tank crews and formed into small regiments for infantry support. The availability of the new crews is positive evidence that the tank crew replacement system was functioning well. The large number of imported tanks in the depot at Tula indicated a plentiful supply.

By July 1944, after heavy fighting during the summer, the supply of Russian tanks was less plentiful. The 260th Heavy Tank Regiment was using five Churchills and only five additional Soviet tanks.[76] Also in July, the 2nd Guard Motorized Brigade of the 3rd Guard Tank Corps had thirty Valentines in its tank regiment.[77] The British tanks, then mounting 75mm guns, were used in the infantry support role. The heavy tank regiments were normally equipped with either KVs or later with the JS. Production of Soviet light tanks had ceased in favor of the SU-76, so the Valentine was being used as a substitute light tank when stocks of the T-70 were not available. During the summer the ground was firm and the narrow tracks on the British tanks would not have been the drawback as during the spring or winter.

By January 1945 the M4A4 Shermans with the powerful 76mm guns were arriving in great numbers. In view of the high quality of the tank and the heavy losses in Soviet tanks, even the best units received Shermans. In January 1945 the 35th Guard Tank brigade had sixty-five Shermans.[78] Also in January, the 1st Guard Mechanized Corps gave all its remaining T-34/85s to the 7th Mechanized Corps and was equipped with Shermans.[79]

An additional source of tanks was the repair of captured German tanks. In 1943, 1,200 captured T-38s, Mk IIIs, and Assault Guns based on the two types of chassis were rebuilt into fully armored SU-76is at Zavod #38 at Gorki. The assault guns served in tank regiments and SU regiments.[80] In April 1944 the 28th Guard Tank Brigade was using two captured Tigers along with thirteen Valentines and thirty-two T-34s.[81]

The allocation of tanks within the Red Army was complicated by changing requirements, varying quality, and the multiplicity of types. Training units used obsolete tanks. A total of 70 BTs and T-26s were still being used in 1943 at the training school near Chelyabinsk.[82] British tanks were widely used for training because their engines were superior to Soviet engines and could endure the long running hours. Some modern Soviet tanks were necessary in the school regiments because of the short time a crew had to acquaint themselves after receiving new tanks from the factories before going to the front. In July 1943 the 2nd Tank Replacement Regiment sent 30 crews to Nishnij-Tagil where they had only a week to work up their new tanks before being sent to the front.[83]

Units either went to the factories for tanks or the tanks were sent to the unit behind the front. The usual method of replacing tank losses was to transfer all tanks with crews from a worn unit to a neighboring unit and withdraw the worn unit to the rear for refit. In January 1945 the 1st Guard Mechanized Corps gave all its T-34/85s to the 7th Mechanized Corps and the former corps went to Stuhlweisenburg, where it received M4A2 Shermans. The cast-off T-34/85s brought the 7th Mechanized up to full strength.[84] Some tanks with or without crews went from the factory to depots instead of being sent directly to units. A tank replacement battalion with 20 KVs formed in Chelyabinsk in 1944 and went to Tula, where it later reinforced the 107th Tank Brigade.[85]

Large tank depots were located at Gorki and Tula. In August 1944 the Tula depot had 400 SU-76s, 40 M4A2 Shermans, 40 Churchills, 60 JSs, and 140 T-34s (a total of 680 tanks) plus many trucks and motorcycles. Tanks came from all the tank factories and from abroad. The depot, located eight kilometers north of Tula in an area twenty-five by twenty-five kilometers, included a firing range where each tank gun was fired six times to ensure its serviceability. The Tula depot also repaired tanks. New units were formed at the depot, although most replacement tanks were sent with crews directly to units at the front.[86]

At Gorki, the 16th Tank Replacement Regiment received foreign tanks, supplied crews, formed the tanks into companies of ten, and sent them to units as needed. No training took place at Gorki. A reserve of five or six companies was usually available ready to be shipped. In November and December 1944 fifteen companies with 150 M4A2 Shermans were sent to the front.[87] The Gorki depot also processed Soviet tanks. The 54th Guard Tank Brigade received twenty new T-34/85s from Gorki in September 1944.[88] The two huge depots held a reserve of more than 1,000 tanks in 1944 ready to be shipped to the front complete with crews, a luxury that the Germans never enjoyed. The reserve made it possible to maintain Soviet tank units near their authorized strength despite heavy losses.

A significant source of replacements was repaired or rebuilt tanks. Before the war the maintenance and repair of tanks was a major problem.

Contributing to the poor state of readiness was the age of the tanks, poor maintenance facilities, lack of spare parts, and multiplicity of types. Of the 22,000 tanks in the Red Army in 1941, 44 percent required rebuilding and 29 percent required replacement of a major component such as an engine or a transmission. The latter was a problem in most armies as designers consistently provided tanks with engines too small and transmissions too weak to absorb the stress of rough handling on broken ground. Spare parts for many types of light tanks were not available because production had ceased. The only source of parts was other disabled tanks.[89]

In June 1941, 50 percent of the tank losses of the 22nd Mechanized Corps resulted from mechanical breakdowns with inadequate repair facilities to make the tanks operational again. Maintenance improved sharply in 1942. The Russians benefited from the primitive quality of their tanks as compared to the Germans. The Russian equipment was easier to operate, easier to produce, and easier to maintain and repair. The Russian repair units needed fewer spare part and other supplies and therefore smaller repair units were necessary. Tank salvage and repair after 1942 was especially well organized by the Red Army.[90] Because of the availability of spare parts, the Russians usually replaced a tank engine or transmission rather than repairing the component and tying up the tank in the workshop for a long period. Despite the good supply of spare parts, the Russians continued to cannibalize damaged tanks.

As the war progressed there was a steady increase in the number of mechanics.[91] Damaged tanks were maintained and repaired at the brigade, corps, and army levels. Each tank brigade had a repair platoon with four trucks. Only minor repairs and routine maintenance were done at the brigade level. The tank corps repair workshops made medium-level repairs.[92] More serious repairs were done in the rear. A report in 1944 stated that of tanks hit by the Germans, 75 percent were a total loss, 10 percent could be repaired at the front, and 15 percent went to factories to be rebuilt.[93] An earlier report in 1943 indicated that 60 percent of the tanks hit by the Germans could be repaired.[94] As long as the tank did not bum and the turret ring was not severely damaged, it could be rebuilt. As more tanks became available from the factories, rebuilding a tank was less likely considering the transportation and the man-hours.

Each front had a tank recovery battalion. Salvage crews with tractors rescued tanks from the battlefield, dragging damaged tanks to the rear for repair.[95] Heavily damaged tanks were dragged to the nearest railroad to be loaded on flatcars and sent to a factory. The tank recovery units used Voroshilov, TSCHTS-60 and 65, and SS-1 tractors, and ZIS-5 and

GAZ-AA trucks. Each unit had about 40 trucks and 100 tractors available to recover tanks.[96]

Need for overhaul deprived a unit of a tank just as surely as battle damage. The Germans estimated that 3 to 4 percent of all their tanks would be out of action while being overhauled in a factory in Germany or in the tank repair centers in Russia. Three to four weeks were required to repair a Mark IV at a factory. A Panther or Tiger required five to six weeks if the spare parts were available. If not available, obtaining the part entailed an additional month. Transport from the front to Germany could take six weeks. Because of the delays, 10 to 12 percent of the total tank force was usually absent in repair. Fremde Heer Ost assumed that the time to make heavy repairs was even longer for the Russians because the distance to the factories was greater and there were fewer rail lines. Therefore, the Germans estimated that from 15 to 20 percent of all Russian tanks were in repair.[97] A few tank status reports captured by the Germans reveal the problem of repair and maintenance. In March 1944 the 6th Mechanized Crops had 35 percent of its tanks in repair.[98] A tank regiment in February 1945 had twenty-one tanks ready for duty, four in a rear-area repair facility, four under repair by the regimental maintenance platoon, and four immobilized for Lack of fuel and left behind, over 35 percent out of action.[99]

The T-34 was a sturdy tank with a strong chassis, but the engine usually needed overhaul after 400 to 500 hours of operating time. If the engine could not be replaced at the front, the tank went to a repair base. Damage to the gun also had to be handled at a repair base. Tanks with heavy damage were cannibalized at the front, making one complete tank out of three or four wrecks.[100] Tank repair factories, called either *Remontbase* (repair base) or *Remontfabrik* (repair factory) were located at Chvastovitschi, Jagodnoje (near Bolkhov), Bryansk, and Novosybkov. The Kolomenski factory, Zavod #38 at Gorki, that produced SU76s also did repair work.[101] After T-70 production ended, light tank replacements were either imported or repaired tanks. In July 1944 the 29th Tank Brigade had one battalion of new T-34s and two light tank battalions, each with twenty old T-70s that had been repaired at the Gorki factory.[102]

The repair system evidently became more important as the war progressed. In January 1945 the 12th Guard Tank Brigade had twenty repaired T-34s and forty new T-34s.[103] The crews disliked repaired tanks because many were earlier models and lacked improvements—for example, the 85mm gun on the T-34. In July 1944 the 222nd Tank Regiment was reduced to three or four tanks, which were given to another regiment and the headquarters and service units plus surviving crew mem-

bers went to the rear where they expected to receive new tanks. To their
disappointment, some of the replacements were older repaired tanks.[104]
Another tank regiment in March 1945 had only twenty-one T-70s, eighteen of which had been repaired[105]

In January 1945 more replacements were available than needed. The
10th Guard Tank Corps had 100 extra tanks, so the older tanks were
culled from the tank brigades and sent to the rear as reserves, which were
soon needed when operations began. By February 13, the corps was short
forty-five tanks.[106] In March 1945 the 31st Tank Crops experienced heavy
losses—about seventy T-34s. A shipment of new tanks from Nishnij-Tagil,
complete with crews, arrived on March 10, 1945. All the losses were
replaced and older tanks with their crews were sent to the corps reserve.[107]

The tank replacement and repair system was functioning smoothly
by late 1942. German estimates of Soviet tank losses for 1942 were 16,197;
for 1943, 17,333; and for 1944, 19,050. Despite the heavy losses inflicted
by the Germans, the Russians maintained their tank units and created
new ones. The heaviest losses had occurred in the early years when the
Germans were advancing rapidly and the Soviets could not salvage damaged tanks. Formation of new units practically ceased after 1943 and new
tanks and crews were used to maintain existing units. Once the Russians
began to advance, the battlefields remained in their possession and they
could salvage tanks. At the same time the Germans were denied this
advantage. A steady flow of the Soviet tanks and crews from the interior
to the front kept the Soviet tank units at strength despite the ever-increas-
ing efficiency of the German antitank weapons. By early 1943 the replacement system was maintaining the Soviet tank units at a high level of
combat effectiveness.

CHAPTER 11

Artillery Doctrine and Organization

A rtillery was the basic striking force of the Red Army. Its mission was to neutralize or destroy enemy fire permitting the infantry and tanks to penetrate the enemy defenses.[1] Soviet theory concerning the employment of artillery differed radically compared to other armies in the use of enormous numbers of guns. By the end of the war there were over 2,000 Russian artillery and mortar regiments of various types plus many separate battalions assigned to rifle divisions, artillery brigades, and other units. The artillery included over 100,000 guns and mortars served by more than 1 million men, one-sixth of the troops on the German Front. This enormous investment of men and material in the artillery was unique to the Red Army.

The Red Army doctrine was that victory would come only through offensive action. Penetration of an elastic defense was the major objective. In 1924 the Red Army held an "All-Union Artillery Conference." Tukhachevskii, an admirer of the German Army and later commander of the Red Army, presented a paper on maneuvers and artillery. This and other papers presented at the conference led to the Field Regulations of 1927, which established the idea of the combined arms offensive.

1. All arms must cooperate throughout the battle. The artillery must continue to provide support after the infantry advances.
2. Artillery fire must be massed.
3. Action must be sudden, taking the enemy by surprise and be flexible as the battle unfolds.[2]

Vladimir Triandafilov published *Character of the Operations of Modern Armies* in 1929, stressing that the artillery accompany the advancing infantry through the defensive zone and that huge quantities of fire were needed to break through the defensive zone. Triandafilov believed that fifty to sixty guns per kilometer would be required, and seventy-five guns per kilometer if enemy artillery had to be suppressed by counter-battery fire. A corps attacking on a five-kilometer front would need 300 guns.

Such concentrations called for a large pool of artillery that could be attached to attacking divisions. This requirement led to the formation of the Stavka reserve artillery in the 1930s, which grew to 110 regiments in June 1941, 255 in December 1941, and over 850 artillery regiments by April 1945[3]

The German theory in the 1930s was that aircraft could be substituted for artillery and that the heavy preparatory barrage was unnecessary. Tanks and self-propelled artillery would support the infantry through the defensive zone. In contrast the Russian Field Regulations of 1936 stressed that massive artillery fire open the way for the tanks and infantry, destroying the machine guns and antitank guns before the tanks and infantry advanced. The artillery was to continue its support through the defensive zone. Following this theory, the Russians produced thousands of guns. In 1937 the Red Army had 9,200 field guns and heavy artillery pieces compared to half that number in the German Army and one-third in the French Army. In June 1941 the Red Army had 67,000 guns and mortars.[4]

Voronov, later chief of artillery, had served as an advisor to the Spanish Republican Army during the Spanish Civil War. His experience there led him to believe that antitank guns were not essential to defeat tanks; that tank defense could be provided by light artillery guns with a low silhouette and a high muzzle velocity; and that such guns could be used both for tank defense (direct fire) and for barrages and infantry support (indirect fire). Direct fire was also to be used to destroy bunkers and strong points during an advance. The great advantages of direct fire were that it was easier to teach to the troops, required less fire-control equipment, and used less ammunition (one or two rounds of direct fire did the work of twenty rounds of indirect fire).[5] Voronov's experience had a profound impact on the design of Russian artillery in the 1930s.

Direct fire required that the gun be near the front line. Only a comparatively lightweight gun could be manhandled forward across the battlefield. Guns of this type were called regimental guns because they were assigned to rifle regiments. Before the war the Russians and the Germans recognized the need for regimental guns to accompany the infantry during the assault to provide direct fire support. In the 1930s the Germans issued to the infantry regiments a very short-barreled 75mm howitzer that could be pushed forward by the troops and used to destroy strong points with direct fire. Late in the war self-propelled guns filled that role, but the Germans never had enough SPs and continued to use the lightweight guns. The Russians also developed a regimental 76mm gun in 1927 with a short barrel.

To provide additional direct fire, the Russians pushed forward the divisional 76mm guns, requiring that the guns be light enough to manhandle. The use of the 76mm divisional guns in direct fire was very effective from 1942 on. In attacks the guns destroyed machine guns and antitank guns that would have slowed the infantry and tanks. The Russians also used medium artillery in the direct-fire role. In January 1943 the 2nd Shock Army used 218 guns in the direct-fire role on a nine-kilometer front, including two 152mm gun-howitzers concealed in deep gun pits from 400 to 900 meters from the German line.[6]

In offensive operations, the artillery had three missions; preparatory, support, and accompany. Preparatory fire was much shorter in duration than the barrages of World War I, which sometimes lasted for days. The Russians first applied massed artillery in November 1942 at the opening of the offensive that surrounded the German 6th Army at Stalingrad.[7] The barrage usually lasted up to two hours. At the beginning of the barrage, the Germans retreated to their bunkers to avoid the storm and then emerged to drive back the attackers. As the war progressed and the Russian artillery increased in strength, the barrages became even shorter—as little as forty minutes. To confuse the Germans, no regular timetable was used. Each operation differed. Lulls were designed to fool the Germans that the barrage was over and that they could leave their shelters and bring up their reserves. Then the fire would begin again. Several lulls were part of every barrage. If the Germans waited too long assuming that it was a lull, the Russians would have a half-hour to approach the German lines without opposition.

The Russian artillerymen did not employ the Time-on-Target technique, a carefully orchestrated system that resulted in all of the shells from many guns arriving simultaneously on a target without warning. The "TOT" technique was used by the Americans, British, and Germans, but the Russians lacked the firecontrol equipment needed. Therefore, they relied on masses of guns (200 to 300 per kilometer) to shock the enemy.[8]

Even a simple fire program employed by the 37th Army in August 1944 in the Jassy-Kishinev operation used lulls to trick the Germans. The program began with three minutes of continuous fire by the corps and army artillery (the breakthrough and long-range groups) followed by twenty-five minutes of direct fire by the close support guns. During that twenty-five minutes, the other groups fired slowly—one or two guns at a time for three minutes—then all the guns fired rapidly for one minute, then slow for five minutes, rapid fire for another minute, slow fire for seven minutes, rapid fire for another minute, and slow fire for two minutes, ending with two minutes of concentrated fire by the army and corps artillery. Ten minutes of slow fire followed, then one minute of rapid fire, ten minutes of no fire at all (presumably the ruse to encourage the Germans to leave their shelters), followed by ten minutes of concentrated fire by the corps and army artillery to demoralize the Germans who had emerged. At this point the infantry and tanks advanced on the German positions that had endured more than two hours of fire.[9]

The Russians would leave channels or gaps in the barrage that permitted the infantry to penetrate into the German defense while the barrage continued in adjoining sectors.[10] The support phase began when the infantry advanced. Direct fire guns arrived less than twenty-four hours before the attack and hid. When the attack began, the guns were wheeled out and joined in the fire. The mass of artillery began a rolling barrage just in front of the infantry and tanks. Some guns were manhandled forward with the infantry to provide direct fire on specific targets.[11]

The final phase began when the German defenses were pierced and the exploitation tank forces advanced. At this point the centralized control of the artillery ceased. Units regained control of their organic artillery and attached light artillery and mortar units. Mobile reserves of antitank guns, engineers, infantry, and heavy field guns shattered tank-supported counterattacks. The accompanying artillery was sufficient to deal with demoralized troops. However, if fresh reserves in prepared positions were encountered, the Russian advance paused until the medium and heavy artillery arrived—a matter of days should the roads be poor. If the roads were good, the artillery stayed with the tanks and maintained the momentum of the attack. Self-propelled artillery provided close artillery support in the closing years of the war.[12]

Artillery played a major role in Soviet defense. A static prepared defense line included three separate zones, each spaced far enough apart so that the Germans had to advance their artillery before the next zone could be attacked. The artillery had five missions as part of the defensive effort. The first was long-range fire supplemented by air attacks on potential troop assembly areas, bridges, command posts, artillery positions, and similar targets that would disrupt an enemy attack. The second mission by medium and heavy artillery was to place a curtain of fire in front of the Soviet positions. As the enemy drew nearer, the light artillery and mortars joined in.

The third defensive mission was a preplanned antitank rolling barrage that moved closer to the Soviet line as the tanks advanced. The fourth mission was a curtain barrage at the leading edge of the defensive zone by all indirect fire guns and mortars to separate the infantry from the tanks. Should tanks penetrate the Soviet defenses, the fifth mission was indirect shelling of the Soviet positions while antitank and antiaircraft guns fired directly at the tanks. All of the artillery had a secondary mission of tank defense. Antitank guns concentrated at the most likely approach of the tanks and other types of guns at the second most likely approach. In addition, mobile antitank reserves with antitank guns. engineers, infantry, and other guns were placed in the path of advancing tanks.[13]

Although the Soviet guns were equal or superior to the German guns, the Russians had two major weaknesses in the first phase of the war, poor fire control, and lack of coordination with the tanks and infantry. The first problem would remain to the end of the war, as the number of regiments and battalions far outstripped the available men who could learn the complex techniques involved in fire control. Coordination with other arms improved as the war progressed.[14]

In February and March of 1942 the Soviet General Staff made a survey of the use of artillery and modified the artillery doctrine based on experience. On January 10, 1942, Stalin had directed that artillery concentrate to support offensive actions and move forward with the advancing infantry and tanks.[15] The General Staff study described the German use of strong points in defense during the Russian winter offensive of 1941–42. When Soviet forces had penetrated the German lines, the Germans drove them back with counterattacks. The Germans were able to make more efficient use of their artillery through forward observers with radios.[16]

The General Staff found many problems with the Russian use of artillery. Lack of adequate reconnaissance left the artillery with insufficient information about enemy defenses to plan their fire. Army artillery plans tended to be too general, with inadequate use of divisional and regimental artillery. There was a lack of coordination among the mortars, regimental guns, and field artillery. The infantry was not trained to help the artillery manhandle guns forward as the troops advanced. Munitions supply was not coordinated and supply roads were not improved before offensives.[17]

Results of the problems were noted in the General Staff study. In March 1942 the 2nd Guard Division crossed the Mius River and established a bridgehead with no regimental guns or antitank guns, which had fallen behind during the advance. The Germans counterattacked with tanks, forcing the infantry to retreat across the river and lose a very valuable bridgehead.[18] Reacting to the study, the 1942 artillery regulations (PS-42) included the need for forward observation posts, sending artillerymen with reconnaissance patrols, and the expansion of counter-battery fire and direct fire.[19] The major improvement was the increase in direct

fire by divisional artillery and continued attempts to move the divisional
and regimental artillery forward with the infantry.[20]

Mobile artillery was needed for mechanized forces exploiting a
breakthrough. Truck-drawn guns had difficulty moving forward with the
tanks. As a partial solution, rockets, mortars, antitank guns, light artillery,
and self-propelled guns moved with the advancing armor while the heavier guns remained in the rear.[21] Mechanized artillery regiments began
forming in late 1942 and a sizable number were available for the Battle of
Kursk.

In July 1943 the Germans lost the initiative and began building complex defense systems, presenting the Russians with new problems. The
defensive zones were eight to ten kilometers deep. To penetrate this
depth required even more artillery—up to seven battalions of artillery to
support a rifle regiment and 150 to 300 guns and mortars per kilometer
of front. At crucial points, the Russian artillery outnumbered the German ten-to-one.[22]

The Germans lacked the forces to man deep defenses and multiple
lines to absorb the weight of the attack. Counterattacks to reestablish the
defensive line after a breakthrough no longer succeeded. The increasing
amount of Soviet mobile artillery repulsed the counterattacks and prevented the formation of new defenses. Most Russian offensives halted
only when the distance from the logistical base delayed supplies.[23]

Soviet artillery technique responded to the change from defense to
offense. In preparing for an offensive, artillery of all types concentrated
in the breakthrough area. The artillery was divided into several groups
related to function. During attacks the available artillery formed three
groups: PP (infantry support), DD (long-range artillery), and breakthrough.[24] At the rear DD groups included heavy guns from the army
artillery or attached artillery divisions. The long-range groups neutralized
enemy artillery and attacked enemy reserves. Breakthrough groups and
counter-mortar groups included howitzer battalions. The PP groups,
including divisional and light artillery and mortars, were attached to rifle
regiments. Mortar groups were formed from divisional, medium, and
heavy mortars. With over 100 mortars employed as a unit, the attacking
Russians were able to overwhelm the German defense paving the way for
the Russian infantry.[25]

In June 1944 the 11th Guard Army had a PP group attached to each
rifle regiment in the first echelon. PP Group 99, attached to the 99th
Guard Rifle Regiment, consisted of two battalions of the 186th Guard
Artillery Regiment (the 84th Guard Division artillery) and the 35th
Guard Artillery Regiment, a divisional artillery regiment of a division in

the second echelon. The 99th Regiment had five battalions of close support artillery for two rifle battalions on the front and one in reserve.

At the divisional level, the 31st Guard Division, parent of the 99th
Regiment, had a breakthrough group including the 101st Howitzer Regiment, the 117th Heavy Howitzer Brigade, and the 316th Heavy Artillery
Battalion. Farther back a DD group consisted of the 114th Gun Artillery
Brigade, and the 523rd Gun Artillery Regiment supported the three regiments of the 31st Guard Division. The division, attacking on a frontage
of only three kilometers, had its organic artillery (twenty 76mm guns and
twelve 122mm guns) plus seventy-two 76mm guns, thirty-six 120mm mortars, twenty-eight 122mm howitzers, twenty-four 122mm guns, fifty
203mm howitzers, and twelve 280mm mortars.[26] This huge inventory of
artillery support (254 guns and mortars) compared to the thirty-six
105mm howitzers and twelve 155mm howitzers plus perhaps twelve to
twenty additional guns that an American division with double the number of riflemen would have spread over a much wider front. The 31st
Guard Division had eighty-five guns and mortars 76mm or larger per
kilometer. In the battle for Berlin in April 1945, the support was even
heavier. The 147th Division had 280 guns and mortars over 76mm per
kilometer![27]

By the time of the Battle of Kursk the Soviets had worked out a comprehensive doctrine for the employment of artillery in defense and had
formed the necessary units to execute the doctrine. Much of the credit
for the victory at Kursk belonged to the artillery. After Kursk the change
to offensive action brought new methods and new units that successfully
overcame all of the German defensive efforts.

The artillery doctrine was reflected in changes in artillery organization. In the mid-1930s the field artillery consisted of 115 artillery regiments (82 divisional, 17 corps, 12 horse, and four regiments assigned to
fortified regions).[28] The Stavka reserve had only twenty-four regiments in
1937. Only 20 percent of the artillery was assigned to corps or armies.
The 1937 table of organization allocated two artillery regiments for each
corps. One corps regiment had a battalion of 122mm guns and two battalions of 152 gun-howitzers. The other regiment had a battalion of
122mm guns and a battalion of 203mm howitzers.[29] In 1938 the Russian
plan for artillery included two regiments for each of ninety-six rifle divisions and two regiments of corps artillery for each of twenty corps.[30] In
1939 the authorized strength for corps artillery was a regiment of 107mm
guns and 152mm howitzers (total thirty-six pieces), a regiment of 152mm
howitzers and 152mm gun-howitzers (thirty pieces), and a battalion of
eighteen 76mm antiaircraft guns.[31]

In the year preceding the German invasion, the Red Army had organized many new independent artillery regiments to implement the doctrine of massive artillery support at critical points. In May 1940 the Stavka reserve included only seven gun regiments, seventeen howitzer regiments, one heavy gun regiment, twenty heavy howitzer regiments, and ten independent battalions.[32] By June 1941 the Stavka reserve had increased to sixty regiments of howitzers and fourteen of guns. The units included 122mm guns, 152mm gun-howitzers, and 203mm howitzers formed in regiments of four battalions with three or four batteries each. The 152mm gun-howitzer regiments had forty-eight guns, while the 203mm howitzers had twenty-four. In addition there were eleven mortar regiments; ten antitank brigades; and some battalions of 210mm guns, 280mm howitzers, and 305mm howitzers.[33]

The artillery was equal to 8 percent of the ground forces in 1941.[34] The number of guns and mortars in the Red Army had increased rapidly from 56,000 in January 1939 to 74,000 in January 1941.[35] From January 1939 to June 1941, the Russians produced 82,000 guns and mortars. By June 1941 the Red Army had a powerful artillery force with 91,493 guns and mortars of all types[36] Excluding mortars and regimental guns, the Germans estimated that the Russians had 18,000 guns on June 22, 1941.

Given the large number of guns available, a complex organization was necessary. In June 1941 most Russian artillery was at the division level, one horse-drawn 76mm gun regiment and one motorized howitzer regiment. The howitzer regiment consisted of two battalions of 152mm howitzers and one battalion of 122mm howitzers. The rifle division also had a battalion of 45mm antitank guns and an antiaircraft battalion of four 85mm guns and twelve 37mm guns.[37]

The table of organization for the corps artillery regiment was two battalions of 152mm howitzers and one battalion of 122mm guns. However, there were not enough regiments to give each rifle corps two regiments. In June 1941 the 6th Corps had only one artillery regiment. After the war began the Red Army doubled the number of corps regiments. The military district formed new corps artillery regiments by taking a cadre from an existing regiment and filling the vacancies with recalled reservists. The guns came from large stocks available in arsenals.

In the first six months of the war the Russians lost a large part of their artillery. The Germans estimated that the Russians lost 15,904 guns, 4,413 antitank guns, and 1,738 antiaircraft guns in the first three months of the war and a further 10,730 guns of all types by the end of the 1941, for a total of over 32,700 guns plus many mortars. The Red Army had only 21,933 guns and mortars on December 1, 1941, compared to 90,000 before the war.[38]

The second phase of the war, from November 1941 to December 1942, was marked by improvisation. The remaining artillery had to be concentrated and used where needed. To accomplish that end, in October 1941 the divisional artillery was reduced to one horse-drawn regiment of 76mm guns. The motorized howitzer regiments from the rifle divisions became army artillery or moved into the strategic reserve. The number of guns and mortars in the rifle division decreased from 280 to 132. A heavy mortar regiment replaced the howitzer regiment in the division. The heavy regimental mortar batteries joined to form a division mortar battalion. A new regimental mortar battery had medium and light mortars. The mortars were easier to produce and to operate.

Taking artillery from the division commander reduced his firepower, but many inexperienced division commanders had made poor use of their resources. In 1942, divisions in defensive positions received sufficient support from their organic artillery regiment. Centralizing the bulk of the artillery made the best use of the available trained gun crews. Artillery regiments that became part of the Stavka reserve also had more time to train.[39]

Faced with a shortage of able senior commanders and staffs, the Russians abolished corps headquarters in late 1941. Artillery previously assigned to the corps became army artillery or Stavka reserve. The armies received an army gun artillery regiment with three battalions armed with 107mm, 122mm, and 152mm guns and 152mm howitzers.[40] With the addition of the former corps artillery regiments and new formations, the Stavka reserve increased to 58 antitank regiments, 101 gun regiments, 68 howitzer regiments, 14 mortar regiments, and 24 regiments and 73 battalions of rocket launchers by the end of 1941.[41] Despite the heavy losses in the opening months of the war, Russian artillery remained a potent force.

Russian artillery strength rapidly recovered as evacuated factories returned to production and others increased their output. On May 1, 1942, the Russians had 43,642 guns and mortars (double the number in December 1941), and 72,505 on November 1, 1942, including regimental guns and mortars.[42] The number of independent artillery regiments expanded rapidly in 1942.[43] The 51st Artillery Regiment formed from December 1941 to March 1942 at Kazan. The officers and NCOs came from various front-line units and the men from hospitals in Kazan and Gorki. At first the regiment had only one 152mm gun for training. In March 1942 the regiment moved to Moscow where it received new guns and trucks. In May 1942 the regiment moved by rail to Kharkov and took part in the withdrawal battles from Kalach back to Stalingrad.[44]

Four 152mm gun regiments were formed at Kirov in March 1942. The guns were new, but the tractors were old Russian agricultural tractors requisitioned from collective farms. In May 1942 the regiments, still short of men and trucks, went to the front. The 1092nd Regiment traveled by rail to the Voronezh Front, arriving on June 15, 1942, and unloaded with the help of a truck battalion. One gun battalion was detached immediately from the regiment and sent to a different sector, suggesting a shortage of artillery.[45]

In May 1942 the artillery reserve consisted of the equivalent of 122 antitank regiments, 177 gun regiments, 149 howitzer regiments, 63 mortar regiments, and 72 Guard mortar regiments. These totals do not include regiments assigned to divisions and armies. By November 1942 the artillery reserve had grown to 240 tank destroyer regiments, 199 gun regiments, 196 howitzer regiment, 83 mortars regiments, 138 Guard mortar regiments, and 253 antiaircraft regiments assigned to the army, exclusive of interior defense antiaircraft regiments assigned to protect economic and industrial targets.[46]

The Stavka reserve (excluding regiments assigned to field armies, corps, and divisions) grew rapidly in this period, as follows:[47]

Type of Regiment	June 41	Dec. 41	May 42	Nov. 42
Antitank	20	58	122	240
Gun	15	101	177	199
Howitzer	64	68	149	196
Mortar	11	14	63	83
Guard Mortar	0	24	72	138
Antiaircraft	0	0	0	253
TOTAL	110	265	583	1,109

After the first year of the war, production exceeded losses in field artillery and antitank guns. Losses of antiaircraft guns dropped to fewer than a thousand per year. In 1942 losses in guns of all types totaled 20,597; in 1943, 23,767; and in 1944, 18,479.[48] Production easily compensated for losses. In the first half of 1942, 14,000 guns of 76mm or more were produced and in the second half of 1942, 15,600.[49] The new guns replaced losses and equipped new independent regiments in 1942. In November 1942 the Red Army had 77,700 guns and mortars.[50]

To strengthen the divisional artillery the organization was revised in December 1942, increasing the number of 120mm mortars from eighteen to twenty-one and 45mm guns from thirty to forty-eight.[51] The increase provided more support for the dwindling strength of the rifle companies. The rifle divisions were receiving their full allotment of artillery. In October 1942, the 270th Rifle Division reformed after the original division was destroyed in the spring of 1942 at Izyum. One of artillery men in the new division transferred from a heavy gun artillery regiment. The 76mm guns came from the 53rd Fortified Region (UR) that served as a cadre unit for the new division. By January 1943 the 270th Division had five batteries of horse-drawn 76mm guns and two batteries of tractor-drawn 122mm howitzers. However, there were only enough horses to pull half the 76mm guns at one time and only three tractors for the six 122mm howitzers. Therefore, the divisional artillery had to move in two stages, limiting the ability of the artillery to move with the infantry.[52]

Even at full strength the divisional artillery was weaker than the German counterpart, but the Red Army had far more nondivisional artillery regiments. In November 1942 there were twenty-five artillery divisions and 1,203 independent artillery regiments and battalions.[53] The artillery divisions were authorized in October to command the large number of independent artillery regiments.[54] Previously the only control came from the corps and field army artillery commanders. In 1941 and early 1942 an army had two to six regiments. By late 1942 armies had twelve to fourteen artillery regiments. At Stalingrad the 5th Tank Army had twenty-nine artillery regiments attached.[55] The artillery divisions originally consisted of eight regiments with 168 guns. The regiments included three with 76mm guns, three with 122mm howitzers, and two with 152mm guns. In December 1942 the regiments formed three brigades—light, howitzer, and gun—and the artillery division received a mortar brigade formed from three or more Stavka reserve mortar regiments. The artillery division then totaled 168 guns and 80 120mm mortars.[56]

The 1st Artillery Division supported the 21st Army on the Southwest Front in November 1942 in the Stalingrad offensive. The division had the 468, 501, and 1189 Light Artillery Regiments (later the 13th Light Artillery Brigade); the 274, 275, and 331 Howitzer Regiments (later the 4th Howitzer Brigade); and the 1162 and 1166 Gun Regiments (later the 6th Gun Brigade).[57] The 12th Artillery Division had organized in October and November 1942 at Tschebarkol. Most of the men were nineteen years old, suggesting that the regiments were also new.[58] The 5th Artillery Division had formed at Yefremov in October 1942 with two 152mm regiments, two 122mm regiments, two 76mm gun regiments, and three 122mm mortar regiments.[59]

The howitzer and gun brigades provided indirect fire in support of the infantry. The light artillery brigade provided indirect fire and direct fire against tanks and defenses such as bunkers and machine gun nests.[60] The light artillery regiments differed from the divisional artillery regiments in that they did not have 122mm howitzer batteries and were motorized instead of horsedrawn. In December 1942 the 49th Light Artillery Brigade of the 16th Artillery Division was formed at Tschigirin with the 1426, 1429, and 1431 Light Artillery Regiments. In late 1943 the regiment had ZIS-3 M1942 76mm guns and a full complement of Studebaker 2.5-ton trucks. The ammunition carried was primarily armor piercing and hollow-charge high-explosive, both designed for antitank work.[61]

Most of the new artillery divisions went to the Stalingrad area along with many independent regiments. The Southwest, Don, and Stalingrad fronts received 75 artillery and mortar regiments, half the Stavka reserve. At the beginning of the offensive the three fronts had 230 artillery and mortar regiments with 13,500 guns and mortars, double the number available for the Battle of Moscow.[62]

After the winter of 1942-43 the Germans could no longer replace their losses in artillery, while the Russians received more weapons of all kinds.[63] In 1943 the Russians produced the following:[64]

45mm antitank gun	19,500
57mm antitank gun	4,000
76mm gun	27,000
122mm howitzer	5,200
152mm gun-howitzer	2,200

The number of artillery units continued to increase in early 1943. In April 1943, sixteen of the artillery divisions were heavily reinforced, becoming artillery breakthrough divisions. The artillery breakthrough division had six brigades instead of four, adding a heavy howitzer brigade (152mm howitzers) and a longrange howitzer brigade (203mm howitzers).[65] The new divisions had a light artillery brigade, a gun brigade, a howitzer brigade, a heavy howitzer brigade, a mortar brigade, and a long-range howitzer brigade with a total of 356 gun and mortars.[66] For counter-battery work to destroy German artillery units, four heavy gun divisions were formed in June 1943. The gun divisions had four brigades of 122mm and 152mm guns.[67]

Given the large number of artillery divisions, a higher headquarters was required to coordinate the fire of several divisions. Artillery breakthrough corps, consisting of two or more artillery breakthrough divisions and a Guard mortar division, were formed in April 1943. Four Guard mortar divisions using the Katusha rocket launchers had formed late in 1942, each able to fire 3,840 projectiles with a weight of 230 tons in one salvo.[68] The breakthrough corps had a total of 712 guns and mortars and 864 rockets. Five artillery corps existed by June 1943.[69] The 3rd Leningrad Counter Battery Corps formed in September 1943, presumably to match the heavy concentration of German artillery around Leningrad. The corps consisted of three gun regiments, a naval rail gun brigade, and guns of the Baltic Fleet.[70]

In June 1943, just before the Battle of Kursk, the Stavka reserve of artillery consisted of 6 artillery corps (including 11 breakthrough artillery divisions, 10 four-brigade divisions, and some three-brigade divisions), 7 Guard mortar divisions, 20 independent artillery brigades, 11 mortar brigades, 50 tank destroyer brigades, and 140 independent artillery and antiaircraft regiments. This enormous force of artillery was in addition to the multitude of regiments assigned to fronts, armies, corps, and divisions! The Red Army had a total of 132,000 guns, mortars, self-propelled artillery pieces, and rocket launchers![71]

Three of the artillery corps were at Kursk and two more were forming in the rear.[72] By July 1943 there were 27 artillery divisions. The individual divisions were assigned to armies. At the Battle of Kursk an unprecedented concentration of artillery awaited the German attack. The Central Front had four artillery corps, an additional artillery division, ten regiments of Guard mortars, fifteen independent artillery and mortar regiments, six self-propelled artillery regiments, ten tank destroyer regiments, and three destroyer brigades. The Fourth Artillery Corps included in the Central Front had two artillery divisions with six brigades and a Guard mortar division with three brigades.[73]

By September 1943 the Germans had located eighteen artillery divisions, four on the Central Front, four on the Bryansk Front, four on the Western Front, two on the Southwest Front, two on the Leningrad Front, one on the Kalinin Front.[74] The heaviest concentration was in the critical center. Only two were in the north and two in the south. The creation of the huge artillery reserve enabled the Russians to concentrate artillery effectively. At Krivoi Rog in late 1943 the Red Army had twenty guns and nine heavy mortars per kilometer, compared to only three guns and ten heavy mortars on the German side.[75]

In 1944 artillery divisions received a heavy mortar brigade with forty-eight 160mm mortars. Later in the year some divisions received an addi-

tional heavy howitzer brigade with 203mm howitzers and a brigade
equipped with the new 100mm antitank guns. In February 1945 the 12th
Artillery Division had the following units:[76]

32nd Howitzer Brigade	3 regiments of 122mm howitzers
41st Gun Brigade	3 regiments of 152mm guns
46th Light Artillery Brigade	3 regiments of 76mm guns
89th Howitzer Brigade	152mm howitzers
104th Heavy Howitzer Brigade	203mm howitzers
125th Heavy Howitzer Brigade	
11th Mortar Brigade	

With the increased availability of guns and mortars, the Russians
assigned more to divisions, corps, and armies. By August of 1943 divisional
artillery had improved considerably. The 1036th Artillery Regiment of the
161st Rifle Division had five batteries of horse-drawn 76mm guns (twenty
guns) and three batteries of tractor-drawn 122mm howitzers (twelve howitzers). The regiment had 414 artillery horses—ample to pull the guns
and supply wagons—and twenty trucks to pull the howitzers and carry supplies.[77] In November 1943 an independent motorized artillery regiment,
the 1101st, had twenty-four Russian TS tractors, twenty-four GAZ-AA
trucks, and seven ZIS-5 trucks to pull its twenty-four guns and carry supplies. The regiment was short forty vehicles, mostly ZIS-5 trucks.[78]

The tank corps in late 1942 had a table of organization that included
a tank destroyer regiment, a 120mm mortar regiment, a 37mm antiaircraft regiment, and a Guard mortar (rocket) battalion with M8 or M13
rocket launchers.[79] In December 1943 the number of guns and mortars
assigned to a tank corps increased from 90 to 152 and to a mechanized
corps from 246 to 252.[80] More artillery regiments were assigned to each
army. In early 1943 army artillery regiments had a table of organization
of two battalions of 152mm gun-howitzers and one battalion of 122mm
guns. In 1943 field army artillery increased to three artillery regiments
and a mortar regiment.[81] In June 1944 the army artillery regiments
joined to form an artillery brigade for each army.[82]

In April 1943 the Red Army reestablished the corps headquarters,
but there was no corps artillery; the artillery continued to be assigned to
armies. In 1944 each rifle corps received three regiments of artillery and
late in the year the regiments formed corps artillery brigades.[83] Independent brigade headquarters were created to command artillery regiments assigned to armies and in 1945 to Guard rifle divisions.[84] The
brigades usually had three regiments, but some later brigades (those

numbered 116 and higher) had four battalions numbered 1 through 4.[85]
In June 1943 an army launching an attack received support from many
attached units: one or two artillery divisions, three artillery regiments,
three tank destroyer regiments, three or four tank or self-propelled
artillery brigades, ten tank or self-propelled artillery regiments, two antiaircraft divisions, and one or two mechanized or tank corps.[86]

In the final eighteen months of the war, the Soviet Union produced
69,400 guns and mortars.[87] German estimates for the breakdown of the
types of guns at the front in Soviet units in March 1944 were:[88]

76mm regimental guns	6,500
76mm guns	17,000
107mm, 122mm, 152mm guns	1,800
122mm, 152mm, 203mm howitzers	9,700
57mm antitank guns	3,100
85mm antiaircraft guns	1,100
37mm antiaircraft guns	3,400
120mm mortars	16,100
M 13 rocket launchers	3,200
82mm mortars	43,000
50mm mortars	31,000

Simultaneously, the German supply of artillery was steadily diminish-
ing, dropping from 70,000 guns and mortars in November 1942 (almost
equal to the Red Army) to only 28,500 in January 1945.[89] In June 1943
the Red Army had 103,100 guns and mortars; in January 1944, 92,600; in
June 1944, 92,600; and in January 1945, 108,000.[90] The Germans estimated Russian monthly production in 1945 as follows[91]

37mm antiaircraft guns	3,756
45mm antitank guns	7,246
57mm antitank guns	2,080
76mm guns	9,118
85mm antiaircraft guns	1,144
122mm guns	1,040
152mm guns	572

The supply of gun and mortars did not always maintain artillery units
at full strength. In March 1944 the 660th Artillery Regiment of the 220th
Rifle Division had three battalions (each two batteries) of 76mm guns
(twenty-four guns), but only one battery of 122mm howitzers (four how-

itzers). American three-axle trucks (probably Studebaker 2.5-ton trucks) replaced the artillery horses and Russian tractors pulled the 122mm howitzers.[92]

On May 31, 1944, the 619th Artillery Regiment of the 179th Rifle Division had sixteen 76mm guns and nine 122mm howitzers, considerably short of its organization table. The regiment had two tractors, three trucks, thirty-three two-horse wagons and eight one-horse wagons. The guns were horse-drawn, including the howitzers, but the regiment had only 264 horses instead of the authorized 618. On the plus side, the regiment had received new M1942 76mm guns and new M1938 122mm howitzers in May 1944.[93]

Rifle regiments were given a considerable amount of artillery and mortars, but shortages of manpower reduced the number of men in artillery components. In September 1944 the 881st Rifle Regiment had two 76mm regimental guns, three 45mm antitank guns, four 120mm mortars, and nine 82mm mortars with a total of 143 officers and men assigned to the artillery. All of the guns were horse-drawn.[94] The table of organization called for four 76mm guns, twelve 45mm guns, and seven 120mm mortars, so the regiment was under strength.[95]

Guard rifle divisions had more artillery. In August 1943 three Guard rifle divisions each had the following artillery:[96]

82mm mortars	54 to 61
120mm mortars	18 to 24
45mm antitank guns	29 to 43
76mm regimental guns	8 to 12
76mm divisional guns	22 to 24
122mm howitzers	all had 12

In 1943 the 26th Guard Rifle Division artillery had twenty-four 76mm guns, twelve 122mm howitzers, twenty-three 120mm mortars, and fifty-nine 82mm mortars.[97] The data confirmed that the Russians had maintained Guard divisions near shtat strength. In December 1944 some rifle divisions received an artillery brigade headquarters to command the divisional artillery consisting of a light artillery regiment, a howitzer regiment, and a mortar regiment.[98]

New artillery regiments continued to form and refit throughout the war, becoming more powerful with new guns and more mobile with American trucks and, for the heavier guns, American tractors. The 64th Howitzer Regiment, in combat since 1941, had been reduced not only by casualties but also by continual demands for cadres for new regiments. In June 1944 the depleted regiment went to the rear. There the regiment received new guns, American Caterpillar tractors to replace Russian tractors, and men from artillery and infantry replacement training regiments.[99] In March 1944 the 615th Howitzer Regiment had twenty-eight M1938 122mm howitzers, twenty-one American International trucks, fourteen Studebakers, seven Russian GAZ-AA trucks, and one Willys Jeep. The regiment had its full complement of guns, and the superior American vehicles replaced Russians trucks and tractors to pull and supply the guns, resulting in a far more mobile regiment.[100]

Determining the number of artillery regiments in the Red Army was confusing. Before the war the Red Army had adopted a numbering scheme for artillery regiments as follows:[101]

Type of Regiment	Number Range
Corps artillery	1–99
Division light artillery	100–199
Division heavy artillery	200–299
Stavka howitzer	300–399
Stavka gun	400–499

This scheme was abandoned in 1941. Regimental numbers were reused, often for a different type of regiment, making it difficult to determine how many regiments were active in 1942. Adding to the problem was a broken series of low numbers denoting antiaircraft regiments. Other antiaircraft regiments were numbered in the higher range of the general artillery sequence.

Another complication came from the duplication of the divisional artillery regiment numbers by army, corps, and Stavka artillery regiments. Still another cause for confusion was the numbering of Guard artillery regiments in a series that included divisional artillery regiments, tank destroyer regiments, antiaircraft regiments, and miscellaneous artillery regiments. Therefore it was possible to find a divisional artillery regiment, a howitzer regiment, an antiaircraft regiment, and a Guard artillery regiment all active at the same time with the same number. The sources sometimes failed to state the complete classification, often leaving out the Guard designation.

German intelligence records were very sketchy for artillery, relying mostly on radio intercepts and captured documents. These factors made it difficult to establish the precise numbers of regiments. The number of artillery regiments continued to expand until the end of the war. The Germans identified over 2,000 artillery regiments as follows:[102]

Type of Regiment	March 1944	June 1944	Sept. 1944	Dec. 1944	March 1945
Division artillery	472	484	491	499	499
Howitzer	190	202	211	208	183
Gun	103	105	111	114	112
Light artillery	57	63	68	65	67
Tank destroyer	342	363	390	386	338
Mechanized artillery	88	120		not in table	
Antiaircraft	255	299	320	330	343
Army	73	76	74	99	66
Heavy mortar	0	13	15	19	18
Mortar	219	229	259	250	261
Guard mortar	127	127	134	129	131
Unlocated division	31	28	20	20	23
Unlocated mortar	0	22	18	14	15
TOTAL	1,957	2,031	2,111	2,133	2,056

The later totals did not include mechanized artillery, but did include mortar and Guard mortar regiments. Artillery brigades originally included three or more individually numbered regiments. The artillery brigades with four battalions would add the equivalent of at least 200 additional artillery regiments to the total.

The Germans used the tables to compute the number of guns and mortars on the front, each regiment being multiplied by the number of guns in its table of organization. Here is an example for March 26, 1944:[103]

76mm field guns	9,484
122mm, 152mm, and 203mm howitzers	10,261
107mm, 122m, and 152mm guns	2,106
57mm antitank guns	2,360
76mm antitank guns	6,424
37mm antiaircraft guns	3,684
85mm antiaircraft guns	1,228
120mm mortars	18,963
M13 rocket launchers	3,456
TOTAL GUNS AND MORTARS	57,966

Similar tables were maintained for higher artillery headquarters:[104]

UNIT	March 1944	June 1944	Sept. 1944	Dec. 1944	March 1945
Artillery Div.	29	29	30	33	39
Antiaircraft Div.	37	49	55	58	64
Guards mortar Div.	4	4	5	5	5
TOTAL DIVISIONS	70	82	90	96	108
Howitzer Bde.	52	57	63	69	76
Gun Bde.	19	24	36	44	49
L. artillery Bde.	18	22	22	20	24
Unknown Bde.	18	17	9	8	17
Tank dest. Bde.	44	45	48	54	53
Mortar Bde.	28	33	33	35	39
Guards mortar Bde.	21	29	26	30	31
TOTAL BRIGADES	200	227	237	260	289

Soviet sources indicated that the Germans were close to the mark. In January 1944 there were 80 artillery, antiaircraft, and mortar divisions and 73 independent artillery and mortar brigades; in June 1944 there were 83 divisions and 93 artillery brigades; and in December 1944 the Red Army had 105 artillery divisions (artillery, antiaircraft, and Guard mortar) and 147 independent brigades (including artillery, tank destroyer, mortar, and Guard mortar.[105] Another Soviet source gave lower figures for January 1945: 89 divisions (including artillery, antiaircraft, and Guard mortar divisions) and 138 independent brigades (including artillery, tank destroyer, mortar, and Guards mortar).[106] By the end of the war the Russians had formed 10 artillery corps, 105 artillery and mortar divisions (including antiaircraft divisions), and 97 independent brigades.[107] In January 1945 there were 1,548 artillery and mortar regiments in the Stavka reserve plus 154 independent brigades and 958 independent regiments in corps and army artillery.[108]

The Germans estimated that the Russians had more than 1 million men in artillery units in February 1945.[109] The allotment of one-sixth of the men on the German Front to the artillery and the allocation of a major part of the industrial capacity to the production of guns and mortars testified to the Soviet belief in the power of the guns. The Soviet artillery was the primary weapon both in offense and defense. Without the artillery the Red Army could not move. By early 1943 the artillery divisions had been formed and a substantial number of independent regiments had been activated. During the last two years of the war new units were formed, but these only added to the massive Russian superiority. The Russian artillery had attained mastery of the battlefield by the time of the Battle of Kursk in July 1943.

CHAPTER 12

Artillery Weapons and Munitions

Artillery was classified according to function: field artillery used by divisions, medium and heavy artillery used by corps and armies, antitank guns to defend against tank attacks, and antiaircraft guns for air defense. The field, medium, and heavy artillery included both guns and howitzers. All were designated by the diameter of the bore, expressed in mm. A 76mm gun had a bore 76 millimeters in diameter and fired a projectile of the same diameter.

A gun had a flat trajectory and long range stemming from its high muzzle velocity. A muzzle velocity from 400 meters per second to more than 1,000 meters per second resulted from a large powder charge, a large chamber to hold the powder, and a long barrel (about 40 caliber) to allow the powder time to burn. The barrel of a gun was measured in calibers: a 40-caliber barrel on a 76mm gun was forty times the diameter of the bore, or three meters.[1]

The howitzer had a lower muzzle velocity resulting from a smaller powder charge. A shorter barrel was sufficient as the powder burned in less time. A typical howitzer had a 27-caliber barrel. The advantage of the howitzer was that it could be fired with a high trajectory over hills and other obstacles. The plunging shell struck the target from a nearly vertical angle, an advantage when shelling troops in dugout shelters. Gun-howitzers were a compromise and the ammunition was often adjustable. By removing some powder, the muzzle velocity decreased, allowing the gun to function as a howitzer.[2]

A mortar had a barrel of 12 caliber or less. Most mortars were simple tubes supported by a bipod and a base plate firing rounds of 50mm, 82mm, or 120mm. The 240mm mortars were heavy artillery pieces with short barrels. The 160mm mortar was mounted on a carriage with wheels and had a recoil system, but retained the base plate.[3]

The Red Army entered World War II with an excellent arsenal of artillery pieces that were designed or improved in the 1930s. The Russians increased the range, the rate of fire, the accuracy, and the destructive force of all of the artillery during this period. The standard Russian divisional gun of World War I was the M1902, similar to the French 75mm gun of the same vintage. In 1930 the M1902 was modernized, resulting in the MO2/30 and the M10/30. The muzzle velocity increased from 595 meters per second to 680 meters per second and range increased from 8,500 meters to 13,170 meters with a 40-caliber barrel. The weight increased from 1,100 kilograms to 1,350.[4] The standard guns before 1930 and the modernized versions were as follows:[5]

Pre-1930 Model	Modernized Version
76mm gun M1902	76mm gun MO2/30
76mm mountain gun M1909	
122mm howitzer M1909/M1910	122mm howitzer M10/30
107mm gun M1910	107mm gun M10/30
152mm howitzer M1910	152mm howitzer M10/30

By January 1932, the Red Army had 14,000 guns. In addition to the modernized guns listed above, the following guns were in production in 1932:[6]

	Weight (kg)	Muzzle Velocity (m/s)	Shell Weight (kg)
76mm regimental gun M1927	780	387	6.2
37mm antitank gun M1930	406	762	.82
45mm antitank gun M1932	520	762	1.54
76mm antiaircraft gun M1931	3,750	815	6.5
122mm gun Al9 M1931/37	7,117	800	24.9
152mm howitzer M1930	2,580	390	40.0
152mm gun M1910/30	7,100	650	43.6
203mm howitzer Bm (long range) M1931	17,700	606	98.4

The Russians also used a few foreign heavy artillery pieces. In the late 1930s a round of designs produced the following new guns:[7]

	Weight (kg)	Muzzle Velocity (m/s)	Shell Weight (kg)
45mm antitank gun M1937	560	760	1.4
76mm mountain gun M1938	785	495	6.2
76mm division gun M1936 F22	1,620	706	6.4

	Weight (kg)	Muzzle Velocity (m/s)	Shell Weight (kg)
76mm division gun M1939 USV	1,483	676	6.1
76mm antiaircraft gun M1938	4,300	815	6.5
85mm antiaircraft gun M1939	4,330	800	9.2
107mm gun M1940 M60	4,000	737	17.1
122mm gun M1931/37	7,117	800	24.9
122mm howitzer M1938	2,250	500	21.7
152mm howitzer M1938	4,156	510	40.0
152mm gun howitzer M1937 ML20	7,130	655	43.5
152mm gun M1935	17,200	880	49.0
210mm gun M1939	61,610	800	135.0
280mm mortar M1939	17,610	356	286.0
305mm howitzer M1939	62,110	530	330.0

The M1927 76mm gun was the M1913 3-inch short gun with a redesigned carriage, making it more mobile. The weapon was light in weight (780 kilograms) with a short 16.5-caliber barrel. Production began in 1928 and continued through 1944. Rifle regiment camion companies used the gun for close support.[8] The M1936 F22 76mm gun was an entirely new weapon designed primarily as divisional artillery, but with a long barrel (51 calibers) and a high muzzle velocity of 706 meters per second, making it an effective antitank gun. Although it weighed 1,620 kilograms, the carriage was not strong enough to absorb the heavy recoil caused by the high muzzle velocity and the 6.4-kilogram shell.[9] The M1939 USV 76mm gun corrected the problems, reducing the length of the barrel to 42 calibers, the muzzle velocity to 676 meters per second, and the weight to 1,483 kilograms, making it easier to move. The new design strengthened the recoil system and the carriage. The gun was economical to produce and functioned well in combat. The M1939 was the standard field gun of the Russian division in 1941.[10]

In 1940 the M1940 M60 107mm gun was designed to provide the corps artillery with a lightweight long-range piece. However, it fell short of expectations and few were made. The recoil was too strong for the carriage. The 122mm gun replaced the 107mm in the corps artillery.[11] In 1941 the organization of the newly formed antitank brigades called for the M1940 107mm as a heavy antitank gun to equip one regiment in each brigade. As only a few 107mm guns were available, the Russians substituted the 85mm antiaircraft gun as an antitank gun. The Germans did capture a few of the 107mm guns.[12]

The M1931 A19 122mm gun was a heavy piece for use as corps and army artillery. In 1937 the carriage was improved and the new gun was designated the M1931/37. Weighing 7,117 kilograms, it was difficult to move, requiring a separate two-wheel limber to support the trail. The twenty-five-kilogram shell and 20,800-meter range were better than average for medium guns. The long 46-caliber barrel and 800-meter-per-second muzzle velocity made it a potent antitank weapon when mounted on a heavy tank chassis, as the JSU-122.[13]

The M1938 M30 122mm howitzer was the standard divisional medium artillery piece also used in corps and army artillery. The 21.8-kilogram shell was average. The howitzer had a short 22.7 caliber barrel, a low muzzle velocity (515 meters per second), and a range of 11,800 meters.[14] The M1938 M10 152mm howitzer fired a 39.9-kilgoram shell 12,400 meters, but weighed only 4,150 kilograms, compared to 5,500 kilograms for a comparable German howitzer. The 508-meter-per-second muzzle velocity was appropriate for a howitzer.[15]

In 1934 the Russians had developed prototypes looking for a weapon to provide longer range than a howitzer without a radical increase in weight. The result was the M1937 ML20 152mm gun-howitzer that had a long 32 caliber barrel and a moderate muzzle velocity of 655 meters per second. It had a long range—17,300 meters, compared to 12,400 meters for the comparable German howitzer with a muzzle velocity of 432 meters per second. The chief of artillery, G. I. Kulik, appointed in 1937, opposed the howitzer, saying it was neither a gun nor a howitzer. Although the piece was in production, Kulik insisted on new trials. The trials were successful and production resumed. The 43.6-kilogram shell was on the heavy side. The piece was very heavy, 7,130 kilograms, making movement and emplacement difficult, but it was much lighter than the M1935 152mm gun (17,200 kilograms) that it replaced.[16]

The Russians designed an entirely new 203mm howitzer in 1931 to serve as the most common heavy artillery of its class. The piece could be towed either assembled or broken down into two loads that made it more maneuverable than most heavy artillery pieces. The range of 18,000 was not much greater than the 152mm gun-howitzer, but the 98.4-kilogram shell made it a potent barrage weapon.[17]

In 1940–41 the Soviets designed the M1941 ZIS-2 57mm antitank gun to replace the 45mm gun. The gun was superior to the German 50mm antitank gun and equal to the British six-pounder. The new gun penetrated 100mm of armor at 1,000 meters. Production difficulties delayed deliveries in 1941. The large powder charge that produced the high muzzle velocity required a long barrel and a substantial chamber, making it far more difficult to manufacture than the 45mm gun.[18]

To provide some measure of the destructive power of artillery, a 76mm shell created a crater one meter in diameter and half a meter deep; a 122mm shell, three meters in diameter and 0.7 meter deep; and a 152mm shell, five meters in diameter and 1.8 meters deep. Assuming that the average shell made a crater two meterse in diameter, seventy-four guns firing a single round destroyed 231 square meters (1 meter × 3.14 = 3.14 square meters × 74 = 231.1 square meters) of a 1,000-square-meter area.[19] Seven shells from each gun could theoretically destroy the entire target allowing for more than 60 percent overlap of craters (7 × 231 = 1,617 square meters).

After June 1941, the Russians developed new guns to cope with the German tanks. To replace the heavy losses in the first six months of the war, and to build the powerful artillery arm called for by Russian tactics, new guns were needed. New guns and mortars introduced after 1942 were:[20]

	Weight (kg)	Muzzle Velocity (m/s)	Shell Weight (kg)
45mm antitank gun	570	820	1.43
57mm antitank gun ZIS-2	1,150	990	3.14
76mm division gun ZIS-3 M1942	1,115	680	6.2
76mm regimental gun OB-25	600	262	6.2
132mm rocket M20			
300mm rocket M30			
152mm howitzer M1943	3,600	510	39.9
100mm gun BS-3 M1944	3,650	887	15.6

The ZIS-3 76mm gun used the carriage of the MI941 ZIS-2 57mm antitank gun and the barrel of the M1939 76mm gun. Simple tubular legs replaced the box-section riveted trail legs which were difficult to manufacture. The ZIS-3 filled many roles: divisional artillery, antitank gun, and tank gun.[21] The weight decreased from the 1,620 kilograms of the M1936 to 1,116 kilograms, a major improvement. The 42.6-caliber barrel and the 680-meter-per-second muzzle velocity increased the range and made it an excellent antitank gun using armor-piercing shot. With a 6.2-kilogram high-explosive shell, it was an efficient field gun.[22]

In 1943 the M1938 152mm howitzer barrel combined with the carriage of the M1938 122mm howitzer produced the M1943 (D 1) 152mm howitzer, reducing the weight to only 3,600 kilograms but still firing a 39.9-kilogram shell. The barrel (25 calibers), muzzle velocity (508 meters per second), and range (12,400 meters) were similar to the M1938.[23] In 1944 the Soviets developed the BS-3 100mm gun with a 60-caliber barrel and a muzzle velocity of 887 meters per second, making it a powerful antitank gun. The Russians employed the following artillery pieces exclusive of antitank guns in 1944:[24]

TYPE	% in use 1944
76mm gun (M1936, M1939, ZIS-3, M1942, M1938)	48
122mm howitzer (M1909/37, M1938)	31
152mm howitzer (M1909/30, M1938)	8
107mm gun (M1940 M60, M1910/30)	1
122mm gun (M1931, M1931/37)	2
152mm gun-howitzer (M1937)	3
152mm gun (M1934, M1935)	3
203mm howitzer (M1931)	4

Production of artillery before the war was at a high level as new guns replaced older designs and the Red Army increased in size. Additional factories, including the Red Putilov Factory, were constructed in the late 1920s and early 1930s to manufacture artillery. By 1940 six major factories produced artillery: the Boishevik and the Kirov Factories (formerly the Putilov works) in Leningrad, the Stalin Machine Works in Kramatorskaya in the Ukraine, the Kalinin Factory #8 in Mytischtsche near Moscow, the Molotov Factory at Perm, and the Ordzhonikidze Factory at Sverdlovsk. Eleven other factories including one or more in Dnepropetrovsk, Mariupol, Nikolayev, Voroshilovsk, Gorki, Kolomna, Moscow, Stalingrad, Magnitogorsk, and Sverdlovsk also made guns along with 22 smaller plants.[25]

A 1943 list of factories producing artillery included most of the above excluding those in occupied territory.[26] The Permsk Machine Factory made 45mm antitank guns, M1938 76mm regimental guns, 122mm guns, and 152mm gun-howitzers also used on the SU-152 and JSU-152. During the war the factory provided artillery for 116 artillery regiments.[27] Factory #183 at Nishnij-Tagil made 250 to 300 76mm guns per month in 1944.[28]

By early 1943 the Russians were manufacturing large numbers of guns and mortars sufficient to replace losses and to equip new units. However, artillery was of no value if there were no shells. During World War I, the armies on the Western Front had used prodigious amounts of shells in barrages that lasted for days. The barrage doctrine carried over from that war to 1939, and large stocks of shells had been accumulated by the major powers before war began. The extreme shortage of shells that marked the beginning of World War I was not repeated. The quick campaigns from 1939 to April 1941 required smaller amounts of munitions, but the Russo-German conflict brought back the era of massive bombardments.

As early as November 1942 the Don Front fired over 180,000 shells in twelve days during the opening phase of the Stalingrad offensive.[29] Later offensives used many more. In 1941 the Russians had considerable capacity for shell production. The German estimate made in January 1941 included fifty shell-producing factories with monthly production as follows:[30]

25mm to 57mm	3,600,000 rounds
76mm to 107mm	700,000 rounds
152mm to 203mm	115,000 rounds
240mm to 406mm	20,000 rounds

Most of the factories were located in the west, seventeen in Leningrad alone. The German occupation severely disrupted production as well, capturing large stocks. Evacuation of factories to the east produced a good supply of shells by early 1942.

Most armies, including the Red Army, had established a unit of fire for each weapon. The unit of fire was a measurement of the number of rounds that might be fired in a given period, perhaps in a few hours in a barrage. The heavier the gun, the fewer rounds that would be fired. In August 1943 the 32nd Guard Rifle Corps artillery fired a 185-minute barrage preceding an attack during which the guns fired between 0.9 and 1.1 units of fire.[31] Another quantity was the "first munitions issue," which specified the number of rounds carried with the gun and in the unit supply column. This number often exceeded a unit of fire. The units of fire for Soviet artillery and the first munitions issue were:[32]

	Unit of Fire (rounds)	First Munition Issue (rounds)
82mm mortar	60	120
120mm mortar	120	40–80
76mm gun	60	140
122mm howitzer	40	80
152mm howitzer	30	40–60
152mm gun	60–80	
203mm howitzer	30–40	

In preparation for the Stalingrad offensive, the Russians accumulated from two to four units of fire. The heavy artillery units carried their supply, while about half the divisional artillery supply was held in army artillery depots. The expenditure rate (in units) was calculated as follows for a weapon with two units of fire:[33]

First day	.75
Second day	.50
Third day	.12
Fourth day	.12
Fifth day	.12
Battle in depth	.37

The actual consumption of ammunition by the three armies of the Don Front from November 19 to November 30, 1942, was huge.[34]

82mm mortar (1,704 mortars)	185,390
120mm mortar (423 mortars)	29,565
45mm gun	68,784
76min regiment gun	27,556
76mm division gun	119,220
122mm howitzer	23,472
152mm howitzer	8,957

These totals were equal to 1.2 to 1.7 units of fire—much less than the two or three units in the plan. The Russians normally used a half-unit of fire per day in quiet sectors. An artillery regiment carried about two units of fire. Of the 140 rounds carried for the 76mm gun, 16 were with the gun, 24 in the battery reserve, 88 in the battalion reserve, 28 at the regimental level, and 70 at the division and corps level.[35]

The Soviets made a heavy buildup of munitions supplies for the counteroffensive at Kursk in July 1943. The 8th Guards Corps had 1.5 to 3.5 units of fire for each weapon and the 3rd Artillery Division supporting the corps had 2.7 units of fire. In the barrage that lasted about one and a half hours, the 82mm mortars fired nearly three units (165 rounds); the 120mm mortars, nearly one unit (110); the 76mm guns, nearly three (165); the 122mm howitzers, nearly four (110); and the 152mm howitzers, nearly three (82). The result was an intense barrage that crushed the German defenses.[36] For another attack a year later in June 1944, three rifle divisions had from 3.2 to 3.5 units of fire for their artillery regiments.[37]

However, this supply was for the initial period of the attack and would not have been expended on the first day.

Although the Red Army fired enormous amounts of ammunition in preparation for an attack, daily use in periods of inactivity was much less. On quiet sectors the Russians fired far less than the Germans even as late as the fall of 1944.[38] Building up munitions supplies for an offensive was a limiting factor in the Soviet offensive pattern, and there may have been a chronic shortage of shells. In a study of shell usage in November 1944, the Germans found that the Red Army had fired an average of two rounds per day from 13,000 guns while the Germans on the Eastern Front fired nine rounds per day from 4,800 guns, using nearly twice as many shells over the ten-day period. On the Western Front, the Germans fired twenty rounds per day from 2,000 guns, while the Allies fired twenty-eight rounds from 3,500 guns. The Germans had used about the same number of shells on each front, but the Allies fired four times as many shells as the Russians and fourteen times as many shells per gun.[39] The Allies, especially the Americans, used enormous quantities of shells daily. The Russians used their guns sparingly except during an attack.

Most of the Russian firing was done by the lighter guns. In 1945 the 3rd Ukrainian Front received 120 carloads of artillery ammunition each day, as follows:

45mm	5%
76mm	65%
122mm	8%
152mm	7%
Rockets	15%

The need for antitank fire was probably the reason for the disproportionate share of light gun ammunition.[40] Another factor was wear on the barrels. The life of a 152mm gun was 800 rounds, while that of a 122mm howitzer was 8,000 rounds. The heavier the gun, the fewer rounds fired before the barrel wore and its range and accuracy deteriorated.[41]

The Soviet rifle division received an average of seventy-six tons of munitions per day in 1943—much less than the 180 tons allocated to a U.S. division slice during normal combat.[42] The Russians tended to conserve on artillery during quiet periods and accumulate stocks of shells for offensives. Most of the Soviet artillery was at the corps, army, front, and Stavka level so that comparison was difficult.

By late 1942 the Red Army had ample stocks of shells to break through the German defenses. Using the Stavka artillery divisions, the Russian high command selected areas to break through at will, and the only limiting factor was the distance the spearheads moved from the rail heads. The quality and quantity of the guns and mortars had improved substantially since the beginning of the war. The only new gun issued in 1944 and 1945 was the 100mm antitank gun. The Red Army had the tools and the munitions in early 1943. The remainder of the war was a matter of carrying out programs overwhelming the German defenses with earth shaking barrages.

Soviet artillery doctrine had matured by early 1943 and munitions supply was adequate to carry out assigned missions. The remainder of the war was a matter of carrying out the program and driving the Germans back in a series of bounds limited more by logistics than any other factor.

CHAPTER 13

The Tank Destroyers

How to stop tanks was one of the most controversial issues of World War II. All nations agreed that a gun was the best method, whether self-propelled, towed, or mounted on a tank. A brief survey of the anti-tank doctrine of the major powers before the war is illuminating. British doctrine was that another tank was the best way to stop a tank. Other nations relied on the towed antitank gun, mines, direct fire by artillery, and indirect fire. During the war the self-propelled tank destroyer was developed, providing a heavier gun than could be carried by a tank of the same weight.

Although military writers disparaged French prewar doctrine because of its failure against the Germans in 1940, the French ideas deserve more careful analysis. They strongly believed that the best defense was the anti-tank gun. The French believed that the tank killing zone should be in front of the main line of resistance (MLR) and placed the antitank gun line at the forward edge of the line. Two additional gun lines were located farther back in the MLR. By dispersing the guns in three lines, all were necessarily weak in view of the limited number of guns available.[1] The major fault in the execution of the doctrine was the poor quality of French antitank guns. The 25mm gun did not have the power, and a new 47mm gun issued in 1939 was scarce. The French used the M1897 75mm field gun as an antitank gun, but it had a low initial muzzle velocity. All three were horse-drawn and too heavy to be easily manhandled. Once an attack began, the guns could not be moved.[2]

U.S. doctrine in the late 1930s followed the French, in that the anti-tank gun was the best defense. General Leslie McNair rejected the idea of the tank's being the best tank destroyer. He believed that the French fail-ure in 1940 was the result of several problems: too few guns, guns with inadequate force, and poor organization. Lacking a good antitank gun, the U.S. army copied the German 37mm gun in 1939.[3] In 1941 there was a reversal in U.S. doctrine. Tank destroyer battalions were formed to seek and destroy enemy tanks. Towed 37mm guns and modernized 75mm guns were the basic weapons, but the doctrine also advocated the use of medium tanks in the tank destroyer role.[4] After North Africa, the Americans invested heavily in self-propelled tank destroyers.

The German doctrine before the war placed great stress on the antitank gun. The Germans developed the 37mm antitank gun which was adequate to deal with most Western tanks in 1940. The Germans used the 88mm antiaircraft gun and field artillery to stop the heavily armored British Matilda. The heavier armor on Russian T-34s and KVs could not be pierced by the German 37mm gun. When the Russians mounted tank attacks with the T-34 in the winter of 1941–42, the Germans experienced severe problems. German defense on the Russian Front in World War II centered on the main line of resistance. Most of the antitank guns were placed behind the HKL to engage any tanks that penetrated into the HKL.[5]

In the 1930s Russian antitank doctrine considered the antitank gun the primary defense. Artillery, natural obstacles, minefields, ditches, and other man made obstacles were secondary. The Russians did not believe in the tank versus tank doctrine unless the conditions were extremely favorable. The 1937 *Artillery Field Manual* emphasized that direct fire by antitank guns was the best method to destroy tanks. The manual suggested a density of six to nine guns per km in a zone two to three kilometers in depth. That estimate proved far short in practice.[6] The Russians determined the number of guns using an equation based on the rate of fire of the antitank guns as well as on the speed of the tanks and other factors. These factors influenced the choice of guns and organization in the Russian antitank defense system.

The effectiveness of an antitank gun was difficult to judge. The purpose of the gun was to penetrate armor, which could be achieved in several ways: by a high-velocity armor-piercing projectile, by a tungsten core shell, or by a shaped charge. The development of the latter two shells improved the performance of antitank guns later in the war.[7]

The high-velocity gun was the mainstay of the Russian defense. Higher velocity, not a heavier projectile, improved penetration. To increase the muzzle velocity of a gun of a given caliber, the designer had to increase the amount of the powder. Increasing the powder required several changes: a larger casing, a larger chamber to fit the larger round, a longer barrel to give the powder time to burn, and a heavier carriage or a more efficient recoil mechanism to absorb the increased recoil. However, all of these changes increased the weight of the gun. A gun weighing over a ton was difficult to move with manpower. The M1937 45mm weighed 560 kg; the M1939 76mm gun weighed 1.48 tons. At 1.25 tons the M1943 57mm gun could still be moved by hand, but with difficulty.[8]

The Russians compared the efficiency of antitank guns according to the number of tanks destroyed.

ENEMY TANKS DESTROYED BY ONE GUN

Antitank Gun	Tanks Destroyed
57mm	3
76mm	2.5
122mm	2
45mm	0.25

Obviously the 57mm was the most effective weapon, and the 45mm was comparatively ineffectual. However, there were many more 45mm guns and they did have a deterrent effect.[9]

In 1930 the Russians copied the German 37mm antitank gun, effective against the thirty to forty millimeters of armor on the existing light tanks. In 1932 the Russians scaled up the gun to 45mm, producing a gun that could pierce forty-two millimeters of armor at 500 meters. Experience in Spain showed the superiority of the 45mm gun against the Mk I German tank.[10] The Russians manufactured 12,200 45mm guns from 1937 to 1940. In June 1941, the Red Army had 14,500 antitank guns and production reached 2,000 per month in 1942.[11]

By 1941 heavier tanks had made the standard Russian 45mm gun marginal. In the same year the Russians scaled up the 45mm to produce the 57mm M1941, which had a muzzle velocity of 990 meters per second and fired a 3.17-kilogram shell. The shell penetrated 100 millimeters of armor at 500 meters.[12] The 57mm gun made the antitank gun line twice as effective with the same number of guns. The new gun doubled the effective range and maintained a high rate of fire because of the light-weight shell. However, production (1,900 in 1943, 2,300 in 1944, and 800 in 1945) never caught up with demand and the 45mm remained in use.[13]

A gun of 76mm was the heaviest one that could be manhandled. In 1936 the Russian designers increased the size of the 76mm powder charge and the length of the barrel. The Model 1936 76mm gun had a high muzzle velocity (706 meters per second) that improved its armor-piercing performance, but the recoil was too heavy for the carriage. The Model 1939 USV 76mm gun became the standard division artillery piece and also the best antitank gun. The gun had a muzzle velocity of 676 meters per second and fired a 6.1-kilogram shell. The armor-piercing shell pierced seventy millimeters of armor at 500 meters.[14]

The Russians tried the 107mm gun that had a satisfactory muzzle
velocity and the shell weight, but the gun was too heavy for the carriage.
In the early months of the war, Russian antitank guns were spread evenly
over the front in a thin defensive zone, six to nine guns per kilometer in
a depth of two or three kilometers.[15] There were too few guns at any
point to stop a German panzer attack. The shortage of guns was partly
responsible, but a doctrine of spreading the guns out at the front rather
than concentrating them in large numbers at likely points also was faulty.

In reaction to the threat posed by massed panzer attacks, the Russians had formed independent antitank brigades. On April 24, 1941, ten
antitank brigades were formed with two regiments each with twenty-four
76mm guns, a battalion with twelve 107mm guns, two battalions with
twelve 85mm guns, an antiaircraft battalion of eight 37mm guns and
thirty-six machine guns, and an engineer mine-laying battalion. The ten
antitank brigades were assigned to the three border military districts in
June 1941. The antitank brigade provided an antitank gun line for five or
six kilometers of front with from twenty to twenty-five guns per kilometer,
three to four times the density achieved by spreading out the guns evenly.
Theoretically each brigade could defend against an attack by one or two
panzer divisions with one gun for each two or three tanks.[16]

The Russians hastened to form new antitank units after the initial
German attack. In August 1941, thirty new antitank regiments were
formed each with sixteen to twenty guns, and an additional forty-two
regiments were formed in the fall. The regiments included 770 37mm
and 85mm antiaircraft guns in place of the scarce antitank guns.[17] When
supplies of guns improved in April 1942, twenty-five new destroyer
brigades were formed with an antitank regiment with three batteries of
45mm guns and four batteries of 76mm guns (a total of twelve 45mm
guns and sixteen 76mm guns), two antitank rifle battalions, a mortar battalion, and an engineer company or battalion[18]

In May 1942 five antitank divisions were formed each with three
destroyer brigades, having a total of forty-eight 76mm guns and thirty-six
45mm guns, about equal to the prewar antitank brigades.[19] The divisions
were short-lived and the destroyer brigades were gradually eliminated
as well. In the summer of 1942 the Red Army formed tank destroyer
brigades, some by reforming the destroyer brigades. The new brigades
consisted of two regiments with twenty-four 76mm guns and a third regiment with either twenty-four 45mm or 57mm guns, a total of forty-eight
76mm guns and twenty-four light caliber guns, almost equal in strength
to the antitank divisions and the prewar antitank brigades.[20] By the end
of 1942 the Red Army had enough tank destroyer units to create antitank

gun lines (referred to as PaK fronts by the Germans, panzer and kanone) where needed. New tank destroyer regiments either independently or in brigades were assigned to the armies in substantial numbers.[21]

The defeats of early 1943 and the appearance of the Tiger tank in November 1942 called for major improvements in the Red Army antitank forces. The Russians created many new tank destroyer regiments and brigades. By the end of 1943 there were more than fifty tank destroyer brigades and twenty-one independent regiments, plus many more regiments assigned to armies and corps, a total of 289 regiments with 6,700 guns.[22] In December 1943 the organization of the tank destroyer regiments was increased to six batteries with a total of twenty-four guns. The tank destroyer brigade then had seventy-two guns, usually twenty-four 45mm guns and forty-eight 76mm guns. Some brigades received a regiment of SU-76s besides the three towed regiments.[23]

Imported American trucks improved the flexibility of the tank destroyer regiments. Regiments using American trucks were completely mobile with the guns towed at high speed on paved roads and then directly into positions cross country, using the six-wheel drive of the American trucks.[24] The mobility provided by the American trucks was essential. During the war two-thirds of the German tank losses resulted from the direct fire of antitank guns and artillery. This achievement resulted from several improvements in policy: massing antitank forces in the decisive sectors, increasing the depth of antitank defense, increasing the activity of each antitank gun, and integrating all of the arms into a single battle formation.[25]

The tank destroyers were effective. At Kursk the artillery accounted for 1,900 tanks of the 3,000 destroyed, according to Soviet sources. The importance the Red Army placed on towed tank destroyers was indicated by the division of the available 76mm guns and 100mm guns. By the end of the war, 73 percent of the artillery regiments were primarily antitank, compared to 27 percent whose primary function was divisional artillery. For each divisional artillery regiment, there were about three antitank regiments.[26]

In 1944 the increasing number of Panthers and Tigers and improved Mk IV tanks called for better antitank guns. A mechanized artillery regiment with SU-85s was added to some tank destroyer brigades in 1944.[27] In May 1944 the 100mm antitank gun was developed, firing a 15.8-kilogram shell with a muzzle velocity of 887 m/s, giving it the ability to penetrate 160 millimeters of armor at 500 meters with a shell heavy enough to ensure destruction of the target. In August 1944 a regiment of 100mm guns substituted for the 57mm gun regiment in the tank destroyer brigades.[28] On January 1, 1945, there were 59 tank destroyer brigades and a total of 350 tank destroyer regiments with an authorized strength of 8,400 guns.[29] During the last four months of the war, the number of tank destroyer regiments continued to increase. The guns were upgraded. The Model 1937 45mm gun was seldom seen as supplies of the 57mm gun improved.

After July 1943 the Russians were on the offensive for the rest of the war. Although the towed antitank gun was a powerful asset to the defense and useful in offense, it presented difficulties during offensive operations. Hooking the gun to its towing vehicle, moving it forward over rough terrain, unhooking, and bringing the gun into position was time-consuming. The most effective form of tank destroyer in offensive situations was the self-propelled gun. The Russians formed nearly equal numbers of regiments of towed and self-propelled tank destroyers. Both types of regiments had multiple roles, fighting tanks and supporting the infantry either with direct or indirect fire. The Red Army made a greater investment in self-propelled artillery than any other army in World War II. The Russian SU-76 was opened topped, lightly armored, and had no turret. The heavier SUs had heavy armor and closed tops. All were used as assault guns, mobile antitank guns, and substitute tanks.

The Germans, Americans, and Russians had differing doctrines for the use of self-propelled artillery. In addition, economic factors created differences that obscured the basic propose of mounting an artillery piece on a tracked chassis. The Germans in 1940 had placed 75mm guns on light tank chassis as self-propelled artillery to accompany the infantry in attack. Others were used to provide direct fire support to the panzer divisions. The Americans began with towed 76mm pack howitzers in the regimental cannon company, then tried 105nun howitzers with short barrels, and finally gave the cannon companies 105rnm howitzers mounted on surplus Grant tank chassis. This design had been developed to provide the armored divisions with mobile artillery, but was not successful as a close support gun.

The Russians developed the SU ZIS-30 with a 57mm antitank gun to supplement antitank defense. The few used at Moscow in August 1941 were not successful.[30] The Russians realized the need for a mobile 76mm gun, both as an infantry support gun and as a tank destroyer. The answer was the SU-76, a 76mm gun on a light tank chassis. The 76mm gun outranged the German 50mm antitank gun and was equal to the 75mm antitank gun. Therefore, the SU-76 could fire on the antitank guns before or at the same time as the antitank guns could fire on it. In July 1942 the Russians had developed three models: the SU-76 (a 76mm gun on a T-60 or T-70 chassis), the SU-122 (a 122mm howitzer on the chassis of a captured German Mk III), and the AA SU-37 (a 37mm antiaircraft gun on a T-60 chassis).[31]

According to the doctrine for mechanized artillery, the guns were to work with tank units, providing direct fire at crucial points and protection for the flanks of a breakthrough. A second function was to escort the infantry. In the second role the guns would destroy machine guns, antitank guns, and enemy tanks, all through direct fire. The only use of indirect fire would be in a defensive situation when the SUs would supplement the artillery supporting the infantry.[32]

The SU-76 was best at providing escort artillery fire. It was not successful in the tank role, as the open top invited grenades and machine gun fire. The armor was thin and the SU had no machine gun. Therefore, it could not drive infantry out of trenches without riflemen for protection, but could destroy bunkers and machine gun nests, making it easier for the infantry to mop up. In the escort role, the SU was especially useful in breaking through the German antitank gun line.

In December 1942, the first mechanized artillery regiments were formed. By the end of December 1942, thirty SU regiments using the SU-76, the AA SU-37, and the SU-122 (now using a T-34 chassis) were authorized.[33] The regiments had four batteries of SU-76s and two batteries of SU-122s, with a total of seventeen SU-76s and eight SU-122s.[34] One or two regiments saw action on the Volkhov Front in January 1943 and two others on the Western Front in March 1943.[35] The mixture of two types of SU in the same regiment was a failure. The two chassis had differing capabilities in moving over rough terrain, and the guns were not appropriate for the same targets. A heavy regiment was also authorized in January 1943 consisting of a KV tank as a command vehicle and six batteries of two SU-152s.[36]

In April 1943, two types of regiments were established: the light regiment with twenty-one SU-76s and the medium regiment with sixteen SU-122s. The table of organization of the medium regiments in March 1943 included four batteries each with four SU-122s and one T-34. The command platoon had a T-34 and six armored cars. In addition there were five personnel carriers, thirty-eight trucks, and four motorcycles. The strength of the regiment was 250 men, five T-34s, and sixteen SU-122s.[37]

The Moscow Military District became the center for the creation of mechanized artillery units. The regiments were formed in two weeks, and five or six mechanized artillery regiments were formed every month during 1943.[38] By July 1943, fifty-three mechanized artillery regiments had been formed. With foreknowledge that the Nazis would attack at Kursk, all available mechanized artillery regiments were sent to that area. The Germans identified twenty-two regiments at Kursk.

At Kursk most of the SU regiments were attached to tank and mechanized corps to provide direct fire support and antitank defense. Others were used with the infantry in the same roles. The SUs were used in four ways: to provide direct support for tank attacks; to establish an antitank gun line behind tanks; to attack strong points, machine gun nests, antitank guns, and tanks; and to provide indirect fire for the infantry in defense.[39]

The Red Army concentrated on a few types. The SU-76 was made by the thousands until the end of the war with slight modifications. Of the 23,000 SUs manufactured, 14,000 were light SUs (with either 76mm or 57mm guns), 4,000 were mediums (with 85mm or 100mm guns or 122mm howitzers), and 5,000 were heavy (with 122mm and 152mm guns).[40]

SU-76 production began in December 1942 in the factories at Gorki and Kirov that had previously produced the T-70 light tank. The SU-76 was based on the T-70 chassis and was easy to manufacture. Production of the T-70 continued for a time, but was soon halted to devote all of the capacity to the SU-76.[41]

The SU-76 mounted the Model 1939 76mm having a comparatively high velocity, which made it satisfactory for all three roles—infantry support, antitank defense, and indirect fire.

The SU-122 with the 122mm howitzer was developed in late 1942 using the T-34 chassis. The SU-122 had the M30 M1938 howitzer with a muzzle velocity of 500 meters per second.[42] The heavy weight of the 21.7-kilogram shell quickly reduced the velocity (and the ability to penetrate armor) and made the gun a poor antitank weapon except at short ranges.[43] Unless a projectile had a high velocity at the point of impact and penetrated the armor, little damage was done to a tank.

In 1943 the SU-85 and an SU-152 were developed to counter the German Tiger tanks. Production of the SU-152 began in March 1943 using an ML-20 (Model 1937) 152mm gun-howitzer on a KV-1S chassis.[44] The ML-20 fired a 43.6-kilogram shell with a muzzle velocity of 655 meters per second. At short range the projectile delivered a powerful blow to even the heaviest tank.[45] Heavy mechanized artillery regiments with twelve SU-152s, three T-34s, and nine armored cars were formed in May 1943.[46] By July 1943 the table of organization of the heavy regiment called for twenty-one SU152s.[47] However, the KV chassis was being replaced by the JS in 1943 and few of the SU152s were made.[48]

The SU-85 tank destroyer, developed late in 1943, mounted a D-5S antiaircraft gun on a T-34 chassis. The gun had a muzzle velocity of 880 meters per second that was maintained for a greater distance because of the lighter weight of the shell. The 85mm gun performed much better in penetrating armor at long range than did the 122mm howitzer.[49] Beginning in August 1943, the SU-85 appeared in mechanized artillery regiments with four batteries, each with four SU-85s.[50]

By November 1943 the original SU-122 with the howitzer was halted.[51] Production of the SU-85 was halted in June 1944 because the same gun was then available on the fully armored T-34/85.[52] The increasing number of Panthers and Tigers in 1944 led to the development of more powerful guns. The new SUs were designed primarily as antitank weapons, the other roles being left to the SU-76s, which continued to come off the assembly lines in increasing numbers.

In 1944 the 100mm antitank gun was mounted on a T-34 chassis to make the SU-100.[53] The SU-100 used a D-10S (antiaircraft designation) or BS-3 (antitank gun) 100mm gun on a T-34 chassis. The BS-3 had a muzzle velocity of 900 meters per second—slightly greater than the 85mm—and fired a 15.6-kilogram shell—much heavier than the 85mm. The 100mm gun pierced 150 millimeters of armor at 1000 meters. powerful enough to destroy any German tank at a range beyond the reach of the German tank gun.[54] The production of the SU-100 was under way at Sverdlovsk in September 1944. The heavy Guard mechanized artillery brigade was equipped with sixty-five SU-100s.[55]

A new JSU-122 using an A-19 Model 31/37 122mm gun on a JS chassis was also developed in 1944. Production began in August 1944 at Chelyabinsk. The A-19 gun was far more powerful than the howitzer used on the SU-122 in 1942 and 1943. The A-19 gun had a muzzle velocity of 800 meters per second compared to only 515 meters per second for the howitzer. The shell was also heavier (25 kilograms compared to 21.8 kilograms). Production was limited: only eight were made in August and seven in September 1944.[56]

The JSU-152 was developed with the Model 1937 ML-20 gun-howitzer similar to the SU-152, but mounted on a JS chassis. The same gun was merely transferred to an improved chassis. The characteristics of the gun remained the same. The change was necessary because production of the KV chassis a: Chelyabinsk was terminated.[57] The JSU-152 and JSU-122 were used by the heavy mechanized artillery regiments until the end of the war.[58]

During 1944 there was a rapid increase in the number of mechanized artillery regiments—twenty-five to thirty were being formed every month in the Moscow District. Every tank and mechanized corps eventually received a light, a medium, and a heavy regiment. Some regiments were reorganized from towed 45mm and 76mm guns to mechanized artillery without change of number. Other regiments were formed using as cadres the headquarters and service components of tank units. The old regiments gave all of their weapons to others at the front and were sent to the Moscow Military District where they received new SUs complete with crews from schools. Other regiments were formed from experienced cadres and new crews. Fremde Heer Ost believed that the mechanized artillery regiments were using the numbers of abolished regiments to confuse the Germans and possibly to reward the new regiments with a tradition and a regimental banner. The Red Army highly valued unit tradition, which may have been the key, rather than the use of cadres drawn from the older regiment.[59]

In the summer of 1944, the Red Army had three types of mechanized artillery regiments: the light regiment with five batteries of four SU-76s plus a command SU-76, an armored car, and forty trucks; the medium regiment with four batteries of four SU-85s, a command T-34, and forty-three trucks; and the heavy regiment with six batteries of two SU-152s, a command tank, an armored car, and forty-five trucks.

The supply of SU-76s had become so plentiful in 1944 that each regiment was given an additional battery of four vehicles. In May a battalion of SU-76s was assigned to some of the Guard rifle divisions and some regular rifle divisions.[60] In late 1944 each tank and mechanized corps had three SU regiments, each with twenty-one vehicles, a total of sixty-three SUs. The cavalry corps had forty-two, one regiment of SU-76s in the light artillery brigade and an independent SU-85 regiment.[61] The rifle corps received a single SU regiment in 1944.[62] In 1945 the light mechanized artillery regiments had twenty-one SU-76s; the medium regiments, sixteen SU-100s or SU-85s; and the heavy regiments, either sixteen JSU-122s or twelve JSU-152s.[63]

The light mechanized artillery brigades with sixty-three vehicles were assigned to tank armies in 1943.[64] The medium brigades formed in late 1944 used the SU-100 and possibly some remaining SU-85s. The single heavy brigade formed in December 1944 had the JSU-152.[65] The mechanized artillery brigades were used almost exclusively in the antitank role. Employed together in a hull-down position on a reverse slope, it would have been a chilling experience to a panzer regiment commander to mount the brow of a hill and suddenly encounter sixty SUs. The lack of a turret meant there was ample room for a large supply of shells and space for the gunners and loaders to work quickly.

Including the units in the Mechanized Artillery and Tank Destroyer brigades and the battalions in the rifle divisions, the Red Army probably had the equivalent of over 300 mechanized artillery regiments at the end of the war with about 7,000 SUs.[66] By April 1945 the Red Army had 241 independent regiments, 119 regiments with SU-76s, 69 medium regiments with SU-85s and SU-100s, and 53 heavy regiments with JSU-122s and JSU-152s. In addition the Red Army had seven light mechanized artillery brigades with SU-57s or SU-76s, four medium brigades with SU-85s, and one heavy brigade with SU-152s. All of the brigades had three battalions with a total of sixty to sixty-five SUs.[67]

In January 1945 the German Army had about 12,000 tanks and assault guns dispersed on three fronts and in noncombat formations. Probably fewer than 10,000 were on the Eastern Front. Facing these vehicles were over 7,000 SUs and over 8,000 antitank guns. Little wonder that German losses in January 1945 alone were 1,375 tanks and assault guns.

By July 1943 the Red Army had developed a powerful balanced antitank force with an effective doctrine. As German tank armor increased in thickness in 1944, the Russians produced heavier guns. With its overwhelming antitank forces, the Red Army no longer feared German tank-supported counterattacks that had turned victory into defeat in 1942 and the spring of 1943. The result was far-ranging advances and rapid conquest of enemy held territory by the Red Army from July 1943 to the end of the war.

Conclusion

By early 1943 the Red Army could defeat the Wermacht without military assistance, but to do so required enormous quantities of advanced weapons and an army of at least 5 million men. The cost in lives would run in the millions. The Americans and especially the British feared heavy casualties. Public opinion in both countries would have balked at a war dragging on for years with millions of casualties. It took a concerted effort by the British and Americans to overcome about a hundred German divisions from 1943 to 1945 after the Germans had been defeated on the Eastern Front.

The question of whether the Russians needed a second front in 1943 is a sequel to the thesis that launching an attack in France was not only possible in 1943 but advantageous to the West, presented in *Second Front Now 1943* (published in 1981). The second front was not essential to the Soviets after early 1943. According to one Soviet historian, "After this [the Battle of Stalingrad] nobody could any longer doubt the ability of the Soviet Army to crush Nazi Germany singlehandedly."[1]

Although the Russians still needed economic assistance from the West after 1943, the military position had shifted to favor the Russians. Incompetent military leaders had been replaced with new young dynamic men. The commissars no longer had dual command; their role was mainly political indoctrination of the troops. The Red Army had developed effective tactics and was superior in numbers to the Germany Army in both weapons and men. The Germans had retained an edge in technical skill and mobility, as demonstrated by Manstein's victories in February 1943, but they lost the initiative at the Battle of Kursk.[2]

It is likely that Stalin did not want a second front in 1943, at least not in France. He feared that U.S. and British forces would not only sweep aside the weak German forces and occupy most of Germany but perhaps even parts of Poland, while the Russians were still fighting east of the Dnieper River. Because he was aware of the political risk of an early collapse of the Germans in the west in 1943, he supported the diversions to Sicily and Italy. Soviet writers believed that the Americans and British

205

launched the second front only after the Red Army had crossed the Soviet border "and it became quite obvious that the Soviet troops would crush Germany without a second front being opened."[3] In other words, the West waited until the Russians had defeated the German army.

In general, most Russians (as opposed to Stalin and his inner circle) would have welcomed the assistance of the West through a second front at any time to reduce casualties. The Soviet interpretation in the 1970s was that the second front, when it came "belatedly," did indeed contribute to "hastening the final defeat of the fascist bloc."[4] During the war the Soviets praised lend-lease and were angry when deliveries by way of Murmansk were interrupted in the crucial phase from June 1942 to mid-1943. However, after the war the Russian interpretation changed. In denigrating the value of lend-lease one author stated that it "did not contribute substantially to the growth of the USSR's military and economic potential during the war."[5]

The threat of an Allied second front was of value to the Russians in 1942 because the uncertainty tied down thirty to forty German divisions in France while the debate went on among Allied leaders. Hitler strengthened the defenses of the French seaports after the Dieppe raid in 1942. However, when Hitler learned of the Casablanca decision in January 1943 not to land that year, he immediately transferred dozens of divisions from France to Russia, his last strategic reserve, to restore the German position after Stalingrad and the withdrawal from the Caucasus. Manstein then had the troops needed to repulse the Soviet offensives in February and March. Although Manstein used these divisions to drive back the Soviet spearheads, by April 1943 the Soviets had achieved a degree of superiority that left no doubt about the outcome on the Eastern Front. A Soviet victory was assured even without a second front. In July the German army was defeated at Kursk, even though the Allied invasion was a year away. The war was lost for Germany on the Eastern Front.

The keys to Soviet success were effective organization of their manpower and production of superior numbers of practical weapons. The period from 1918 to 1941 marked the development of doctrine and organization that were implemented in the mobilization in 1941. The mobilization was an outstanding accomplishment. Regardless of anecdotes of cavalry without saddles and many other shortages, the new divisions went into the field and halted the German Army in December 1941. In 1941–42, the emphasis was on replacing the rifle formations destroyed by the Germans and mobilizing new divisions. Few of the Soviet divisions formed after June 1941 had more than six months training before entering combat. General George Marshall was ridiculed by the British for claiming that a hundred U.S. divisions could be created in less than eighteen months after Pearl Harbor and trained well enough to take on the Germans in 1943. The Russians created over 400 divisions in far less time that did defeat the Germans with a far smaller industrial base and far lower educational levels.

Most Russian divisions were created in the second half of 1941 and the first six months of 1942 to conclude the mobilization scheme and to replace destroyed divisions. The divisions destroyed by the Germans were replaced with new divisions bearing the old numbers. By late 1942 the mobilization of the Red Army was complete. The Soviets drafted enough recruits from 1943 on to maintain the army on the German Front at more than 6 million men. The number of rifle divisions remained at about the same level for the remainder of the war, although they were reduced in strength to make maximum use of manpower in supporting units. As the number of riflemen declined, the number of heavy weapons and machine pistols increased. More and more men were added to the artillery and tank forces. In the last year of the war the service element was increased to cope with the lengthening supply lines.

All of the manpower policies were functioning effectively by early 1943, providing the Red Army with a superior number of well-trained and adequately equipped formations. Despite heavy losses to the well-entrenched Germans, the Russians were able to sustain their units with a steady stream of replacements to maintain combat effectiveness. The mobilization system established training camps throughout the Soviet Union. The drafting organization produced and trained an annual class of 2 million or more eighteen-year-olds as well as returning the wounded to service and picking up men in the liberated territory. Rather than having exhausted the available manpower in 1945, the Russians diverted men to serving heavy weapons and tanks and even returned some to civilian life.

The armored forces were paramount on the Eastern Front. The Soviet tank organizations were developed over a long period from 1918 to 1941 while new tanks were designed and produced both before and during the war. From the end of 1941 through 1942 an intense effort rebuilt the tank force, first with light tanks from the automotive factories and then medium and heavy tanks from the former tractor factories. Production reached 2,000 per month in late 1942 and then leveled off. The evolution of Soviet tank units during the first two years of the war and the creation of an effective replacement and training system resulted in an armored force superior in numbers and quality to the German Army in early 1943.

The Red Army relied on artillery to overcome the German defenses. During the 1930s major improvements had been made in the weapons and organization of the artillery. During 1942 the artillery arm began its steady expansion. The overwhelming superiority of the Red Army artillery was manifest by early 1943. The tank destroyer force had increased sharply from mid-1942 and leveled off by mid-1943. The self-propelled artillery regiments that performed two roles—close support artillery fire and antitank defense—began slowly at the end of 1942, had a spurt in early 1943 in preparation for Kursk, and had a major expansion in 1944 and 1945 when the bulk of new regiments formed were mechanized artillery.

Many Western writers believed that the Germans were defeated by massed attacks of poorly equipped riflemen. In 1941, and to a lesser degree in 1942, the Red Army actually relied on superior manpower to counter German skill and equipment. The change in emphasis in late 1942 and early 1943 from rifle divisions to tanks, artillery, and self-propelled guns has been underestimated. In 1943 Soviet doctrine changed. Firepower, rather than manpower, was called on to win battles. The number of weapons in the rifle division increased as the number of riflemen decreased. Manpower was diverted into hundreds of new artillery, self-propelled artillery, and tank regiments. The number of guns and tanks assigned to units was increased. Although the number of men at the front remained somewhat constant, the number of weapons increased dramatically. More men were serving heavy weapons and fewer were assigned to rifle companies. At the end of the war one-sixth of the Russians on the Eastern Front were in artillery units.

Furthermore, the Soviets did not have unlimited manpower. Although there were 200 million Soviet citizens versus only 80 million Germans, the Germans had the assistance of allied European nations, whereas the Soviet Union lost 60 million people to German occupation in the first six months of the war. Germany was extremely wasteful and inefficient in its management of both industrial and human resources. While the Russians extracted the last drop from their potential resources, the Germans only "talked" of total war until late in 1943. The Soviet government from the very beginning demanded incredible sacrifices from its civilians. Practically all available human and industrial capacity was devoted to winning the war, stripping the civilian economy of all but the bare essentials. The men sent to the front were replaced in the factories and on the farms by women, old men, and children. In contrast, German women were not employed in industry to any appreciable extent and factories worked only one shift.

Given the lack of overwhelming manpower, the Soviets countered the highly skilled German Army with masses of weapons. In addition to Russian's own production, its allies made a substantial contribution to defeating the Germans with the air war and lend-lease supplies, although the major share of lend-lease arrived after the war had been won in 1943. During the crucial period from June 1942 to November 1943 only four convoys arrived in the north as German ships, submarines, and aircraft prevented deliveries. The Far Eastern route and the Persian Gulf route had to be developed and had slow beginnings. Lend-lease provided the Russians with trucks, locomotives, rails, and goods that otherwise would have absorbed much of Soviet productive capacity, but the weapons were made by the Russians.

The keys to victory were the organization and supply of the Red Army. Both had to be accomplished in the most cost-effective manner. Perhaps the most powerful ingredient was the Russian ability to reduce every weapon and organization to its minimum. The choice was either a single beautiful tank with excellent optics and comfortable crew facilities or four ugly giants. The Germans opted for technical excellence and lost the production battle.

The Russians not only won the battle of production but also developed an efficient military organization that placed the fruits of production in the right place at the right time. The production methods were learned from the Americans, but the organization was homegrown. Faced with the competing need for resources in building the economy in the 1930s, the Russians delayed development of their army until the late 1930s. Untrained and equipped with obsolete weapons, the Red Army suffered disastrous defeats in 1941 and 1942, but by early 1943, training, organization, and equipment were equal or superior to the German army.

The Russian people sacrificed and fought because of their love of country and hatred of the invaders. There was little enthusiasm for the Communist Party and the socialist system. The Communist leadership could take little credit for the victory. The Stalinist purge of the late 1930s had deprived the army of its trained officer corps and was a direct cause of many of the Russian defeats in 1941. Communist ideology destroyed the productive capacity of the country not once but twice—first after the Revolution in 1917 when the middle class was eliminated and then in the 1930s when the new managerial class was purged along with the army officers. Technical assistance by the United State and other Western countries played the major role in Soviet production. All of the big tank factories were built under U.S. supervision in the 1930s.

Despite the German concentration in the east in 1943, the Red Army was clearly in control. The Russians did not need a second front in 1943, but a second front before 1944 would have been advantageous to the West. The postwar implications are enormous. The iron curtain would have been drawn many kilometers east had the West rather than the Russians taken Berlin. Instead of the Western Allies having a tenuous communication with Berlin, a restored Polish government might have relegated the Russians to a restricted line through a hostile Poland to an occupation zone in Germany. How many Jewish lives would have been spared had the war in Europe ended in the spring of 1944?

Notes

PREFACE

1. The term *database* will be used to refer to the computer file of 6,150 unit histories plus other hard-copy files with related material, including, for example, more than thirty binders with data extracted from the FHO microfilm and other sources.
2. *Velikai Otechestvevennaia Voena Entsiklopediia, 1941–1945* (Moscow, 1985), passim.
3. OKH Generalstab des Heers, Abt. Fremde Heer Ost (1k), National Archives Microfilm Publication T78, passim.
4. Robert G. Poirier and Albert Z. Conner, *Red Army Order of Battle in the Great Patriotic War* (Navato, Calif.: Presidio Press, 1985), passim.

INTRODUCTION

1. K. Malanin, "Razvitie Organizatsionnik Form Sukoputhik Voist v Velikoi Otechestvennoi Voine," *VIZh*, August 1967, p. 28; G. F. Krivosheev, *Grif Sekretnosti Sniat: Poteri Vooruzennix sil SSSR v Voinax Boevix Deistviiax i Voennix Konfliktax* (Moscow: Voennoe Izdatelistvo, 1993), pp. 130–31.
2. James F. Dunnigan, ed., *The Russian Front* (London: Arms and Armour Press, 1978), p. 83.
3. Alexander Werth, *Russia at War* (New York: Discus Books, 1970), p. 176. At the end of June 1941 each provincial Party committee was ordered to provide from 500 to 5,000 Communists for service. A total of 95,000 party members were mobilized and 58,000 were sent to the army. In addition, the first *Opolchenye* workers battalions were formed in late June.
4. Ibid., p. 265.
5. Ibid., p. 198.
6. Ibid., pp. 212–13.

CHAPTER 1: SOVIET MILITARY DOCTRINE

1. David M. Glantz, *From the Don to the Dnepr: Soviet Offensive Operations, December 1942–August 1943* (London: F. Cass, 1991), p. 1.
2. Vitaly Rapoport and Yuri Alexeev, *High Treason: Essays on the History of the Red Army, 1918–1938* (Durham, N. C.: Duke University Press, 1985), pp. 13, 173, 177.
3. Ibid., pp. 13, 173, 177.
4. Ibid., pp. 15, 180.
5. Ibid., p. 184.

6. John Erickson, *The Road to Stalingrad: Stalin's War with Germany* (New York: Harper & Row, 1975), pp. 26–27.

7. Rapoport and Alexeev, pp. 14, 181; A. B. Kadishev, *Voprosi Strategii i Operativnogo Iskusstva v Sovetskii Voennik Trudak (1917–1940)* (Moscow: Voennoe Izdatelistvo, 1965), p. 18.

8. Seweryn Bialer, ed., *Stalin and His Generals: Soviet Military Memoirs of World War II* (New York: Pegasus, 1969), pp. 57–58.

9. Ibid., p. 58.

10. Theodore H. Makhine, *L'Armee Rouge* (Paris: Payot, 1938), pp. 296–97; Erickson, *Stalingrad*, p. 26.

11. Rapoport and Alexeev, pp. 263–63.

12. Bialer, pp. 89–90.

13. M. V. Zakharov, "On the Eve of World War II (May 1938–September 1939)," *Soviet Studies in History* 23, No. 3 (Winter 1984–85), pp. 85, 94.

14. Ibid., p. 98.

15. M. V. Zakharov, *General'nyi shtab v Predvoennye Gody* (Moscow: Voenizdat, 1989), pp. 111–31.

16. Rapoport and Alexeev, p. 281; Erickson, *Stalingrad*, p. 26.

17. Bialer, p. 60.

18. Mark Harrison, *Soviet Planning in Peace and War, 1938–1945* (Cambridge, England: Cambridge University Press, 1985), pp. 60–61; Werth, p. 142; Bialer, pp. 60–61.

19. U. S. War Department, *Handbook of German Military Forces TM-E 30–451* (Washington, D. C.: GPO, 1945), p. IV-5.

20. Timothy A. Wray, *Standing Fast: German Defensive Doctrine on the Russian Front During World War II, Prewar to March 1943*, Combat Studies Institute Research Survey No. 5 (Fort Leavenworth, Kansas: U. S. Army Command and General Staff College, 1987), p. 25.

21. Ibid., pp. 14–15; *German Handbook*, pp. IV, 20–23; G. F. Biryukov and G. Melnikov, *Antitank Warfare* (Moscow: Progress Publishers, 1972), p. 55.

22. Wray, p. 16–17.

23. Bryan I. Fugate, *Operation Barbarossa* (Novato, Calif.: Presidio Press, 1984), pp. 50–51.

24. Bialer, pp. 60–63.

25. Werth, p. 158.

26. Wray, pp. 42–47; Fugate, pp. 51–53.

27. Wray, p. 21.

28. Ibid., p. 47.

29. Ibid., p. 23.

30. Michael Parrish, ed., *Battle for Moscow: The 1942 Soviet General Staff Study* (Washington, D. C.: Pergamon-Brassey's, 1989), p. 3.

31. Wray, pp. 57–62, 68–69, 90–92; Werth, pp. 260, 262; Parrish, p. 2.

32. Erickson, *Stalingrad*, pp. 291–92; Wray, pp. 91–92; *Istoriya Velikoy Otechestvennoy Voyny Sovetskogo Soyuza, 1941–45*, 6 vols. (IVOVSS hereafter) (Moscow: Voyennoye Izdatelistvo, 1960–63), II, 359; Parrish, pp. 1, 3–4.

33. Wray, p. 100; Parrish, pp. 3–4.

34. Wray, pp. 101–2.

35. Erich von Manstein, "The Development of the Red Army, 1942–1945," in Basil Liddell Hart, *The Red Army* (New York: Harcourt, Brace, 1956), p. 142.

36. Wray, p. 106; Parrish, pp. 8–9.

37. Wray, pp. 109–10.

38. Ibid., p. 116.

39. Ibid., p. 118.

40. FHO, CGR, H 3/191, November 24, 1942, Roll 556, Frame 565.

41. Ibid., Frames 570–79.

42. Fritz Bayerlein, "The Armoured Forces," in Liddell Hart, *Red Army*, p. 307.

43. Glantz, *From Don*, pp. 367–68.

44. Ivan Parotkin, ed., *Battle for Kursk* (Moscow: Progress Publishers, 1974), p. 161; Glantz, *From Don*, p. 217.

45. Parotkin, p. 162.

46. Ibid., p. 164.

47. Ibid., pp. 165–66.

48. Ibid., pp. 167–68. *Geschichte des Grossen Vaterlandischen Krieges der Sowietunion*, 8 vols. (Berlin: Deutscher Militarverlag, 1964), VI, p. 282. [hereafter *IVOVSS* (German)].

49. *VOVE*, p. 798.

50. *IVOVSS* (German), VI, p. 296.

51. Glantz, *From Don*, p. 219.

CHAPTER 2: CREATING THE RED ARMY, 1918–41

1. A. A. Egorovskii, I. V. Tutarinov, et al., *Istoria Ural'skogo Voennogo Okauga* (Moscow: Voennoe Izdatelistvo, 1970), p. 118.

2. J. M. Mackintosh, "The Red Army 1920–1936," in Liddell Hart, *Soviet Army*, pp. 54–56. The totals do not agree as information came from a variety of sources.

3. David M. Glantz, "Soviet Mobilization in Peace and War, 1924–1942, A Survey," *Journal of Soviet Studies* 5 (September 1992), pp. 9–10.

4. N. V. Piatnitskii, *Krasnia Armia, SSSR* (Paris: N. V. Piatnitskii, 1931), p. 217. The author lists 31 active divisions and 41.5 territorial divisions with a total complement of 337,100 men.

5. Mackintosh in Liddell Hart, pp. 57–59.

6. Public Record Office, WO 33, 1461, January 1, 1937; Makhine, p. 29; Egorovskii, pp. 118, 127.

7. Makhine, p. 29; Mackintosh in Liddell Hart, p. 62.

8. Glantz, "Soviet Mobilization," p. 13; Piatnitskii, p. 217.

9. Order of Battle, March 1, 1937. WO 33 1461 PRO.

10. Mackintosh in Liddell Hart, p. 62.

11. Harrison E. Salisbury, *The 900 Days: The Siege of Leningrad* (New York: Avon Books, 1970), p. 135–36; Alan Clark, *Barbarossa: The Russian-German Conflict, 1941–45* (New York: New American Library, 1966), p. 55; Mackintosh in Liddell Hart, p. 63.

12. FHO, CGR, H 3/83.3a, January 1, 1940, Roll 550, Frame 793.

13. Mackintosh in Liddell Hart, pp. 86–87.

14. S. M. Shtemenko, *The Soviet General Staff at War* (Moscow, Progress Publishers, 1970), p. 15; WO 33 1655A, January 15, 1940, PRO.

15. WO 33, 1655A, January 15, 1940, PRO.
16. Egorovskii, p. 118.
17. A. A. Grechko, *The Armed Forces of the Soviet Union* (Moscow: Progress Publishers, 1977), p. 55; FHO, CGR, H 3/83.3a, January 1, 1941, Roll 550, Frame 789.
18. Grechko, *Armed Forces*, p. 52.
19. WO 33, 1655A, January 15, 1940, PRO.
20. Erickson, *Stalingrad*, p. 14.
21. Shtemenko, *Soviet General Staff*, pp. 15–17.
22. Erickson, *Stalingrad*, p. 8.
23. Ibid., pp. 15–16.
24. Ibid., p. 17.
25. Ibid., pp. 18–23.
26. Ibid., p. 25; N. Ye. Eliseyev and I. M. Nagayev, "Germanskiy Militarizm i legenda o Œpreventivnoy voyne' Gitlerovskoy Germanii protiv SSSR," *VIZh*, 3 (March) 1991, pp. 5–7. The article is an edited copy of a report signed by Voroshilov in May 1940. The Germans estimated that the Red Army had 151 rifle divisions, 31 cavalry divisions, 6 mechanized corps, and 36 mechanized brigades in July 1940.
27. Viktor A. Anfilov, *Proval Blitskriga* (Moscow: Nauka, 1974), p. 192.
28. Eliseyev and Nagayev, pp. 4–7.
29. E. I. Zuzina, "Iz Arkivov Ministerstva Oboroni SSSR," VIZh, January 1992, p. 28.
30. FHO, CGR, H 3/83.3a, January 15, 1941, Roll 550, Frame 746.
31. FHO, CGR, H 3/83.3a, January 1, 1941, Roll 550, Frame 792.
32. Shtemenko, *Soviet General Staff*, p. 30.
33. V. N. Kiselev, "Upriame Fakti Nachala Voini," *VIZh*, February 1992, pp. 2122.
34. Fugate, Barbarossa, p. 50. Much of the Red Army data in this work comes from Prof. James Goff and is based on forty years of research in Russian publications; Erickson, *Stalingrad*, p. 122.
35. S. P. Ivanov, *The Initial Period of the War: A Soviet View* (Washington, D. C.: GPO, 1986), p. 179.
36. Anfilov, *Blitskriga*, pp. 194–96.
37. Ivanov, *Initial Period*, p. 178.
38. Anfilov, *Blitskriga*, pp. 200–201.
39. Louis Rotundo, "The Creation of Soviet Reserves and the 1941 Campaign," *Military Affairs* 50, No. 1 (January 1986), p. 23. The data are based on Prof. James Goff's research. Glantz, "Soviet Mobilization," p. 31; Anfilov, *Blitskriga*, pp. 112–19. A German estimate (made in 1943) was higher: 247 rifle, mountain, and motorized divisions (compared to 229 above), 65 tank divisions, and 23 cavalry divisions. In a later calculation made in 1944, the Germans revised their estimate for Soviet rifle divisions available against the German Army on June 22, 1941 (not including the Far Eastern forces). They assumed 225 rifle divisions, 65 tank divisions, and 20 cavalry divisions. FHO, CGR, H 3/468.2, September 9, 1943, Roll 564, Frame 942; FHO, CGR, H 3/1774, June 1, 1944, Roll 589, Frame 240.

CHAPTER 3: WARTIME MOBILIZATION

1. Rapoport and Alexeev, pp. 339–41.
2. Erickson, *Stalingrad*, p. 225; Rapoport and Alexeev state 2.9 million lost out of 5 million, p. 343.
3. Erickson, *Stalingrad*, p. 174.
4. Salisbury, *900 Days*, p. 147.
5. Albert Seaton, *The Russo-German War, 1941–45* (New York: Praeger, 1970), p. 99; Trevor N. Dupuy and Paul Martell, *Great Battles on the Eastern Front: The Soviet-German War, 1941–1945* (Indianapolis: Bobbs-Merrill, 1982), p. 11.
6. K. F. Skorobogatkin et al., *50 Let Vooruzhennykh Sil SSSR* (Moscow: Voenizdat, 1968), p. 273; Grechko, *Armed Forces*, pp. 59–60; *VOVE*, p. 452.
7. James M. Goff, "Evolving Soviet Force Structure, 1941–1945: Process and Impact," *Journal of Soviet Military Studies* 5, 3 (September, 1992), pp. 375, 381.
8. A. A. Grechko, *Godi Voini* (Moscow: Voennoe Izdatelistvo, 1976), pp. 165–66.
9. USSR Reports, Military Affairs, June 26, 1978, #3051, p. 38.
10. M. I. Kazakov, "Sozdanie i Ispool'zobanie Strategicheskik Rezervov," *VIZh*, December 1972, #12, Table 1, p. 47; Skorobogatkin, p. 273. Grechko, *Armed Forces*, pp. 59–60.
11. Erickson, *Stalingrad*, p. 174.
12. Fugate, p. 59.
13. Klaus Reinhardt, *Die Wende vor Moskau* (Stuttgart: Deutsche Verlag-Anstalt, 1972), p. 75.
14. K. I. Bukov, et al., *Bumva za Moskvi* (Moscow: Izdatelistvo, "Moskovskii Rabochii," 1985), p. 22.
15. Reinhardt, p. 75.
16. Included were the 10th, 26th, 57th (later 28th), 39th, 58th, 59th, 60th, 61st, 1st Shock, 20th, and 24th; Rotundo, "Soviet Reserves," p. 25.
17. F. Golikov, "Rezervnaia Armiia Gotovitsia K zashite Stolits," *VIZh* 8, No. 5 (May 1966), pp. 67–76; Reinhardt, p. 201.
18. Vladimir Sevruk, compiler, *Moscow-Stalingrad, 1941–1942* (Moscow: Progress Publishers, 1974), p. 42; Erickson, *Stalingrad*, pp. 239–40.
19. Kazakov, "Sozdanie," p. 49; the Stavka reserve peaked in December, as shown here:

	Oct. 41	Nov. 41	Dec. 41	Jan. 42	Feb. 42	Mar. 42	Apr. 42
Armies	3	8	1	2	2	2	
Rifle divisions	4	22	44	8	8	13	25
Cavalry divisions	3	8	14	1			
Rifle brigades			13	3	7		

20. Bukov, p. 33.
21. FHO, CGR, H 3/1774, June 1944, Roll 589, Frame 240.
22. Goff, p. 381.
23. Glantz, "Soviet Mobilization," p. 350.

24. Poirier and Connor, pp. 182–83.

25. James Lucas, *War on the Eastern Front, 1941–1945: The German Soldier in Russia* (New York: Bonanza Books, 1979), pp. 48–49.

26. FHO, CGR, H 3/468.1, May 7, 1942, Roll 564, Frame 848.

27. FHO, CGR, H 3/1039, August 2, 1942, Roll 580, Frame 927.

28. Erickson, *Stalingrad*, pp. 335–36.

29. Erickson, *Stalingrad*, p. 336; Werth, pp. 367–68; *IVOVSS*, II, pp. 406–15.

30. Most of the information concerning the reserve armies came from the computer database. As the armies were committed to combat they were given new numbers (64th, 60th, 63rd, 6th, 62nd, 1st Guard, 38th, 66th, 24th, and 5th Shock). The 38th, 6th, and 24th were numbers of armies destroyed in previous battles; Walter Kerr, *The Secret of Stalingrad* (New York: Playboy Press, 1979), pp. 36–41; Erickson, *Stalingrad*, p. 335.

31. Kerr, pp. 103, 105.

32. T. F. Vorontsov et al., *Ot Volshskik Stepei do Austriskik Alip* (Moscow: Voennoe Izdatelistvo, 1971), p. 6.

33. Ibid., pp. 7–8.

34. Ibid., p. 9.

35. Louis C. Rotundo, *Battle for Stalingrad: The 1943 Soviet General Staff Study* (Washington, D.C.: Pergamon-Brassey's, 1989), p. 6.

36. FHO, CGR, H 3/1039, August 2, 1942, Roll 580, Frame 927.

37. Burkhart Muller-Hillebrand, *Das Heer 1933–1945* (Frankfurt am Main: E. S. Mittler & Sohn, 1959–1969), Vol. 3, p. 108.

38. FHO, CGR, H 3/78, March 11, 1945, Roll 550, Frame 13. *IVOVSS* (German), VI, p. 230. Numbers of rifle brigades was determined by a survey of unit histories in the database.

39. Georgi K. Zhukov, *Marshal Zhukov's Greatest Battles* (New York: Harper & Row, 1969), pp. 217–18, 490–91.

CHAPTER 4: MANPOWER

1. Hubert P. Van Tuyll, *Feeding the Bear: American Aid to the Soviet Union, 1941–1945* (New York: Greenwood Press, 1989), p. 74.

2. Harrison, p. 137.

3. Ibid., pp. 142–43.

4. Ibid., p. 143.

5. Dupuy, *Great Battles*, p. 3; Van Tuyll, p. 75.

6. Harrison, p. 138; Theo J. Schulte, *The German Army and Nazi Policies in Occupied Russia* (Oxford: Berg, 1989), p. 181; Krivosheev, p. 143.

7. FHO, CGR, H 3/1506, February 10, 1945, Roll 587, frame 18. The FHO estimates were as follows:

Class of 1924	1,900,000
Class of 1925	2,200,000
Class of 1927	2,200,000

The estimate of 1926 was included with other data; FHO, CGR, H 3/1704, 1944, Roll 588, Frame 211.

8. Birth-rate statistics are from B. Urlanis, *Wars and Population* (Moscow: Progress Publishers, 1971), p. 255, and B. R. Mitchell, *European Historical Statistics, 1750–1970* (London: MacMillan Press, 1978), p. 31. The second column, Boys in 1931, is from Makhine, p. 31. The third and fourth columns are from FHO, CGR, H 3/464, March 5, 1942, Roll 564, Frame 812.

9. Mitchell, pp. 7, 31; Urlanis, passim; Gehlen speech, FHO, CGR, H 3/1039, June 9, 1942, Roll 580, frame 857. Data on the birth rate for 1921 to 1927, the pertinent years, has not been located.

10. Holland Hunter and Janusz M. Seymour, *Faulty Foundations: Soviet Economic Policies, 1928–1940* (Princeton, N.J.: Princeton University Press, 1992), pp. 30–31.

11. Dunnigan, *Russian Front*, p. 71.

12. V. S. Kozurin, "O Chislennosti Naseleniia SSSR," *VIZh* 2 (February 1991), p. 23. 8.8 million were added to the Ukraine, 4.7 million to the White Russian Republic, .5 million came from Finland, 2.3 millions Moldavians came from Roumania, 2.9 million Lithuanians, 2.0 million Latvians, and 1.1 million Estonians.

13. FHO, CGR, H 3/1039, June 9, 1942, Roll 580, Frames 855–57; Steven J. Zaloga, *The Red Army*, Men at Arms Series, #216, p. 7.

14. FHO, CGR, H 3/468.1, March 1, 1942, Roll 564, Frame 802; Krivosheev, p. 143.

15. Manual of the Red Army Replacement System, FHO, CGR, H 3/89, December 1943, Roll 462, Frame 6441494; H 3/64.2, April 5, 1944, Roll 460, Frame 6438464; H 3/77, August 13, 1943, Roll 549, Frame 981.

16. N. N. Golovine, "The Red Army," *The Infantry Journal* 4 (July–August 1936), p. 303.

17. FHO, CGR, H 3/468.1, October 31, 1941, Roll 564, Frame 794.

18. FHO, CGR, H 3/464, March 5, 1942, Roll 564, Frame 812.

19. FHO, CGR, H 3/1039, June 9, 1942, Roll 580, Frames 855–57.

20. FHO, CGR, H 3/193, June, 1943, Roll 556, Frame 787.

21. FHO, CGR, H 3/1521, September 5, 1944, Roll 587, Frame 287.

22. FHO, CGR, 14 3/1506, February 10, 1945, Roll 587, Frame 14.

23. *IVOVSS* (German), VI, pp. 52, 230; A. A. Grechko, *Liberation Mission* (Moscow: Progress Publishers, 1975), p. 80; Skorobogatkin, et al., pp. 343, 361–62.

24. FHO, CGR, H 3/1508, January 1945, Roll 587, Frame 26.

25. S. M. Shtemenko, *General Staff*, p. 284; Krivosheev, pp. 130–31. During World War I the Germans had mobilized 19.5 percent out of a population of 67.8 million

26. WO 33/1829 January 1, 1945, PRO.

27. FHO, CGR, H 3/64.2, June 10, 1944, Roll 460, Frame 6438386.

28. *IVOVSS* (German), VI, p. 149; Lucas, p. 57; FHO, CGR, H 3/1508, February 2, 1945, Roll 587, Frame 24; FHO, CGR, H 3/1506, February 10, 1945, Roll 587, Frame 14.

29. FHO, CGR, H 3/65, February 28, 1944, Roll 460, Frame 6438746.

30. Harrison, p. 138.

31. Ibid., p. 139.

32. Werth, p. 695.

33. Louis Ely, *The Red Army Today* (Harrisburg: Military Services Publishing Co., 1953), p. 28.

34. In August and September 1943, Red Army divisions opposed to Army Group Center received from 1,000 to 3,000 replacements per month. The mechanized brigades had all losses replaced, while one tank brigade received 40 tanks and two others, "full" replacements. FHO, CGR, H 3/503, September 1943, Roll 566, Frame 1202; Krivosheev, p. 143.

35. WO 33/1829 January 1, 1945, PRO.

36. In April 1944 the 21st Army at Kalinin was reforming divisions that had been worn down in combat. Replacements of the classes of 1923 through 1925 (19 to 21 years of age) were received from Siberia, the Far East, and Central Asia and added to the divisions. The process of rebuilding took four weeks. FHO, CGR, H 3/73, April 7, 1944, Roll 549, Frame 711.

37. CGR, FHO, H 3/1508, January 1945, Roll 587, Frame 26.

38. I. G. Pavlovskii, *Sukhoputniye Voyska SSSR* (Moscow: Voenizdat, 1985), p. 117.

39. John P. Cole and F. C. German, *A Geography of the USSR: The Background of a Planned Economy* (London: Butterworths, 1984), p. 91; J. A. Newth, "The Soviet Population: Wartime Losses and the Postwar Recovery," *Soviet Studies* 15, no. 3 (January 1964), pp. 345–47; Rapoport and Alexeev, p. 358; V. T. Eliseev and S. N. Mikhalev, "Tak Skoliko Zhe Ludei mi Poteriali v Voine?" *VIZh* 7 (July 1992), pp. 31–33; Warren W. Eason, "The Soviet Population Today: An Analysis of the First Results of the 1959 Census," *Foreign Affairs* 37 (July 1959), pp. 598–606; Alec Nove, *An Economic History of the USSR* (New York: Penguin Books, 1982), p. 286; Schulte, p. 181; Krivosheev, pp. 130–31.

40. Urlanis, pp. 261, 287.

41. Ibid., p. 289.

42. Ibid., pp. 284–89.

43. Makhine, pp. 45–46.

44. FHO, CGR, H 3/1508, February 10, 1945, Roll 587, Frame 18; H 3/1521, September 5, 1944, Roll 587, Frame 287.

45. FHO, CGR, H 3/1508, February 23, 1945, Roll 587, Frame 23.

46. Andrei I. Eremenko, *Stalingrad, Zapiski Komanduyushchego Frontom* (Moscow: Voenizdat, 1961), p. 417.

47. Erickson, Stalingrad, p. 384. Erickson based his conclusion on Eremenko.

48. Werth, pp. 425–26.

49. FHO, CGR, H 3/64.2, February 27, 1944, Roll 460, Frame 6438505.

50. FHO, CGR, H 3/118, March 12, 1945, Roll 552, Frame 227.

51. U. S. S. R. Central Statistical Board of the USSR Council of Ministers, National Economy of the U.S.S.R. Statistical Returns (Moscow: Foreign Languages Publishing House, 1957), p. 18.

52. Ibid., p. 17.

53. Gunther Blumentritt, "The State and Performance of the Red Army, 1941," in Liddell Hart, *The Soviet Army*, p. 134.

54. Ely, p. 25; Werth, p. 8.

55. Werth, p. 7.

56. V. Drozdov and A. Korkeshkin, *The Soviet Soldier* (Moscow: Progress Publishers, 1980), pp. 79–80; Erickson, *Stalingrad*, p. 175.

57. FHO, CGR, H 3/67, Roll 460, Frame 6439041.

58. Seaton, Russo-German War, p. 295.
59. FHO, CGR, H 3/464, Roll 564, Frames 37, 40, 88, 122, 155, and 209.
60. FHO, CGR, H 3/64.2, August 30, 1944, Roll 460, Frame 6438465.
61. FHO, CGR, H 3/64.2, June 10, 1944, Roll 460, Frame 6438386.
62. F. W. Mellenthin, *Panzer Battles* (New York: Ballantine Books, 1976), p. 221.
63. Drozdov and Korkeshkin, p. 94.
64. Erickson, *Stalingrad*, p. 173.
65. FHO, CGR, H 3/67, February 23, 1943, Roll 460, Frame 6438969.
66. FHO, CGR, H 3/69, March 29, 1944, Roll 549, Frame 87.
67. FHO, CGR, H 3/69, March 29, 1944, Roll 549, Frame 87; H 3/69, March 11, 1944, Roll 549, Frame 84.
68. Pavlovskii, p. 117.

CHAPTER 5: THE EVOLUTION OF THE RIFLE DIVISION
1. FHO, CGR, H 3/64.2, June 1, 1944, Roll 460, Frame 6438398.
2. Kent Greenfield, et al., *Organization of Ground Combat Troops* (Washington, D.C.: Department of the Army, 1947), p. 351.
3. Martin van Creveld, *Fighting Power* (Westport, Conn.: Greenwood Press, 1982), p. 56.
4. Goff, p. 378.
5. VOVE, VI, p. 282; FHO, CGR, H 3/104; Comparison Chart, September 1943, Roll 551, Frame 118.
6. Zakharov, "Eve of World War II," pp. 95, 98.
7. *VIZh*, February 1988, p. 28.
8. Ivanov, *Initial Period*, p. 179; Skorobogatkin, p. 235; S. A. Tiushkevich, ed., *Sovetskie Vooruzhennye Sily* (Moscow: Voenizdat, 1978), p. 235; Pavlovskii, p. 109; Anfilov, *Blitskriga*, p. 125.
9. Tiushkevich, *Vooruzhennye Sily*, p. 235.
10. *VIZh*, March 1988, p. 28.
11. Pavlovskii, p. 109; Viktor A. Anfilov, *Bessmertnii Podvig Issledovanie Kanuna i Pervogo Etapa Velikoi Otechestvennoi Voini* (Moscow: Nauka, 1971), p. 115.
12. Erickson, *Stalingrad*, p. 173; Tiushkevich, *Vooruzhennye Sily*, p. 277.
13. CGR, FHO, H 3/83.2, Roll 550, Frame 590.
14. Tiushkevich, *Vooruzhennye Sily*, p. 307.
15. Ibid., p. 277.
16. Ibid., p. 280; Dunnigan, *Russian Front*, p. 98.
17. Malanin, p. 32; Tiushkevich, *Vooruzhennye Sily*, p. 278.
18. Seaton, *Russo-German War*, p. 291; CGR, FHO, H 3/64.2, March 20, 1944, Roll 460, Frame 6438439; *IVOVSS* (German), VI, p. 281; Erickson, *Stalingrad*, p. 307.
19. Konstantin K. Rokossovsky, *Velikaia Pobdea Na Volga* (Moscow: Voennoe Izdatelistvo, 1965), p. 77.
20. Pavlovskii, p. 109; Malanin, p. 34; Tiushkevich, *Vooruzhennye Sily*, p. 315.
21. IVOVSS (German), VI, p. 282.
22. FHO, CGR, H 3/126, December 24, 1942, Roll 552, Frame 946.
23. FHO, CGR, H 3/104, January 25, 1943, Roll 551, Frame 346.
24. N. I. Krilov, et al., *Naustrecho Pobede Boevoi Puti 5–i Armii* (Moscow: Izdatelistvo Nauka, 1970), p. 156.

25. FHO, CGR, H 3/64.2, November 20, 1943, Roll 460, Frame 6438599; H 3/64.2, March 20, 1944, Roll 460, Frame 6438439; H 3/64.2, July 21, 1944, Roll 460, Frame 6438399; H 3/104, October 8, 1943, Roll 551, Frames 218–32; Glantz, *From Don*, p. 220.

26. Walter S. Dunn, Jr., *Second Front Now 1943* (University, Ala.: University of Alabama Press, 1980), p. 134.

27. FHO, CGR, H 3/64.2, Roll 460, Frame 6438439.

28. FHO, CGR, H 3/64.2, February 1, 1944, Roll 460, Frame 6438563.

29. Lucas, p. 57.

30. FHO, CGR, H 3/64.2, December 24, 1943, Roll 460, Frame 6438585.

31. FHO, CGR, H 3/64.2, Dec. 22, 1943, Roll 460, Frame 6438595.

32. FHO, CGR, H 3/64.2, March 6, 1943, Roll 460, Frame 6438493.

33. FHO, CGR, H 3/64.2, Dec 24, 1943, Roll 460, Frame 6438587.

34. FHO, CGR, H 3/384, November 16, 1944, Roll 562, Frame 1050; H 3/63, August 10, 1944, Roll 459, Frame 6437547.

35. FHO, CGR, H 3/64.1, Roll 460, Frame 6438162.

36. FHO, CGR, H 3/64.2, July 25, 1944, Roll 460, Frame 6438339.

37. FHO, CGR, H 3/64.1, October 26, 1944, Roll 460, Frame 6438267.

38. IVOVSS (German), VI, p. 282.

39. Militarakademie M. V. Frunze, *Der Durchbruch der Schutzenverbande Durch Eine Vorbereitete Verteidigung* (Berlin: Ministeriumus fur Nationale Verteidigung), p. 130; Grechko, *Liberation Mission*, p. 100.

40. FHO, CGR, H 3/65, February 19, 1944, Roll 460, Frame 6438736.

41. FHO, CGR, H 3/65, May 8, 1944, Roll 460, Frame 6438736.

42. FHO, CGR, H 3/64.2, June 11, 1944, Roll 460, Frame 6438388.

43. FHO, CGR, H 3/64.2, Roll 460, Frame 6438551.

44. FHO, CGR, H 3/118, October 15, 1944, Roll 552, Frames 377–79.

45. John Erickson, *The Road to Berlin* (Boulder, Colo.: Westview Press, 1983), p. 81.

46. *IVOVSS* (German), VI, p. 157.

47. *IVOVSS* (German), VI, p. 155.

48. *VOVE*, p. 690; Pavel A. Kurochkina, Obshevoiskovaia Armiya v. Nastuplenii (Moscow: Voenizdat, 1966), Chart I; Pavlovskii, p. 109.

49. FHO, CGR, H 3/64.1, March 11, 1945, Roll 460, Frames 6438170–77.

50. FHO, CGR, H 3/64.2, March 20, 1944, Roll 460, Frame 6438439, and Jan. 26, 1945, Frame 6438530.

51. FHO, CGR, H 3/64.1, March 11, 1945, Roll 460, Frame 6438170.

52. FHO, CGR, H 3/64.1, March 22, 1945, Roll 460, Frame 6438204.

53. FHO, CGR, H 3/118, February 16, 1945, Roll 552, Frame 162.

54. FHO, CGR, H 3/64.1, March 11, 1945, Roll 460, Frame 6438168.

55. Krilov, p. 404.

56. FHO, CGR, H 3/64.1, March 16, 1945, Roll 460, Frame 6438167.

57. Erickson, *Berlin*, p. 622.

58. FHO, CGR, H 3/64.1, March 5, 1945, Roll 460, Frame 6438182.

59. FHO, CGR, H 3/64.1, February 10, 1945, Roll 460, Frame 6438215.

CHAPTER 6: THE REPLACEMENT SYSTEM

1. In the German blitzkriegs of 1939, 1940, and early 1941, neither replacements nor unit rebuilding required serious attention because the German losses were inconsiderable. The Germans first faced major problems in Russia.
2. FHO, CGR, H 3/468.1, May 1942, Roll 564, Frame 855.
3. Grechko, *Armed Forces*, pp. 123–24.
4. Drozdov and Korkeshkin, p. 63; Grechko, *Armed Forces*, p. 124.
5. Grechko, *Armed Forces*, p. 125.
6. Georg Tessin, *Verbände und Truppen der Deutschen Wehrmacht und Waffen-SS im Zeiten Weltkrieg, 1939–1945* (Osnabrück: Biblio Verlag, 1973), VII, p. 131.
7. FHO, CGR, H 3/64.2, November 15, 1944, Roll 460, Frame 6438390.
8. Grechko, *Armed Forces*, p. 125.
9. Drozdov and Koreshkin, p. 114.
10. FHO, CGR, H 3/64.1, December 16, 1944, Roll 460, Frame 6438239.
11. FHO, CGR, H 3/65, Roll 460, Frame 6438831.
12. FHO, CGR, H 3/64.2, March 6, 1944, Roll 460, Frame 6438493.
13. Werner Haupt, *Die 260.Infanterie-Division, 1939–1944* (Bad Nauheim: Podzun, 1970), p. 187.
14. FHO, CGR, H 3/65, May 8, 1944, Roll 460, Frame 6438736.
15. Grechko, *Liberation Mission*, p. 92.
16. FHO, CGR, H 3/64.1, March 3, 1945, Roll 460, Frame 6438198.
17. Seaton, *Russo-German War*, pp. 18, 99.
18. FHO, CGR, H 3/64.2, November 19, 1944, Roll 460, Frame 6438684.
19. U. S. War Department, *TM 30–430 Handbook on USSR Military Forces* (Washington, D.C.: GPO, 1946), II, p. 26.
20. Drozdov and Koreshkin, p. 94. In the United States in 1940, 50 percent of the men entering the army were high school graduates. United States, Department of Commerce, *Historical Statistics of the United States: Colonial Times to 1957* (Washington, D.C.: GPO, 1960), pp. 214, 207.
21. FHO, CGR, H 3/468.1, May 1942, Roll 564, Frame 855.
22. Blumentritt, p. 135.
23. FHO, CGR, H 3/104, February 6, 1944, Roll 551, Frame 121.
24. FHO, CGR, H 3/123.1, September 2, 1943, Roll 552, Frame 528 and May 17, 1944, Roll 552, Frame 518.
25. FHO, CGR, H 3/1726, 1943, Roll 589, Frame 31.
26. Tiushkevich, *Armed Forces*, p. 346; *Ordena Lenina Moskovskii Voennii Okrug* (Moscow: Voenizdat, 1977), p. 318.
27. WO 33 1829, January 1, 1945, PRO.
28. FHO, CGR, H 3/191, August 29, 1942, Roll 556, Frame 596.
29. FHO, CGR, H 3/1079, November 1943, Roll 581, Frame 723.
30. Josef P. Goebbels, *The Goebbels Diaries, 1942–43* (New York: Universal Award House, 1971), p. 320; FHO, CGR, H 3/178, March 17, 1943, Roll 556, Frame 459.
31. FHO, CGR, H 3/193, 1943, Roll 556, Frame 787.
32. FHO, CGR H 3/1508, February 10, 1945, Roll 587, Frame 19.
33. FHO, CGR, H 3/89, Red Army Manual, December 1943, Roll 462, Frame 6441494.

34. FHO, CGR, H 3/64.1, March 22, 1945, Roll 460, Frame 6438204.
35. FHO, CGR, H 3/89, Red Army Manual, Roll 462, Frame 6441494.
36. *IVOVSS* (German), III, pp. 35–36.
37. FHO, CGR, H 3/64.1, November 19, 1944, Roll 460, Frame 6438249.
38. FHO, CGR, H 3/64.2, June 6, 1944, Roll 460, Frame 6438405.
39. FHO, CGR, H 3/64.2, June 1, 1944, Roll 460, Frame 6438398 and March 17, 1944, Roll 460, Frame 6438476.
40. FHO, CGR, H 3/89, Red Army Manual, December 1943, Roll 462, Frame 6441494.
41. FHO, CGR, H 3/468.1, February 25, 1942, Roll 564, Frame 802.
42. Kerr, p. 53.
43. Kerr, p. 189.
44. Ibid., p. 194.
45. Erickson, *Stalingrad*, pp. 384, 294.
46. FHO, CGR, H 3/64.2, After Action Report, November 23, 1943, Roll 460, Frame 6438505.
47. FHO, CGR, H 3/64.2, April 1944, Roll 460, Frame 6438464.
48. FHO, CGR, H 3/64.2, December 24, 1943, Roll 460, Frame 6438587. H 3/89, Red Army Manual, December 1943, Roll 462, Frame 6441494.
49. FHO, CGR, H 3/69, Roll 549, Frame 51.
50. FHO, CGR, H 3/104, February 6, 1944, Roll 551, Frame 154.
51. FHO, CGR, H 3/1079, November 1943, Roll 581, Frame 735.
52. FHO, CGR, H 3/1079, November 1943, Roll 581, Frame 726,
53. FHO, CGR, H 3/1079, November 1943, Roll 581, Frame 760.
54. FHO, CGR, H 3/1079, December 1943, Roll 581, Frame 687.
55. FHO, CGR, H 3/118, October 15, 1944, Roll 552, Frame 379.
56. Erickson, *Stalingrad*, p. 323.
57. Kerr, pp. 148, 170.
58. FHO, CGR, H 3/64.2, May 5, 1944, Roll 460, Frame 6438424.
59. FHO, CGR, H 3/118, September 1, 1944, Roll 552, Frame 82.
60. FHO, CGR, H 3/118, October 15, 1944, Roll 552, Frame 379.
61. FHO, CGR, H 3/178, February 27, 1945, Roll 556, Frames 233–35. WO 3: 1829, January 1, 1945, PRO.
62. Lucas, p. 57.
63. FHO, CGR, H 3/113A, March 18, 1942, Roll 551, Frame 662.
64. Erickson, *Stalingrad*, p. 283.
65. FHO, CGR, H 3/67, February 23, 1943, Roll 460, Frame 6438986.
66. Grechko, *Armed Forces*, p. 187.
67. Dunnigan, *Russian Front*, p. 73.
68. Grechko, *Armed Forces*, p. 190; FHO, CGR, H 3/89, Red Army Manual, December 1943, Roll 462, Frame 6441494; Dunnigan, *Russian Front*, p. 73.
69. FHO, CGR, 11 3/69, October 24, 1944, Roll 460, Frame 6438809.
70. FHO, CGR, H 3/89, Red Army Manual, Roll 462, Frame 6441493.
71. Drozdov and Korkeshkin, p. 69.
72. FHO, CGR, H 3/67, February 23, 1943, Roll 460, Frame 6438968.
73. Grechko, *Armed Forces*, pp. 190–91.
74. FHO, CGR, H 3/123.1, May 29, 1944, Roll 552, Frames 504–505.
75. Tiushkevich, *Vooruzhennye Sily*, p. 330.
76. Tiushkevich, *Vooruzhennye Sily*, p. 330.

77. Zhukov, p. 218.
78. FHO, CGR, H 3/64.2, November 27, 1944, Roll 460, Frame 6438389.
79. FHO, CGR, H 3/64.2, February 1, 1944, Roll 460, Frame 6438563.
80. FHO, CGR, H 3/68.1, December 22, 1943, Roll 460, Frame 6439595.
81. FHO, CGR, H 3/64.2, November 15, 1944, Roll 460, Frame 6438389.
82. FHO, CGR, II 3/77, Roll 549, Frame 817.
83. Erickson, *Stalingrad*, p. 283.
84. FHO, CGR, 3/65, February 28, 1944, Roll 460, Frame 6438746.
85. FHO, CGR, H 3/77, February 18, 1945, Roll 549, Frame 821.
86. Ely, p. 28.
87. *IVOVSS* (German), VI, p. 253.
88. FHO, CGR, H 3/113A, June 6, 1942, Roll 551, Frame 662.
89. Kerr, p. 186.
90. *IVOVSS* (German), VI, p. 253.
91. Tiushkevich, *Armed Forces*, p. 326.
92. FHO, CGR, H 3/64.2, February 18, 1944, Roll 460, Frame 6438549.
93. FHO, CGR, H 3/64.2, March 20, 1944, Roll 460, Frame 6438439.
94. FHO, CGR, H 3/64.2, February 1, 1944, Roll 460, Frame 6438563.
95. FHO, CGR, H 3/65, September 30, 1944, Roll 460, Frames 6438809–12.
96. FHO, CGR, H 3/64.1, March 11, 1945, Roll 460, Frame 6438170.
97. FHO, CGR, H 3/64.1, March 22, 1945, Roll 460, Frame 6438204.
98. Goebbels, p. 320; Lucas, p. 57.
99. FHO, CGR, H 3/64.1, November 25, 1944, Roll 460, Frame 6438253.

CHAPTER 7: FORMATION OF THE TANK FORCE

1. *USSR Report, Military Affairs, June 12, 1986, Provisional Field Regulations for the Red Army* (Washington, D.C.: Foreign Broadcast Information Service, 1986), pp. 2–3.
2. Gerhard Forster and Nikolaus Paulus, *Abri der Geschichte der Panzerwaffe* (Berlin: Militarverlag der Deutschen Demokratischen Republik, 1977), pp. 93–95; Rudolf Steiger, *Armour Tactics in the Second World War* (New York: Berg, 1991), p. 36; Provisional Field Regulations, p. 4.
3. Steiger, p. 36.
4. Ibid., pp. 16–17, 31–32.
5. Ibid., pp. 41, 44.
6. Ibid., pp. 45–46.
7. Forster and Paulus, p. 95.
8. J. W. Wheeler-Bennett, *The Nemesis of Power* (New York: St. Martin's Press, 1964), pp. 125–26.
9. Ibid., pp. 119–25.
10. T. N. Dupuy, *A Genius for War: The History of the German Army and General Staff from 1807 through 1945* (London: MacDonald and Jane's, 1977), p. 215; Wheeler-Bennett, p. 128.
11. Dupuy, *A Genius for War*, p. 216; Steven J. Zaloga and James Granden, *Soviet Tanks and Combat Vehicles of World War Two* (London: Arms and Armour Press, 1984), pp. 42–43; Walter K. Nehring, *Die Geschichte der Deutschen Panzerwaffe 1916 bis 1945* (Berlin: Proplylaen Verlag, 1969), pp. 42–43; Wheeler-Bennett, pp. 129–31.

12. Nehring, *Anlage* (appendix with separate pagination), pp. 9–10; Albert Seaton and Joan Seaton, *The Soviet Army, 1918 to the Present* (New York: New American Library, 1986), pp. 84–85. Seaton did not consider the cooperative effort important to either country.

13. Dupuy, *Genius for War*, p. 215; Wheeler-Bennett, p. 128.

14. Kenneth Macksey, *Guderian: Creator of the Blitzkrieg* (New York: Stein and Day, 1976), p. 64; Nehring, pp. 115–16, *Anlage*, p. 10.

15. Nehring, pp. 116–17.

16. Zaloga and Granden, *Soviet Tanks*, p. 43.

17. Nehring, pp. 44–45, 78–80, *Anlage*, p. 13.

18. Zaloga and Granden, *Soviet Tanks*, pp. 38–39.

19. Ibid., Soviet Tanks, p. 48.

20. Antony C. Sutton, *Western Technology and Soviet Economic Development*, 3 vols. (Stanford: Institution Press, 1968–1973), II, pp. 241, 243.

21. Sutton, II, p. 243.

22. Zaloga and Granden, *Soviet Tanks*, pp. 47–52; Krivosheev, pp. 357–58.

23. Sutton, II, pp. 241, 243; Zaloga and Granden, *Soviet Tanks*, pp. 47–52.

24. Erickson, *Stalingrad*, p. 771.

25. Zaloga and Granden, *Soviet Tanks*, pp. 66–67.

26. Ibid., pp. 111, 113; I. M. Golushko, *Tanki Ozhivali Vnov* (Moscow: Voenizdat, 1974), pp. 3–5. Sutton, II, p. 241.

27. Erickson, *Stalingrad*, p. 771.

28. Sutton, II, p. 243

29. Ibid., II, p. 243.

30. Forster and Paulus, pp. 93–95; Zaloga and Granden, *Soviet Tanks*, p. 46.

31. R. A. Savushkin, *Razvitie Sovetskikh Vooruzhennykh sil i Voennogo Iskusstva y Mezhvoennyi Period 1921–1941* (Moscow: Lenin Military-Political Academy, 1989), p. 32; I. M. Anan'ev, *Tankovie Armii v Nastuplenii* (Moscow: Voenizdat, 1988), p. 24; Forster and Paulus, p. 95; Erickson, *Stalingrad*, p. 32.

32. Savushkin, p. 32.

33. Tiushkevich, *Armed Forces*, p. 188; Erickson, *Stalingrad*, pp. 32–33; Shtemenko, *General Staff*, p. 9.

34. A. Ryzhakov, "K Voprosi o Stroitel'stve Bronetankovich Voisk Krasnoi Armii v 30–e Gody," *VIZh* 8 (August 1968), p. 106; Anfilov, *Bessmertnii*, p. 105; Anan'ev, p. 25; Forster and Paulus, p. 95.

35. Ryzhakov, p. 107.

36. Ibid., p. 107.

37. Ibid., p. 108.

38. Savushkin, p. 33; Forster and Paulus, p. 95.

39. Tiushkevich, *Armed Forces*, p. 200.

40. Ryzhakov, p. 108.

41. Steven J. Zaloga and James Granden, *Soviet Heavy Tanks* (London: Osprey, 1981), p. 5

42. A. I. Bedniasin, et al., *Kievski Krasnoznamennii Istorik Karasnoznamennogo Kievskogo Voennogo Okruga 1919–1972* (Moscow: Voennoe Izdatelistvo, 1974), p. 115.

43. Ryzhakov, p. 109.

44. Erickson, *Stalingrad*, pp. 768–70; I. E. Krupchenko, *Sovetskiye Tankovye Voyska 1941–1945* (Moscow: Voyennoye Izdatelistvo, 1973), p. 12; Anfilov, *Blitskriga*, p. 117; Anfilov, *Bessmertnii*, p. 105; Anan'ev, p. 25.

45. Forster and Paulus, p. 97; E. Nikutin, "KPSS i Stroitelistvo Sovetskii Vooruzhennykh sil v Mezvoennie Period," *VIZh* 10 (October 1977), p. 98. Nikutin says fifteen mechanized regiments in cavalry divisions and eighty-three tank battalions and companies in rifle divisions in early 1936.

46. Bedniasin, p. 124.

47. Tiushkevich, *Armed Forces*, p. 200; Forster and Paulus, p. 97.

48. Erickson, *Stalingrad*, p. 26; Anfilov, *Bessmertnii*, pp. 105–106. The commission that presented the recommendation to Stalin included Pavlov, G. I. Kulik, S. M. Budyenny, B. Shaposhnikov, S. K. Timoshenko, K. A. Meretskov, L. E. Mechlis, and E. A. Shadenko.

49. Earl F. Ziemke and Magna E. Bauer, *Moscow to Stalingrad: Decision in the East* (New York: Military Heritage Press, 1988), p. 10. The purge began in the summer of 1937 and by the end, all of the military district and corps commanders, most of the division and brigade commanders, and half the regimental commanders had been removed. Erickson, *Stalingrad*, p. 32; Anan'ev, p. 26.

50. Krupchenko, *Sovetskiye Tankovye*, p. 12; Tiushkevich, *Armed Forces*, p. 238.

51. Anfilov, *Bessmertnii*, p. 107; Krupchenko, *Sovetskiye Tankovye*, p. 12; Anfilov, *Blitskriga*, p. 118; Tiushkevich, *Armed Forces*, p. 238.

52. Ryzhakov, p. 110.

53. Ibid., p. 110.

54. Erickson, *Stalingrad*, p. 26; Tiushkevich, *Armed Forces*, p. 238.

55. Anfilov, *Blitskriga*, p. 118.

56. M. Kazakov, *Nad Karoi Bylykh Srazhenii* (Moscow: Izdatelistvo, 1965) in Bialer, pp. 143–44.

57. *IVOVSS* (German), VI, p. 279. Tiushkevich, *Armed Forces*, p. 239.

58. Zaloga and Granden, *Soviet Tanks*, p. 9; *VOVE*, p. 470; Fugate, p. 36; Krupchenko, *Sovetskiye Tankovye*, pp. 13–14; Malanin, p. 29.

59. Skorobogatkin, p. 251.

60. L. M. Sandalov, "Podgotovka Voisk 4–i Armii k Otragenio Fashistskoi Agressii," *VIZh* 11 (November, 1988), p. 6.

61. Tiushkevich, *Armed Forces*, p. 239.

62. Ziemke and Bauer, *Stalingrad*, p. 11; Krupchenko, *Sovetskiye Tankovye*, p. 10.

63. Anfilov, *Blitskriga*, pp. 118, 126; Tiushkevich, *Armed Forces*, p. 229.

64. Ziemke and Bauer, *Stalingrad*, p. 11.

65. Tiushkevich, *Armed Forces*, p. 230; Shtemenko, *General Staff*, p. 28.

66. Erickson, *Stalingrad*, p. 63; *IVOVSS*, I, pp. 475–76.

67. *IVOVSS*, I, pp. 475–76.

68. Tiushkevich, *Armed Forces*, p. 239.

69. B. A. Semidetko, "Istorii Porazeniia v Belorussia," *VIZh* 4 (April 1989), p. 25.

70. V. P. Krikunov, "Kuda Delici Tanki," *VIZh* 11 (November 1988), p. 29.

71. V. P. Krikunov, "Prostaia Arifmetika V. V. Shlikova," *VIZh* 4 (1989), pp. 4142; Semidetko, p. 25; K. C. Moskalenko, *Na Ugo-zamadnum Napravlenii 1941–1943* (Moscow, 1973), p. 51.

72. Mueller-Hillebrand, III, p. 275.

73. Krupchenko, *Sovetskie Tankovye*, p. 114.
74. Krivosheev, pp. 357–58.
75. Salisbury, *900 Days*, p. 124.
76. Zaloga and Granden, *Soviet Tanks*, p. 13.

CHAPTER 8: ORGANIZATION OF THE TANK FORCES
 1. *IVOVSS* (German), VI, p. 279.
 2. Liddell Hart, *Soviet Army*, pp. 286, 306; Zaloga and Granden, *Soviet Tanks*, pp. 17, 129.
 3. Zaloga and Granden, *Soviet Tanks*, p. 125.
 4. O. A. Losik, *Stroitel'stvo i Boyevoye Primeneniye Sovetskikh Tankovykh Voysk v Gody Velikoy Otechestvennoy Voyne* (Moscow: Voenizdat, 1979), p. 24.
 5. *IVOVSS* (German), VI, p. 279.
 6. Liddell Hart, *Soviet Army*, pp. 300–301.
 7. Ibid., p. 302.
 8. Ibid., p. 304; Losik, p. 24; *VOVE*, p. 704.
 9. Liddell Hart, *Soviet Army*, p. 304.
10. Zaloga and Granden, *Soviet Tanks*, p. 19; *VOVE*, p. 704.
11. Zaloga and Granden, *Soviet Tanks*, p. 25; *VOVE*, p. 704.
12. Losik, p. 24; Liddell Hart, *Soviet Army*, pp. 301, 304; Zaloga and Granden, *Soviet Tanks*, pp. 27–30; *VOVE*, p. 704.
13. Losik, p. 46.
14. Bukov, p. 47.
15. Tiushkevich, *Armed Forces*, p. 281; Skorobogatkin, p. 270.
16. FHO, CGR, H 3/104, March 18, 1943, Roll 551, Frame 334; Zaloga and Granden, *Soviet Tanks*, p. 146; Anan'ev, pp. 38–39; Kurochkina, p. 206; Losik, p. 46.
17. Golushko, pp. 27, 35.
18. FHO, CGR, H 3/104, March 18, 1943, Roll 551, Frame 334; Zaloga and Granden, pp. 23, 147; Losik, pp. 46–47.
19. Zaloga and Granden, *Soviet Tanks*, p. 147; Losik, pp. 47–48.
20. FHO, CGR, H 3/1521, October 1944, Roll 587, Frame 351; Losik, p. 48.
21. Anan'ev, p. 39; Losik, pp. 46–47.
22. *VOVE*, p. 113; Skorobogatkin, p. 270.
23. Losik, p. 48.
24. Golushko, pp. 27, 35.
25. V. V. Tarnov, "Parad Izumivshii Mir," *VIZh* 1 (January 1989), p. 68.
26. *IVOVSS* (German), VI, p. 279.
27. Zaloga and Granden, *Soviet Tanks*, p. 24.
28. FHO, CGR, H 3/1521, October 1944, Roll 587, Frame 351; Zaloga and Granden, *Soviet Tanks*, p. 147.
29. Losik, pp. 48–49.
30. FHO, CGR, H 3/197, February 20, 1942, Roll 556, Frame 976.
31. Anan'ev, p. 39.
32. FHO, CGR, H 3/197, March 27, 1942, Roll 556, Frame 1043.
33. Losik, p. 51.
34. FHO, CGR, H 3/104, March 18, 1943, Roll 551, Frame 334; H 3/104, June 6, 1942, Roll 551, Frame 381; H 3/104, June 25, 1942, Roll 551, Frame 381; Zaloga and Granden, *Soviet Tanks*, p. 23.

35. FHO, CGR, H 3/197, March 17, 1942, Roll 556, Frame 1021.
36. Losik, pp. 51–52.
37. Anan'ev, p. 51.
38. Malanin, p. 33; Anan'ev, pp. 50–51; Tiushkevich, *Vooruzhennye Sily*, p. 281: Losik, pp. 50–51.
39. V. F. Tolubko and N. I. Barishev, *Na Uznom Flange* (Moscow: Izdatelistvo, "Nauka," 1973), p. 11.
40. *VOVE*, pp. 705–706; Erickson. *Stalingrad*, p. 341.
41. FHO, CGR, H 3/126, June 1942, Roll 552, Frame 903.
42. Zaloga and Granden, *Soviet Tanks*, p. 148; Erickson, *Stalingrad*, p. 382.
43. Tolubko and Barishev, pp. 14–15.
44. Ibid., pp. 18–19.
45. Tiushkevich, *Vooruzhennye Sily*, p. 281.
46. Glantz, *From Don*, p. 7.
47. Anan'ev, p. 56; Losik, p. 60.
48. Anan'ev, p. 56.
49. Ibid., p. 57.
50. Ibid., pp. 57–58.
51. Tiushkevich, *Vooruzhennye Sily*, p. 281; *IVOVSS* (German), VI, p. 280; Losik, p. 55.
52. Anan'ev, p. 59; Seaton, *Russo-German War*, p. 290.
53. Anan'ev, pp. 59–60.
54. Ibid., p. 58; Losik, p. 54; *VOVE*, p. 113; Seaton, *Russo-German War*, p. 240; Skorobogatkin, p. 305; *IVOVSS* (German), VI, p. 280.
55. Anan'ev, pp. 58–59.
56. Erickson, *Stalingrad*, p. 382.
57. Ibid., p. 341.
58. Losik, p. 53; Zaloga and Granden, *Soviet Tanks*, p. 148; Anan'ev, p. 39; FHO, CGR, H 3/1521, October 1944, Roll 587, Frame 351.
59. Tolubko and Barishev, p. 25.
60. Ibid., p. 26; Moskalenko, p. 265.
61. Losik, pp. 57–58.
62. Tolubko and Barishev, p. 34.
63. Ibid., p. 42.
64. Losik, p. 57; Malanin, p. 33.
65. Losik, p. 57; Malanin, p. 33; Anan'ev, p. 52.
66. A. P. Riazanskii, *V Ogne Tankovik Srajenii* (Moscow: Izdatelistvo, 1975), pp. 12–16.
67. Ibid., p. 18.
68. Ibid., p. 34.
69. Tolubko and Barishev, p.48; *VOVE*, p. 444; Zaloga and Granden, *Soviet Tanks*, p. 149.
70. *VOVE*, p. 445; Tolubko and Barishev, p. 173; FHO, CGR, H 3/123.1, Roll 552, Frame 443.
71. FHO, CGR, H 3/67, February 21, 1943, Roll 460, Frame 6438922. Anan'ev, p. 52; Losik, p. 58.
72. FHO, CGR, H 3/67, September 30, 1943, Roll 460, Frame 6438961; August 24, 1943, Roll 460, Frame 6438911; August 19, 1943, Roll 460, Frame 6438917.

73. *VOVE*, p. 470; FHO, CGR, H 3/67, February 21, 1943, Roll 460, Frame 6438922.

74. FHO, CGR, H 3/67, February 23, 1943, Roll 460, Frames 6438968–70; Krivosheev, pp. 357–58.

75. FHO, CGR, H 3/67, February 23, 1943, Roll 460, Frames 6438971–73.

76. Vorontsov, pp. 19–20.

77. Losik, p. 98.

78. Glantz, *From Don*, p. 8.

79. FHO, CGR, H 3/104, June 25, 1942, Roll 551, Frame 381.

80. Losik, pp. 56, 58.

81. Zaloga and Granden, *Soviet Tanks*, p. 24; FHO, CGR, H 3/124, December 29, 1943, Roll 552, Frame 817; H 3/123.1, October 25, 1944, Roll 552, Frame 475.

82. FHO, CGR, H 3/123.2, November 1942 and March 7, 1943, Roll 552, Frames 850 and 854.

83. Losik, p. 58; SVE, VII, p. 764.

84. Losik, p. 58.

85. FHO, CGR, H 3/174, December 30, 1942, Roll 556, Frames 225–26; H 3/104, December 10, 1942, Roll 551, Frame 359.

86. Zaloga and Grandsen, *Soviet Tanks*, p. 25.

87. Ibid., p. 26.

88. *VOVE*, p. 113; Losik, p. 59, gives higher numbers used.

89. Erickson, *Berlin*, p. 83; Losik pp. 70–71; *IVOVSS* (German), VI, p. 280; FHO, CGR, H 3/468.2, June 5, 1943, Roll 564, Frame 1069.

90. *VOVE*, p. 113; Losik, p. 59, gives the higher numbers used.

91. Erickson, *Berlin*, p. 83; Losik pp. 70–71; *IVOVSS* (German), VI, p. 280; FHO, CGR, H 3/468.2, June 5, 1943, Roll 564, Frame 1069; Krivosheev, pp. 357–58.

CHAPTER 9: REFINING THE TANK FORMATIONS

1. Parotkin, p. 169.
2. Losik, p. 114.
3. Ibid., p. 109.
4. Ibid., p. 112; Rokossovsky, *Velikai*, p. 436.
5. Malanin, p. 35.
6. Anan'ev, p. 65.
7. Ibid., p. 66.
8. Ibid., p. 60.
9. Ibid., p. 68.
10. Ibid., p. 57.
11. Ibid., p. 57.
12. Ibid., pp. 68–69.
13. Ibid., pp. 66–67; *VOVE*, p. 785.
14. Anan'ev, pp. 67–68.
15. Losik, pp. 71–72; Riazanskii, p. 54; Anan'ev, pp. 66–67.
16. Anan'ev, p. 67.
17. Ibid., p. 64; Losik, pp. 71–72.
18. Tiushkevich, *Armed Forces*, p. 318; Skorobogatkin, p. 334; Anan'ev, p. 75.
19. Anan'ev, p. 74.

20. Ibid., pp. 80–81; Losik, p. 65.

21. Anan'ev, p. 81; Losik, pp. 65–66.

22. Anan'ev, pp. 78, 80–81; Losik, p. 64.

23. Anan'ev, p. 78.

24. Ibid., pp. 78–79.

25. Skorobogatkin, p. 335; Tiushkevich, *Armed Forces*, p. 318; Losik, pp. 67–68; Anan'ev, p. 82; Malanin, p. 35.

26. Malanin, p. 35; Losik 64; Anan'ev, pp. 79–80.

27. Andrei I. Eremenko, *Gody Vozmeddia* (Moscow: Nauka, 1969), p. 111.

28. FHO, CGR, H 3/67, December 23, 1942, Roll 460, Frame 6438835.

29. Anan'ev, p. 79; FHO, CGR, H 3/67, February 21, 1943, Roll 460, Frame 6438922.

30. Anan'ev, p. 80.

31. FHO, CGR, H 3/67, March 30, 1943, Roll 460, Frame 6438917.

32. FHO, CGR, H 3/67, 1944, Roll 460, Frame 6438955 and August 18, 1943, Roll 460, Frame 6438917; H 3/104, Roll 551, Frames 199–202.

33. FHO, CGR, H 3/67, August 18, 1943, Roll 460, Frame 6438917; September 9, 1943, Roll 460, Frame 6438910.

34. FHO, CGR, H 3/67, September 10, 1943, Roll 460, Frame 6438961; August 24, 1943, Roll 460, Frame 6438911; August 19, 1943, Roll 460, Frame 6438917.

35. FHO, CGR, H 3/45, September 10, 1943, Roll 460, Frame 6436961.

36. FHO, CGR, H 3/67, August 24, 1943, Roll 460, Frame 6438911.

37. Parotkin, pp. 170, 177–78.

38. Krupchenko, *Sovetskie Tankovye*, p. 120.

39. Parotkin, p. 178.

40. Ibid., pp. 170–72.

41. Ibid., pp. 173–74.

42. Ibid., p. 122.

43. FHO, CGR, H 3/67, September 10, 1943 and October 22, 1943, Roll 460, Frame 6438911; November 6, 1943, Roll 460, Frame 6438912.

44. FHO, CGR, H 3/67, December 12, 1943, Roll 460, Frame 6438906.

45. FHO, CGR, H 3/67, February 5, 1944, Roll 460, Frame 6438951.

46. FHO, CGR, H 3/67, May 23, 1944, Roll 460, Frame 6438944.

47. Losik, p. 67; Anan'ev, p. 83.

48. Anan'ev, p. 81; Losik, p. 66.

49. Anan'ev, p. 81.

50. Ibid., pp. 78–79; FHO, CGR, H 3/104, October 1943, Roll 551, Frames 15860; Malanin, p. 35; Losik, p. 65; Zaloga and Granden, *Soviet Tanks*, p. 149.

51. Skorobogatkin, p. 335; Losik, p. 77; Malanin, p. 35.

52. S. P. Platanov, ed., *Bitva za Leningrad, 1941–1944* (Moscow: Voenizdat, 1964), pp. 314–15.

53. Tiushkevich, *Vooruzhennye Sily*, p. 319; Malanin, p. 35; *VOVE*, p. 281.

54. Tiushkevich, *Vooruzhennye Sily*, p. 350.

55. Anan'ev, p. 69.

56. Ibid., pp. 75–76; Losik, p. 74.

57. Anan'ev, p. 83.

58. Tiushkevich, *Vooruzhennye Sily*, p. 391.

59. Anan'ev, pp. 81–82; Losik, pp. 64, 66–67; FHO, CGR, H 3/123.1, June 9, 1944, Roll 552, Frame 497.
60. Zaloga and Granden, *Soviet Tanks*, p. 172; Malanin, p. 37.
61. *VOVE*, p. 113; Tiushkevich, Vooruzhennye Sily, p. 391; Malanin, p. 37.
62. FHO, CGR, H 3/1337, July 27, 1944, Roll 585, Frame 362.
63. G. T. Zavision and P. A. Kornushin, *I na Tikom Okeane* (Moscow: Voennoe Izdatelistvo, 1967), p. 55.
64. Losik, p. 65.
65. FHO, CGR, H 3/67, August 26, 1944, Roll 460, Frame 6438934.
66. The First Mechanized Corps had Sherman tanks in 1945 with a JS heavy tank unit attached to provide antitank protection; FHO, CGR, H 3/320, February 20, 1945, Roll 561, Frame 971.
67. Losik, p. 75.
68. David M. Glantz, *August Storm: Soviet Tactical and Operational Combat in Manchuria, 1945* (Combat Studies Institute, Fort Leavenworth, Kans.: U.S. Army Command and General Staff College, 1983), p. 54.
69. FHO, CGR, H 3/68.1, Roll 460, Frame 6439068A.
70. Glantz, *August Storm*, p. 55; FHO, CGR, H 3/123.1, March 3, 1945, Roll 552, Frame 442.
71. Riazanskii, pp. 140, 156, and 165.
72. FHO, CGR, H 3/1774, Roll 589, Frame 244.
73. Anan'ev, p. 74.
74. *VOVE*, p. 113; Tiushkevich, *Vooruzhennye Sily*, p. 347.
75. Tiushkevich, *Vooruzhennye Sily*, p. 391.

CHAPTER 10: TANK AND CREW REPLACEMENTS AND TRAINING

1. Krivosheev, pp. 357–58.
2. Mueller-Hillebrand, III, p. 274.
3. FHO, CGR, H 3/123.2, September 12, 1943, Roll 553, Frame 823.
4. FHO, CGR, H 3/123.2, May 26, 1944, Roll 552, Frames 781–82.
5. V. Zelenskii, "Podgotovka Mladshik Tankovik Spetsialistov v Godi Velikoi Otechestvennoi Voini," *VIZh*, September 1981, p. 72.
6. Krivosheev, pp. 312, 357–58.
7. Erickson, *Berlin*, p. 83; Mueller-Hillebrand, III, p. 274.
8. Seaton, *Russo-German War*, pp. 348–49.
9. FHO, CGR, H 3/123.2, September 30, 1943, Roll 552, Frame 816; Krivosheev, pp. 370–71.
10. Mueller-Hillebrand, III, p. 274.
11. FHO, CGR, H 3/104, January 1, 1944, Roll 551, Frame 155; Krivosheev, p. 358.
12. FHO, CGR, H 3/123.2, May 26, 1944, Roll 552, Frames 781–82.
13. FHO, CGR, H 3/320, February 20, 1945, Roll 561, Frame 966.
14. FHO, CGR, II 3/320, January 1945, Roll 561, Frame 967.
15. FHO, CGR, H 3/320, Roll 561, Frame 964.
16. Zaloga estimated the growth of tanks and self-propelled artillery vehicles from 13,600 in June 1944 to 17,000 in December 1944 and a drop to 14,000 in April 1945; Zaloga and Granden, *Soviet Tanks*, p. 223.
17. FHO, CGR, H 3/123.2, Report from 18th Army, August 8, 1944, Roll 552, Frame 763.

18. FHO, CGR, H 3/123.2, May 26, 1944, Roll 552, Frames 781–82.
19. FHO, CGR, H 3/123.2, February 24, 1945, Roll 552, Frame 658.
20. FHO, CGR, H 3/123.2, February 13, 1945, Roll 552, Frame 664.
21. FHO, CGR, H 3/123.2, February 1945, Roll 522, Frame 679.
22. FHO, CGR, H 3/123.2, May 26, 1944, Roll 552, Frame 781.
23. Tolubko, pp. 18–19.
24. Ibid., pp. 25–26.
25. FHO, CGR, H 3/1337, May 3, 1944, Roll 585, Frame 142.
26. FHO, CGR, H 3/1339, Roll 585, Frame 366.
27. FHO, CGR, H 3/1337, Roll 585, Frame 122.
28. FHO, CGR, H 3/1337, March 19, 1944, Roll 585, Frame 122.
29. Losik, pp. 79–81.
30. Ibid., p. 83.
31. Mellenthin, *Panzer Battles*, p. 221.
32. Anan'ev, p. 48–49.
33. FHO, CGR, H 3/77, November 29, 1943, Roll 549, Frames 838 and 981.
34. FHO, CGR, H 3/77, Roll 549, Frame 982.
35. FHO, CGR, H 3/77, Roll 549, Frame 981.
36. FHO, CGR, H 3/77, November 29, 1943, Roll 549, Frame 838; H 3/1337, May 1944, Roll 585, Frame 138.
37. FHO, CGR, H 3/1337, July 25, 1944, Roll 585, Frame 366.
38. FHO, CGR, H 3/1337, July 25, 1944, Roll 585, Frame 366.
39. FHO, CGR, H 3/77, Roll 549, Frame 986.
40. FHO, CGR, H 3/77, September 10, 1943, Roll 549, Frame 981.
41. FHO, CGR, H 3/77, September 10, 1943, Roll 549, Frame 981.
42. FHO, CGR, H 3/1337, Roll 585, Frame 152; Anan'ev, p. 48.
43. FHO, CGR, H 3/1337, April 30, 1944, Roll 585, Frame 155.
44. FHO, CGR, H 3/77, November 29, 1943, Roll 549, Frame 838.
45. FHO, CGR, H 3/77, Roll 549, Frame 982.
46. FHO, CGR, H 3/77, Roll 549, Frame 986.
47. FHO, CGR, H 3/1337, July 25, 1944, Roll 585, Frame 366.
48. FHO, CGR, H 3/1337, April 30, 1944, Roll 585, Frame 155.
49. FHO, CGR, H 3/67, February 23, 1943, Roll 460, Frames 6438968–73.
50. FHO, CGR, H 3/67, February 23, 1943, Roll 460, Frame 6438972.
51. SVE, p. 400; FHO, CGR, H 3/123.1, March 1944, Roll 552, Frame 512; H 3/330, Roll 562, Frame 56; Erickson, *Berlin*, p. 83; Zaloga and Granden, *Soviet Tanks*, p. 219.
52. Zaloga and Granden, *Soviet Tanks*, p. 219; Erickson, *Berlin*, p. 84.
53. SVE, p. 400; FHO, CGR, H 3/123.1, March 1944, Roll 552, Frame 512; H 3/330, Roll 562, Frame 56; Erickson, *Berlin*, p. 83; Zaloga and Granden, *Soviet Tanks*, p. 219.
54. FHO, CGR, H 3/1689, Roll 578, Frame 1140.
55. FHO, CGR, H 3/828, Roll 578, Frame 1140; H 3/1337, 1943, Roll 585, Roll 132; Eremenko, *Stalingrad*, pp. 460–62.
56. Andrei I. Eremenko, *Na Zapadnom Napravlenii* (Moscow: Voenizdat, 1959), p. 183.
57. Joan Beaumont, *Comrades in Arms: British Aid to Russia, 1941–1945* (London: Davis-Poynter, 1980), p. 152.
58. Ibid., p. 153.

59. FHO, CGR, H 3/1337, 1943, Roll 585, Frame 131.
60. FHO, CGR, H 3/828, Roll 578, Frame 1140.
61. Forster, p. 171; *VOVE*, p. 704.
62. Forster, p. 263.
63. FHO, CGR, H 3/828, Roll 578, Frame 1140; H 3/1337, April 13, 1944, Roll 585, Frame 180.
64. FHO, CGR, H 3/123.1, April 22, 1944, Roll 552, Frame 513.
65. FHO, CGR, H 3/123.1, March 7, 1944, and May 10, 1944, Roll 552, Frame 512.
66. Eremenko, Stalingrad, p. 418–19.
67. FHO, CGR, H 3/123.2, November 6, 1942, Roll 552, Frame 854.
68. FHO, CGR, H 3/123.2, January 20, 1943, and March 7, 1943, Roll 552, Frames 850–51.
69. FHO, CGR, H 3/123.2, June 3, 1943, Roll 552, Frame 844; July 1, 1943, Roll 552, Frame 842.
70. FHO, CGR, H 3/123.2, December 29, 1943, Roll 552, Frame 817.
71. FHO, CGR, H 3/123.1, October 25, 1944, Roll 552, Frame 475.
72. Werner Haupt, *Heeresgruppe Mitte, 1941–1945* (Dorheim: Verlag HansHennings Podzun, 1968), p. 177.
73. FHO, CGR, H 3/1337, March 1944, Roll 585, Frame 126.
74. Tolubko and Barishev, pp. 136, 138.
75. FHO, CGR, H 3/1337, April 12, 1944, Roll 585, Frame 122.
76. FHO, CGR, H 3/1337, July 25, 1944, Roll 585, Frame 348.
77. FHO, CGR, H 3/67, July 17, 1944, Roll 460, Frame 6438942.
78. FHO, CGR, H 3/68.1, January 31, 1945, Roll 460, Frame 6439070.
79. FHO, CGR, H 3/320, February 20, 1945, Roll 561, Frame 962.
80. Zaloga and Granden, *Soviet Tanks*, p. 180.
81. A. Vassilevsky, *Moscow Stalingrad, 1941–1942: Recollections, Stories, Reports* (Moscow: Progress Publishers, 1974), p. 143.
82. FHO, CGR, H 3/77, Roll 549, Frame 981.
83. FHO, CGR, H 3/77, Roll 549, Frame 981.
84. FHO, CGR, H 3/320, February 20, 1945, Roll 561, Frames 962–63.
85. FHO, CGR, H 3/1337, May 7, 1944, Roll 585, Frame 207.
86. FHO, CGR, H 3/123.1, August 25, 1944, Roll 552, Frame 540.
87. FHO, CGR, H 3/77, January 31, 1945, Roll 549, Frame 824.
88. FHO, CGR, H 3/123.2, January 20, 1945, Roll 552, Frame 694.
89. Zaloga and Granden, *Soviet Tanks*, p. 9.
90. Manstein, p. 152; Erickson, *Stalingrad*, p. 225.
91. Ely, p. 53.
92. FHO, CGR, H 3/123.2, September 16, 1944, Roll 552, Frame 716.
93. FHO, CGR, H 3/123.2, May 29, 1944, Roil 552, Frame 782.
94. FHO, CGR, H 3/123.2, December 31, 1943, Roll 552, Frame 813.
95. Erickson, *Stalingrad*, p. 225.
96. FHO, CGR, H 3/104, February 1944, Roll 551, Frame 114.
97. FHO, CGR, H 3/123.2, May 7, 1944, Roil 552, Frame 783.
98. FHO, CGR, H 3/123.2, March 17, 1944, Roll 552, Frame 792.
99. FHO, CGR, H 3/123.2, February 1945, Roll 552, Frame 677.
100. FHO, CGR, H 3/123.2, 1944, Roll 552, Frame 792.
101. SVE, p. 348; FHO, CGR, H 3/77, November 29, 1943, Roll 549, Frame 838.

102. FHO, CGR, H 3/1337, July 1944, Roll 585, Frame 362.
103. FHO, CGR, H 3/123.2, January 27, 1945, Roll 552, Frame 686.
104. FHO, CGR, H 3/1337, July 12, 1944, Roll 585, Frame 157.
105. FHO, CGR, H 3/123.2, March 25, 1945, Roll 552, Frame 630.
106. FHO, CGR, H 3/123.2, February 14, 1945, Roll 552, Frame 697.
107. FHO, CGR, H 3/258, March 19, 1945, Roll 561, Frame 65.

CHAPTER 11: ARTILLERY DOCTRINE AND ORGANIZATION

1. TM 30–430, V-48.
2. Chris Bellamy, *Red God of War* (London: Brassey's Defence Publishers, 1986), p. 45.
3. Ibid., pp. 46, 49.
4. Ibid., pp. 47–48.
5. Ibid., p. 48; Ely, pp. 64–66; Harold J. Gordon, "Artillery," in Liddell Hart, *The Soviet Army*. p. 357.
6. Ely, pp. 64–67.
7. Ibid., p. 70.
8. Gordon, p. 354.
9. Bellamy, p. 56.
10. Gordon, p. 358; Ely, p. 76.
11. Gordon, pp. 358–59.
12. Ibid., pp. 359–60; Steiger, p. 51.
13. Gordon, pp. 361–62.
14. Ibid., p. 347.
15. Bellamy, p. 49.
16. Parrish, pp. 43–44.
17. Ibid., pp. 44–45.
18. Ibid., p. 46.
19. Bellamy, p. 50; Parrish, pp. 49–50.
20. Parrish, p. 52.
21. Gordon, p. 352.
22. Ibid., pp. 350–51.
23. Ibid., p. 352.
24. Glantz, *From Don*, p. 8; Gordon, p. 353.
25. Parrish, p. 48; TM 30–430, V-52–53.
26. Bellamy, p. 59.
27. Ibid., pp. 59, 53; G. E. Peredeliskii, *Artilleriia v Bou i Operatsii* (Moscow: Voennoe Izdatelistvo, 1980), pp. 130–35.
28. Tiushkevich, *Vooruzhennye Sily*, p. 228; Konstantin P. Kazakov, *Vsegda S Pekhotoi Vsegda S Tankami* (Moscow: Voenizdat, 1969), p. 8; V. G. Grabin, *Druzie Pobedi* (Moscow: Izdatelistvo, 1989), pp. 31–34.
29. FHO, CGR, H 3/78, February 21, 1945, Roll 550, Frame 15.
30. Zakharov, "Eve of World War II," p. 95.
31. Tiushkevich, *Vooruzhennye Sily*, p. 237.
32. N. Y. Eliseyev, "Germanskiy Militarizm," *VIZh* 3 (March 1991), p. 6.
33. Tiushkevich, *Vooruzhennye Sily*, p. 237.
34. *VOVE*, p. 68; Tiushkevich, *Vooruzhennye Sily*, pp. 198, 237; M. K. Sekirin, *V Plamenm Srakenii Boevoi Puti 13–i Armii* (Moscow: Voennoe Izdatelistvo, 1973), p. 13; FHO, CGR, H 3/78, February 21, 1945, Roll 550, Frames 18–19; Anfilov, *Blitskriga*, pp. 127, 249.

35. B. L. Vannikov, "Iz Zapisok Narkoma Vooruzheniia," *VIZh* 2 (February 1962), p. 78; N. E. Medvedev, "Artilleria RVGK v. Pervom Periode Voini," *VIZh* 10 (October 1987), p. 85; Kasakov, *Vsegda,* pp. 8–9.

36. Tiushkevich, *Vooruzhennye Sily,* p. 228; Pavlovskii, p. 107. The second source gives the total as 67,335 including regimental guns and mortars.

37. FHO, CGR, H 3/78, February 21, 1945, Roll 550, Frame 15.

38. Pavlovskii, p. 107.

39. FHO, CGR, H 3/374, September 1944, Roll 562, Frame 977; Erickson, *Stalingrad,* p. 226; Gordon, pp. 348–49.

40. FHO, CGR, H 3/78, February 21, 1945, Roll 550, Frames 21–22.

41. VOVE, p. 65; Medvedev, p. 85; Konstantin P. Kazakov, *Artillerii i Raketi* (Moscow: Voenizdat, 1968), p. 75.

42. Pavlovski, p. 107. German estimates were much lower. On May 1, 1942, the Germans estimated Russian artillery strength had increased to 9,543 guns and by November 1, 1942, to 15,000; FHO, CGR, H 3/340, 1945, Roll 562, Frame 161; H 3/191, 1942, Roll 556, Frame 582.

43. The 1091st, 1092nd, 1093rd, and 1094th were formed together in March 1942. In May 1942, after the Soviet disaster as Izyum, the 1092nd was sent by rail to the Voronezh Front, even though it was not completely equipped with trucks and was short of men. The gun tractors were old and had been requisitioned from collective farms. FHO, CGR, H 3/69, May 6, 1943, Roll 549, Frame 108.

44. FHO, CGR, H 3/78, January 1945, Roll 550, Frame 35.

45. FHO, CGR, H 3/69, May 6, 1943, Roll 549, Frame 108.

46. Medvedev, "Artillerii," p. 85.

47. Ibid., p. 85.

48. FHO, CGR, H 3/340, 1944, Roll 562, Frame 161; H 3/123.1, March 13, 1945, Roll 552, Frame 248.

49. Erickson, *Stalingrad,* p. 375.

50. *IVOVSS* (German), VI, p. 230.

51. Tiushkevich, *Vooruzhennye Sily,* p. 316.

52. FHO, CGR, H 3/69, May 6, 1943, Roll 549, Frame 108.

53. Konstantin P. Kazakov, "Razvitiye Sovetskoy Artillerii v Godi Velikoy Otechestvennoy Voyny," *VIZh* 11 (November 1975), p. 14.

54. Erickson, *Berlin,* p. 80.

55. Kazakov, "Razvitiye," p. 15.

56. FHO, CGR, H 3/104, May 30, 1943, Roll 551, Frame 325; Skorobogatkin, p. 335; Malanin, p. 34; *VOVE,* p. 63.

57. A. C. Domank, et al., *Rezerva Verkovnogo Glavno-Komandovaniia* (Moscow: Voyennoye Izdatelistvo, 1987), p. 4.

58. FHO, CGR, H 3/69, May 18, 1943, Roll 549, Frame 111.

59. FHO, CGR, H 3/69, January 26, 1943, Roll 549, Frame 105.

60. FHO, CGR, H 3/69, March 18, 1943, Roll 549, Frame 121.

61. FHO, CGR, H 3/69, February 26, 1944, Roll 549, Frame 43.

62. *IVOVSS* (German), III, p. 25; Erickson, *Stalingrad,* p. 448.

63. *IVOVSS* (German), VI, p. 246.

64. FHO, CGR, H 3/123.1, May 28, 1944, Roll 552, Frame 284.

65. Malanin, p. 37.

66. Skorobogatkin, p. 335; Malanin, p. 36.
67. *VOVE*, p. 63; FHO, CGR, H 3/69, August 25, 1943, Roll 549, Frame 81; Kazakov, "Razvitiye," p. 16.
68. Erickson, *Berlin*, pp. 80–81.
69. Malanin, p. 35.
70. *VOVE*, p. 65; Bellamy, p. 50.
71. Malanin, p. 36; Kazakov, "Razvitiye," p. 16; Skorobogatkin, p. 335.
72. Skorobogatkin, p. 336.
73. Vasiliki I. Kazakov, *Artilleriia Ogono* (Moscow: Izd-vo, 1972), pp. 110, 117.
74. FHO, CGR, H 3/104, September 15, 1943, Roll 551, Frame 260.
75. FHO, CGR, H 3/193, December 11, 1943, Roll 556, Frame 732.
76. FHO, CGR, H 3/1799, 1945, Roll 590, Frame 86.
77. FHO, CGR, H 3/64.2, August 28, 1943, Roll 460, Frame 6438622.
78. FHO, CGR, H 3/69, November 5, 1943, Roll 549, Frame 94.
79. FHO, CGR, H 3/78, February 21, 1945, Roll 550, Frame 21.
80. Tiushkevich, *Vooruzhennye Sily*, p. 316.
81. Erickson, *Berlin*, pp. 80–81.
82. FHO, CGR, H 3/78, February 21, 1945, Roll 550, Frame 22; Malanin, p. 37.
83. Tiushkevich, *Vooruzhennye Sily*, p. 346; FHO, CGR, H 3/78, February 21, 1945, Roll 550, Frame 21.
84. *VOVE*, p. 63.
85. *VOVE*, p. 63; Erickson, *Berlin*, p. 80.
86. Glantz, *From Don*, p. 220.
87. Tiushkevich, *Vooruzhennye Sily*, p. 342; Skorobogatkin, pp. 390–91.
88. FHO, CGR, H 3/123.1, August 16, 1944, Roll 552, Frames 493–96.
89. *IVOVSS* (German), VI, p. 230.
90. *IVOVSS* (German), VI, p. 230. Skorobogatkin has slightly different totals: November 1942 72,500; July 1943 98,790; pp. 343, 362.
91. FHO, CGR, H 3/1339, 1943, Roll 585, Frames 376–78.
92. FHO, CGR, H 3/64.2, March 15, 1944, Roll 460, Frame 6438486.
93. FHO, CGR, H 3/64.2, September 3, 1944, Roll 460, Frame 6438400.
94. FHO, CGR, H 3/64.2, September 17, 1944, Roll 460, Frame 6438308.
95. FHO, CGR, H 3/64.2, April 4, 1944, Roll 460, Frame 6438617.
96. Militarakademie, p. 99.
97. Ibid., p. 62.
98. Malanin, p. 38.
99. FHO, CGR, H 3/78, November 1944, Roll 550, Frame 35.
100. FHO, CGR, H 3/69, March 11, 1944, Roll 549, Frame 84.
101. FHO, CGR, H 3/78, Roll 550, Frame 19.
102. FHO, CGR, H 3/78, March 1, 1945, Roll 550, Frame 6.
103. FHO, CGR, H 3/277, March 26, 1944, Roll 561, Frame 382.
104. FHO, CGR, H 3/118, March 1, 1945, Roll 552, Frame 241.
105. *VOVE*, p. 66; *IVOVSS*, IV, pp. 25–26, 125.
106. Tiushkevich, *Vooruzhennye Sily*, p. 346.
107. *VIZh* 11 (November 1977), p. 52.
108. Kasakov, *Vsegda*, p. 208.
109. FHO, CGR, H 3/118, February 1945, Roll 552, Frame 67.

CHAPTER 12: ARTILLERY WEAPONS AND MUNITIONS

1. Small-bore weapons were referred to by the diameter of the bore plus the word caliber, but this usage had no relationship to the length of the barrel. For example, a .50–caliber machine gun could have a barrel of any length. The ".50" referred only to the diameter of the bullet.
2. Kazakov, *Artilleriia*, pp. 108–109.
3. Ibid., pp. 110–11.
4. *Illustrated Encyclopedia of 20th Century Weapons and Warfare*, 24 vols. (New York: Columbia House, 1969), p. 1331; FHO, CGR, H 3/82, December 1, 1941, Roll 550, Frame 398; Arthur G. Volz, "Soviet Artillery Weapons: II 1918–41," *Soviet Armed Forces Review Annual* 11 (1987–88), p. 303.
5. Kazakov, *Artilleriie*, p. 64; Grabin, p. 31; *Illustrated Encyclopedia*, p. 1331.
6. *Illustrated Encyclopedia*, p. 1344.
7. Kazakov, *Artilleriie*, p. 65; Bellamy, p. 132; Tiushkevich, *Vooruzhennye Sily*, p. 187; *Illustrated Encyclopedia*, p. 1334; Volz, "Soviet Artillery, 1918–41," pp. 316, 318.
8. *Illustrated Encyclopedia*, pp. 1333–34, 1339; FHO, CGR, H 3/82, December 1, 1941, Roll 550, Frame 398; Volz, "Soviet Artillery, 1918–41," p. 301; Krivosheev, p. 343.
9. *Illustrated Encyclopedia*, pp. 1334, 1336; Krivosheev, p. 343.
10. Ibid., pp. 1334, 1336; Vannikov, p. 78.
11. Tiushkevich, *Vooruzhennye Sily*, p. 237.
12. FHO, CGR, H 3/340, October 23, 1944, Roll 562, Frame 85; H 3/78, January 1, 1944, Roll 550, Frame 47; Viktor A. Anfilov, *Krushenie Pokhoda Gitlera na Moskva, 1941* (Moscow: Nauka, 1989), p. 51; Volz, "Soviet Artillery," 1918–41," p. 310.
13. Brian Blunt and Tolley Taylor, *Brassey's Artillery of the World* (New York: Bonanza Books, 1979), p. 49; Volz, "Soviet Artillery, 1918–41," p. 304.
14. Blunt and Taylor, p. 50; *Illustrated Encyclopedia*, pp. 1334, 1336.
15. Blunt and Taylor, p. 57; *Illustrated Encyclopedia*, pp. 1343–44.
16. Blunt and Taylor, p. 55; *Illustrated Encyclopedia*, pp. 1343–44; Vannikov, p. 79.
17. *Illustrated Encyclopedia*, p. 1344.
18. Kazakov, *Artilleriie*, p. 65; Volz, "Soviet Artillery, 1918–41," p. 311.
19. Ibid., p. 127.
20. Kazakov, *Artillerii*, p. 82; *Illustrated Encyclopedia*, p. 1331; Krivsoheev, p. 348.
21. Blunt and Taylor, p. 32; *Illustrated Encyclopedia*, pp. 1334, 1336.
22. Blunt and Taylor, p. 32; *Illustrated Encyclopedia*, pp. 1334, 1336.
23. Blunt and Taylor, p. 56; *Illustrated Encyclopedia*, p. 1344.
24. FHO, CGR, H 3/340, October 23, 1944, Roll 562, Frame 85.
25. FHO, CGR, H 3/1689, September 1940, Roll 587, Frames 810 ff.
26. FHO, CGR, H 3/1339, 1943, Roll 585, Frames 376–78.
27. *VOVE*, p. 554.
28. FHO, CGR, H 3/818, August 1944, Roll 578, Frame 562.
29. Rotundo, *Stalingrad*, p. 210.
30. FHO, CGR, H 3/83.3b, Die Kriegswehrmacht der Union der Sozialistischen Sowietrepubliken, January 1, 1941, p. 3, Roll 587, Frame 810 ff.
31. Militarakademie, p. 104.
32. Militarakademie, p. 64; FHO, CGR, H 3/374, September 1944, Roll 562, Frame 986; H 3/380, November 16, 1944, Roll 562, Frame 1057.

33. Rotundo, *Stalingrad*, p. 203.
34. Ibid., p. 210.
35. TM 30–430, VII-13–14; FHO, CGR, H 3/64.2, March 15, 1944, Roll 460, Frame 6438486.
36. Militarakademie, p. 65.
37. Ibid., p. 178.
38. Gordon, p. 357.
39. FHO, CGR, H 3/118, November 11–20, 1944, Roll 552, Frame 265.
40. FHO, CGR, H 3/73, Roll 549, Frame 542.
41. FHO, CGR, H 3/340, October 1944, Roll 562, Frame 72.
42. Dunn, p. 174.

CHAPTER 13: THE TANK DESTROYERS
1. Robert A. Doughty, "French Antitank Doctrine, 1940: The Antidote that Failed," *Military Review* 56 (May 1976), p. 38.
2. Ibid., pp. 41–43.
3. Christopher R. Gabel, *Seek, Strike, and Destroy: U.S. Army Tank Destroyer Doctrine in World War II*, Combat Studies Institute, #12 Leavenworth Papers (Fort Leavenworth, Kans.: U. S. Army Command and General Staff College, 1985), pp. 5–8.
4. Ibid., pp. 10–13.
5. Biryukov and Melnikov, p. 54.
6. Gordon, p. 349. Biryukov and Melnikov, p. 53.
7. Biryukov and Melnikov, pp. 40–41.
8. *VOVE*, p. 285; Budur, p. 79.
9. Biryukov and Melnikov, p. 42.
10. Ibid., pp 38–39.
11. F. Samsanov, "Iz Istorii Razvitiya Sovetskoi Artillerii," *VIZh* 11 (November 1971), p.   65.
12. *Illustrated Encyclopedia*, p. 1331; Budur, p. 79.
13. FHO, CGR, H 3/1007, May 25, 1944, Roll 580, Frame 301; Krivosheev, pp. 353–54.
14. Budur, p. 79; FHO, CGR, H 3/340, October 23, 1944, Roll 562, Frame 80.
15. Biryukov and Melnikov, pp. 53, 55.
16. Moskalenko, p. 238; Tiushkevich, *Armed Forces*, p. 237; Budur, pp. 80–81: *VOVE*, p. 283; Sandalov, pp. 3–10; Anfilov, *Bessmertnii*, p. 117; Anfilov, *Blitskriga*, p. 127.
17. *VOVE*, p. 67; Budur, p. 81; Skorobogatkin, p. 270; Kazakov, "Razvitiye," p. 13.
18. FHO, CGR, H 3/113, August 5, 1942, Roll 551, Frame 699; H 3/69, April 25, 1942, Roll 549, Frame 244; H 3/374, Roll 562, Frame 1016; Budur, p. 81: Malanin, p. 33.
19. Budur, p. 81; FHO, CGR, H 3/1007, February 1944, Roll 580, Frame 303; H 3/374, Roll 562, Frame 1015.
20. FHO, CGR, H 3/468.2, October 2, 1943, Roll 564, Frame 1007; H 3/104, Roll 551, Frame 246; *VOVE*, pp. 67, 310.
21. Budur, pp. 82–83; *VOVE*, p. 285.
22. *VOVE*, pp. 67, 285.
23. Malanin, p. 36.
24. Biryukov and Melnikov, pp. 45–46.

25. Ibid., p. 55.
26. *VOVE*, p. 67.
27. *VOVE*, p. 285.
28. FHO, CGR, H 3/340, January 22, 1945, Roll 562, Frame 126; VOVE, p. 285; Budur, p. 83.
29. Samsanov, "Iz Istoria," p. 65.
30. Losik, p. 26.
31. N. Popov, "Razvitie Samokhodnoi Artillerii," *VIZh* 1 (January 1977), p. 27.
32. FHO, CGR, H 3/104, November 29, 1943, Roll 551, Frame 236; H 3/104, October 8, 1943, Roll 551, Frame 234.
33. Krupchenko, p. 117; Popov, "Razvitie," p. 28.
34. *VOVE*, p. 631; Popov, "Razvitie," p. 28. The Germans had evidence of a February 1943 table of organization for the regiment with three batteries of four SU-122s, two batteries of four SU-76s, and a command unit of six T-34s and six armored cars; FHO, CGR, H 3/104, November 5, 1943, Roll 551, Frame 194; Anan'ev, p. 80, lists another alternative organization: two batteries of SU-76s and three batteries of SU-122s. The variation is a clear indication that the doctrine was still being developed.
35. Popov, "Razvitie," p. 28.
36. Ibid., p. 28; Anan'ev, p. 80.
37. FHO, CGR, H 3/104, October 8, 1943, Roll 551, Frame 235; Popov, "Razvitie," p. 28; Losik, p. 61; Malanin, p. 34.
38. *Moskovskii Voennii Okrug*, p. 319.
39. FHO, CGR, H 3/104, October 8, 1943, Roll 551, Frames 234–37.
40. *VOVE*, p. 64; Krivosheev, p. 358.
41. FHO, CGR, H 3/340, September 5, 1944, Roll 562, Frame 145.
42. *Illustrated Encyclopedia*, p. 1336.
43. *VOVE*, p. 516.
44. Zaloga and Granden, *Soviet Tanks*, p. 26; Popov, "Razvitie," p. 28.
45. *VOVE*, p. 516.
46. *VOVE*, p. 631; Zaloga and Granden, Soviet Tanks, p. 163; FHO, CGR, H 3/104, November 5, 1943, Roll 551, Frames 194–99.
47. Zaloga and Granden, *Soviet Tanks*, p. 165.
48. Ibid., p. 26.
49. *VOVE*, p. 64.
50. Zaloga and Granden, *Soviet Tanks*, p. 181; Popov, "Razvitie," p. 29.
51. FHO, CGR, H 3/123.1, November 5, 1943, Roll 553, Frame 508.
52. Zaloga and Granden, *Soviet Tanks*, p. 181.
53. *VOVE*, p. 631; Popov, "Razvitie," p. 29.
54. *VOVE*, pp. 64, 516.
55. Zaloga and Granden, *Soviet Tanks*, p. 183.
56. FHO, CGR, H 3/340, February 4, 1945, Roll 562, Frame 135; Malanin, p. 38.
57. *VOVE*, pp. 64, 516.
58. Malanin, p. 38.
59. FHO, CGR, H 3/78, July 1944, Role 550, Frame 274.
60. The 62nd Guard Rifle Division had the 69th Mechanized Artillery Battalion and the 252nd Rifle Division had the 110th Mechanized Artillery Battalion; FHO, CGR, H 3/123.2, December 24, 1944, Roll 552, Frame 464; Losik, p. 62.

61. Popov, "Razvitie," p. 30.

62. Malanin, p. 38.

63. FHO, CGR, H 3/123.1, March 1945, Roll 552, Frame 435; Malanin, p. 38.

64. *VOVE*, p. 630.

65. Zaloga and Granden, *Soviet Tanks*, p. 31; Losik, p. 62; Popov, "Razvitie," p. 30, states that the heavy brigade was formed in March 1945 and used the JSU122.

66. FHO, CGR, H 3/123.2, March 3, 1945, Roll 552, Frame 616; *VOVE*, p. 631.

67. *VOVE*, p. 630; Popov, "Razvitie," pp. 30–31, states that the light SU brigades were equipped with SU-76s.

CONCLUSION

1. Andrei Grechko, "An Historic Victory," in *Soviet Studies on the Second World War* (Moscow: USSR Academy of Sciences, 1976), p. 12.

2. Beaumont, p. 144.

3. Semyon Khromov and Nikolai Shishov, "Military Alliance of the Peoples Against Fascism," in Grechko, *Soviet Studies*, p. 125.

4. Pyotr Fedoseyev, "The Soviet Union's Victory in the Great Patriotic War and the Course of World History," in Grechko, *Soviet Studies*, p. 38.

5. Fedoseyev in Grechko, *Soviet Studies*, p. 50.

Select Bibliography

Anan'ev, I. M. *Tankovie Armii v Nastuplenii*. Moscow: Voenizdat, 1988. Andronikov, Nikolaii, and W. D. Mostowenko. *Die Roten Panzer: Geschichte der Sowjetischen Panzertruppen, 1920–1960*. Munich: J. F. Lehmann, 1963.

Anfilov, Viktor A. *Bessmertnii Podvig Issledovanie Kanuna i Pervogo Etapa Velikoi Otechestvennoi Voini*. Moscow: Nauka, 1971.

———. *Proval Blitskriga*. Moscow: Nauka, 1974.

Beaumont, Joan. *Comrades in Arms: British Aid to Russia, 1941–1945*. London: Davis-Poynter, 1980.

Bedniasin, A. I., et al. *Kievskii Krasnoznamennii Istorik Krasnoznamennogo Kievskogo Voennogo Okruga, 1919–1972*. Moscow: Voennoe Isdatelistvo, 1974. Bellamy, Chris. *Red God of War*. London: Brassy's Defence Publishers, 1986. Bialer, Seweryn, ed. *Stalin and His Generals: Soviet Military Memoirs of World War II*. New York: Pegasus, 1969.

Biryukov, G. F., and G. Melnikov. *Antitank Warfare*. Moscow: Progress Publishers, 1972.

Bukov, K. I., et al. *Bumva za Moskvi*. Moscow: Izdatelistvo, "Moskovskii Rabochii," 1985.

Clark, Alan. *Barbarossa: The Russian-German Conflict, 1941–45*. New York: New American Library, 1966.

Cole, John P., and F. C. German. *A Geography of the U.S.S.R.: The Background of a Planned Economy*. London: Butterworths, 1984.

Domank, A. S., et al. *Rezerva Verknovnogo Glauno Komandovaniia*. Moscow: Voyennoye Isdatelistvo, 1987.

Dunn, Walter S., Jr. *Second Front Now 1943*. University, Ala.: University of Alabama Press, 1980.

Dunnigan, James F., ed. *The Russian Front*. London: Arms and Armour Press, 1978.

Dupuy, Trevor N. *A Genius for War: The History of the German Army and General Staff from 1807 through 1945*. London: MacDonald and Jane's, 1977.

Dupuy, Trevor N., and Paul Martell. *Great Battles on the Eastern Front: The Soviet-German War, 1941–1945*. Indianapolis, Ind.: Bobbs-Merrill Company, 1982.

Ely, Louis B. *The Red Army Today*. Harrisburg: Military Services Publishing Co., 1953.

Eremenko, Andrei I. *Gody Vozeddiia*. Moscow: "Nauka," 1969.

———. *The Arduous Beginning*. Moscow: Progress Publishers, 1966.

———. *Na Zapadnom Napravienii*. Moscow: Voenizdat, 1959.

———. *Stalingrad, Zapiski Komanduyushchego Frontom*. Moscow: Voenizdat, 1961.

Erickson, John. *The Road to Berlin*. Boulder, Colo.: Westview Press, 1983.

————. *The Road to Stalingrad: Stalin's War with Germany.* New York: Harper & Row, 1975.

Fremde Heer Ost. *Truppen-Upersicht und Kriegsliederungen Rote Armee Stand August 1944.* Captured German Records. National Archives.

Forster, Gerhard, and Nikolaus Paulus. *Abri der Geschichte der Panzerwaffe.* Berlin: Militarverlag der Deutschen Demokratischen Republik, 1977.

Fugate, Bryan I. *Operation Barbarossa.* Novato, Calif.: Presidio Press, 1984. Gabel, Christopher R. *Seek, Strike, and Destroy: U. S. Army Tank Destroyer Doctrine in World War II.* Combat Studies Institute, No. 12, Leavenworth Papers, Fort Leavenworth, Kans.: U.S. Army Command and General Staff College, 1985.

Geschichte des Grossen Vaterländischen Krieges der Sowjetunion. 8 vols. Berlin: Deutscher Militärverlag, 1964.

Glantz, David M. *From the Don to the Dnepr: Soviet Offensive Operations, December 1942–August 1943.* London: F. Cass, 1991.

Grechko, A., et al. *Soviet Studies on the Second World War.* Moscow: USSR Academy of Sciences, 1976.

————. *The Armed Forces of the Soviet Union.* Moscow: Progress Publishers, 1977.

————. *Godi Voini.* Moscow: Voennoe Izdatelistvo, 1976.

————. *Liberation Mission.* Moscow: Progress Publishers, 1975.

————. *Vooryuzennie Sili Sovetskogo Gosyarstva.* Moscow: Voyennoye Isdatelistvo, 1975.

Harrison, Mark. *Soviet Planning in Peace and War, 1938–1945.* Cambridge, England: Cambridge University Press, 1985.

Hunter, Holland, and Janusz M. Seymour. *Faulty Foundations: Soviet Economic Policies, 1928–1940.* Princeton, N.J.: Princeton University Press, 1992.

Istoriya Velikoy Otechestvennoy Voyny Sovetskogo Soyuza, 1941–1945. 6 vols. Moscow: Voyennoye Isdatelistvo, 1960–63.

Istoriya Vtoroi Mirovoi Voyny, 1939–1945. 12 vols. Moscow: Voyennoye Isdatelistvo, 1973–82.

Ivanov, S. P. *The Initial Period of the War: A Soviet View.* Soviet Military Thought Series, No. 20. Washington, D C.: U.S. Government Printing Office, 1986.

Kazakov, Konstantin P., ed. *Artilleriia i Raketi.* Moscow: Voenizdat, 1968.

Kehrig, Manfred. *Stalingrad: Analyse und Dokumentation Einer Schlacht.* Stuttgart: Deutsche Verlags-Anstalt, 1974.

Kerr, Walter. *The Secret of Stalingrad.* New York: Playboy Press, 1979. Krupchenko, I. E., et al. *Sovetskiye Tankovye Voyska.* Moscow: Voyennoye Izdatelistvo, 1973.

Krivosheev, G. F. *Grif Sekretnosti Sniat: Poteri Vooruzennix sil SSSR v Voinax Boevix Deistviiax i Voennix Konfliktax.* Moscow: Voennoe Izdatelistvo, 1993. Kurochkina, Pavel A. *Obshevoiskovaia Armiya v Nastuplenii.* Moscow: Voyenizdat, 1966.

Liddell Hart, Basil H. *The Other Side of the Hill: The German Generals Talk.* New York: Berkley Publishing Corp., 1958.

————. *The Red Army.* New York: Harcourt, Brace, 1956.

Losik, O. A. *Stroitelstvo i Boyevoye Primeneniye Sovetskikh Tankovykh Voysk v Gody Velikoy Otechestvennoy Voyne.* Moscow: Voyenizdat, 1979.

Lucas, James. *War on the Eastern Front, 1941–1945: The German Soldier in Russia.* New York: Bonanza Books, 1979.

Makhine, Theodore H. *L'Armee Rouge.* Paris: Payout, 1938.

Militärakademie M. W. Frunse. *Der Durchbruch der Schutzenverbände durch eine Vorbereitete Verteidigung.* Berlin: Ministerium für Nationale Verteidigung, 1959.

Parotkin, Ivan, ed. *The Battle of Kursk.* Moscow: Progress Publishers, 1974. Parrish, Michael, ed. *Battle for Moscow: The 1942 Soviet General Staff Study.* Washington, D. C.: Pergamon-Brassey's, 1989.

Pavlovskii, I. G. *Sukhoputniye Voyska SSSR.* Moscow: Voyenizdat, 1985. Peredeliskii, G. E., et al. *Artilleriia v Bou i Operatsii.* Moscow: Voennoe Izdatelistvo, 1980.

Poirier, Robert G., and Albert C. Conner. *Red Army Order of Battle in the Great Patriotic War.* Novato, Calif.: Presidio Press, 1985.

Rapoport, Vitaly, and Yuri Alexeev. *High Treason: Essays on the History of the Red Army, 1918–1938.* Durham, N. C.: Duke University Press, 1985.

Reinhardt, Klaus. *Die Wende vor Moskau.* Stuttgart: Deutsche Verlag-Anstalt, 1972.

Rotundo, Louis C., ed. *Battle for Stalingrad: The Soviet General Staff Study.* Washington, D. C.: Pergamon-Brassey's, 1989.

Salisbury, Harrison E. *The 900 Days: The Siege of Leningrad.* New York: Avon Books, 1970.

Seaton, Albert. *The Battle for Moscow, 1941–1942.* New York: Stein and Day, 1971.

———. *The Russo-German War, 1941–45.* New York: Praeger, 1970.

———. *Stalin as Warlord.* London: B. T. Batsford Ltd., 1976.

Seaton, Albert, and Joan Seaton. *The Soviet Army, 1918 to the Present.* New York: New American Library, 1986.

Shtemenko, S. M. *The Last Six Months.* Garden City, N.Y.: Doubleday & Co., 1977.

———. *The Soviet General Staff at War, 1941–1945.* Moscow: Progress Publishers, 1970.

Skorobogatkin, K. F., et al. *50 Let Voorezhennykh sil SSSR.* Moscow: Voyenizdat, 1968.

Sovetskaya Voyennaya Entsiklopediya. 8 vols. Moscow: Voyennoye Izdatelistvo, 1976–1980.

Steiger, Rudolf. *Armour Tactics in the Second World War.* Studies in Military History. New York: Berg, 1991.

Stolfi, Russel H. S. *Hitler's Panzers East: World War II Reinterpreted.* Norman: University of Oklahoma Press, 1992.

Sutton, Antony C. *Western Technology and Soviet Economic Development.* 3 vols. Stanford: Hoover Institution Press, 1968–73.

Tiushkevich, Stepan A., ed. *Sovetskie Vooruzhennye Sily.* Moscow: Voenizdat, 1978.

———. *The Soviet Armed Forces.* Washington, D. C.: U.S. Government Printing Office, 1985.

Tiushkevich, Stepan A., et al. *Filosofia i Voennaia Istoriia.* Moscow: Nauka, 1979.

Tolubko, V. F., and N. I. Barishev. *Na Uznom Flange.* Moscow: Izdatelistvo, "Nauka," 1973.

U.S. War Department. *Handbook of German Military Forces.* Technical Manual 30–451. Washington, D. C.: U.S. Government Printing Office, 1945.

———. Military Intelligence Division. *German Military Intelligence, 1939–1945.* Frederick, Md.: University Publications of America, 1984.

———. *Handbook on USSR Military Forces.* November 1945 Technical Manual 30–430. Washington, D. C., U.S. Government Printing Office, 1946.

U. S. S. R. Central Statistical Board of the USSR Council of Ministers. *National Economy of the U.S.S.R. Statistical Returns.* Moscow: Foreign Languages Publishing House, 1957.

Urlanis, B. *Wars and Population.* Moscow: Progress Publishers, 1971.

Van Tuyll, Hubert P. *Feeding the Bear: American Aid to the Soviet Union, 1941–1945.* New York: Greenwood Press, 1989.

Vassilevsky, A., et al. *Moscow Stalingrad, 1941–1942: Recollections, Stories, Reports.* Moscow: Progress Publishers, 1974.

Velikai Otechestvennia Voina 1941–1945 Entsiklopediya. Moscow: Sovetskia Entsiklopediya, 1985.

Werth, Alexander. *Russia at War.* New York: Discus Books, 1970.

Wheeler-Bennett, J. W. *The Nemesis of Power.* New York: St. Martin's Press, 1964.

Wray, Timothy. *Standing Fast: German Defensive Doctrine on the Russian Front during World War II. Prewar to March 1943.* Combat Studies Institute Research Survey No. 5. U. S. Army Command and General Staff College. Washington, D.C.: U.S. Government Printing Office, 1987.

Zakharov, M. V. *Generalnyi Shtab v Predvoennye Gody.* Moscow: Voenizdat, 1989.

Zaloga, Steven J., and James Granden. *Soviet Tanks and Combat Vehicles of World War Two.* London: Arms and Armour Press, 1984.

Zhukov, Georgi K. *Marshal Zhukov's Greatest Battles.* New York: Harper & Row, 1969.

Ziemke, Earl F., and Magna E. Bauer. *Moscow to Stalingrad: Decision in the East.* New York: Military Heritage Press, 1988

———. *The Soviet Juggernaut.* Morristown, N. J.: Silver Burdett Co., 1988.

Index

Stackpole Military History Series

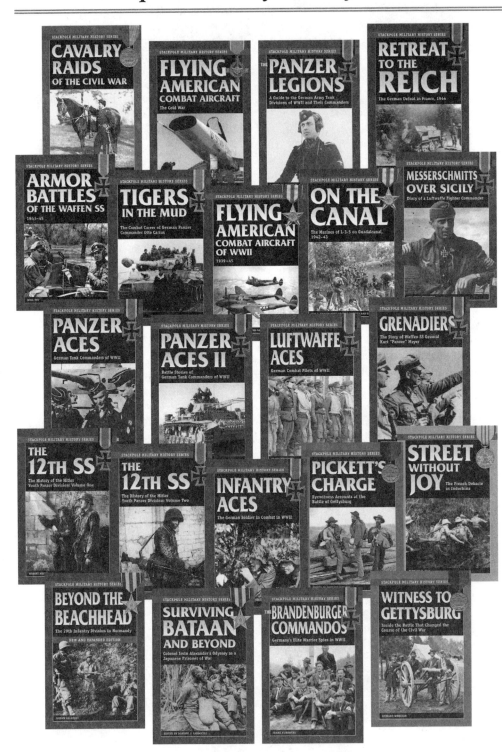

Real battles. Real soldiers. Real stories.

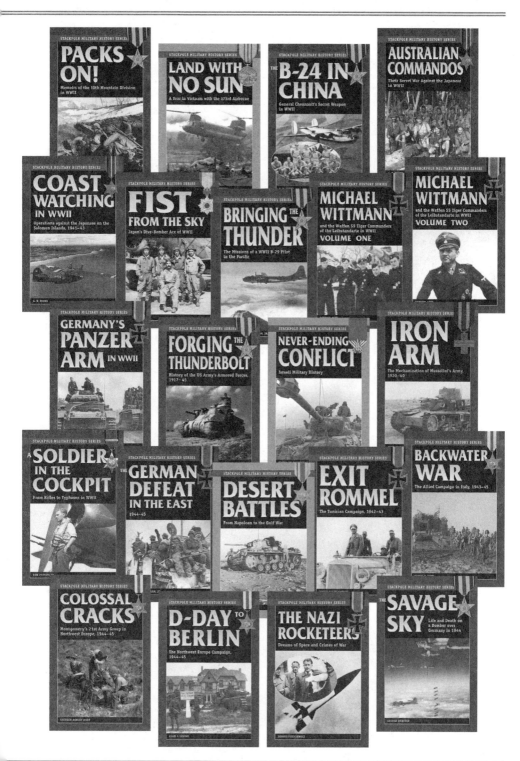

Stackpole Military History Series

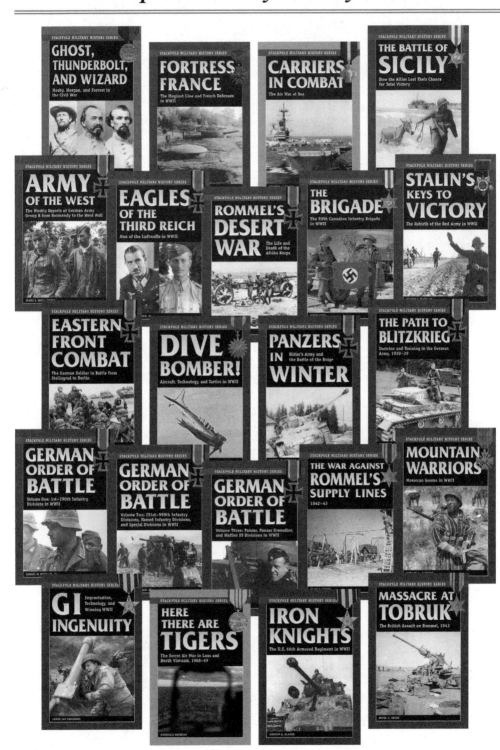

Real battles. Real soldiers. Real stories.

Stackpole Military History Series

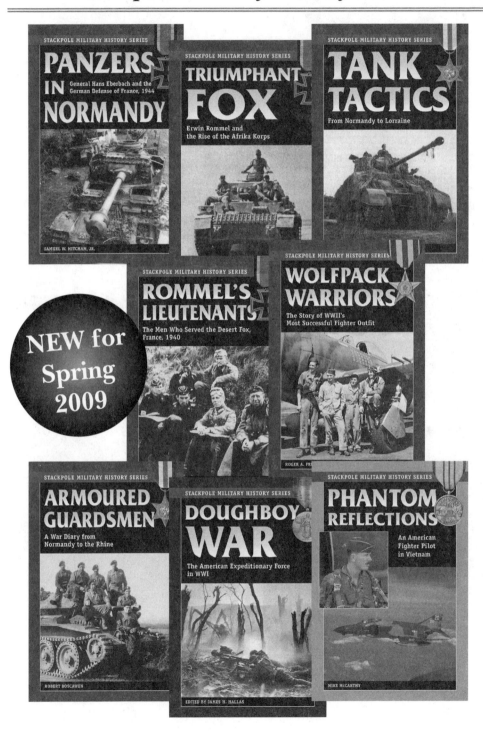

STACKPOLE MILITARY HISTORY SERIES

PANZERS IN NORMANDY
General Hans Eberbach and the German Defense of France, 1944
SAMUEL W. MITCHAM, JR.

STACKPOLE MILITARY HISTORY SERIES

TRIUMPHANT FOX
Erwin Rommel and the Rise of the Afrika Korps

STACKPOLE MILITARY HISTORY SERIES

TANK TACTICS
From Normandy to Lorraine

STACKPOLE MILITARY HISTORY SERIES

ROMMEL'S LIEUTENANTS
The Men Who Served the Desert Fox, France, 1940

STACKPOLE MILITARY HISTORY SERIES

WOLFPACK WARRIORS
The Story of WWII's Most Successful Fighter Outfit
ROGER A. FR

NEW for Spring 2009

STACKPOLE MILITARY HISTORY SERIES

ARMOURED GUARDSMEN
A War Diary from Normandy to the Rhine
ROBERT BOSCAWEN

STACKPOLE MILITARY HISTORY SERIES

DOUGHBOY WAR
The American Expeditionary Force in WWI
EDITED BY JAMES H. HALLAS

STACKPOLE MILITARY HISTORY SERIES

PHANTOM REFLECTIONS
An American Fighter Pilot in Vietnam
MIKE McCARTHY

Real battles. Real soldiers. Real stories.

STACKPOLE MILITARY HISTORY SERIES

GOODWOOD

The British Offensive in Normandy, July 1944

IAN DAGLISH

STACKPOLE MILITARY HISTORY SERIES

DESTINATION NORMANDY

Three American Regiments on D-Day

STACKPOLE MILITARY HISTORY SERIES

EXPENDABLE WARRIORS

The Battle of Khe Sanh and the Vietnam War

BRUCE B. G. CLARKE

STACKPOLE MILITARY HISTORY SERIES

D-DAY DECEPTION

Operation Fortitude and the Normandy Invasion

STACKPOLE MILITARY HISTORY SERIES

RED STAR UNDER THE BALTIC

A Soviet Submariner in WWII

NEW for Spring 2009

STACKPOLE MILITARY HISTORY SERIES

HITLER'S NEMESIS

The Red Army, 1930–45

WALTER S. DUNN, JR., WITH A FOREWORD BY DAVID GLANTZ

STACKPOLE MILITARY HISTORY SERIES

PENALTY STRIKE

The Memoirs of a Red Army Penal Company Commander, 1943–45

ALEXANDER V. PYL'CYN

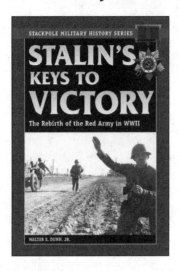

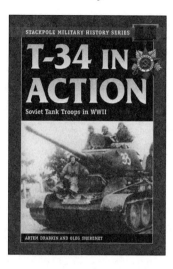

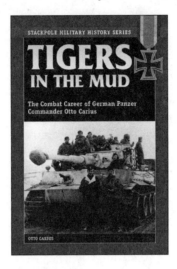

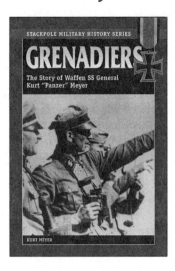

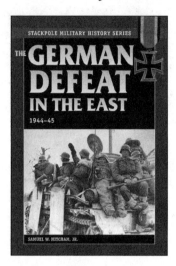

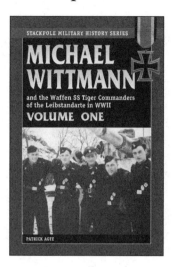
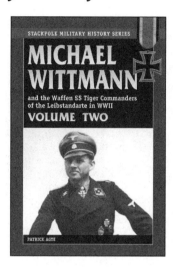